SHARED PROSPERITY
IN A FRACTURED WORLD

Shared Prosperity in a Fractured World

A New Economics for the Middle Class, the Global Poor, and Our Climate

Dani Rodrik

PRINCETON UNIVERSITY PRESS

PRINCETON AND OXFORD

Published by Princeton University Press
41 William Street, Princeton, New Jersey 08540
99 Banbury Road, Oxford OX2 6JX

press.princeton.edu

GPSR Authorized Representative: Easy Access System Europe - Mustamäe tee 50, 10621 Tallinn, Estonia, gpsr.requests@easproject.com

All Rights Reserved

ISBN 9780691268316
ISBN (e-book) 9780691268330

Library of Congress Control Number: 2025939526

British Library Cataloging-in-Publication Data is available

Editorial: Joe Jackson and Rebecca Binnie
Production Editorial: Jaden Young
Jacket Design: Heather Hansen
Production: Erin Suydam
Publicity: James Schneider and Kate Farquhar-Thomson
Copyeditor: Jennifer McClain

This book has been composed in Adobe Text and Gotham

Printed in the United States of America

10 9 8 7 6 5 4 3 2 1

In memory of my mother and father

CONTENTS

SHARED PROSPERITY
IN A FRACTURED WORLD

Introduction

IN SEARCH OF DEMOCRACY, PROSPERITY, SUSTAINABILITY

We want to live in societies that are free, a world without poverty, and a climate that is hospitable. We want, in brief, democracy, prosperity, and sustainability. How can we achieve all three, in a global economy that has become more conflictual, is rapidly moving away from its previously established norms and arrangements, and faces a fragile geopolitical context marked by US-China rivalry? How can we render them compatible, when so many policy currents are at cross-purposes, moving us away from the other goals even when they appear to advance one of them? These are the questions that lie at the heart of this book.

Democracy, prosperity, and sustainability are among the most significant challenges the world faces at present. Climate change is widely accepted today as an existential threat. It is a truly global problem, though its adverse effects will be highly uneven around the world, with low-income countries the hardest hit. The broad outlines of what needs to be done to mitigate and adapt to climate change have long been known. The conventional approach emphasizes global agreements on reduction of carbon and other greenhouse gases along with financial and technological assistance to poor nations, but progress on this agenda has proved elusive. Even where there has been progress, we are seeing the emergence of a messy patchwork of local, national, or regional green policies that lack overall coherence and often appear to shift the costs of adjustment to others.

Democratic backsliding in the US, Europe, and many other countries poses a danger of a different sort, as an existential threat to our freedoms. In November 2024, American voters reelected as their president Donald Trump, who has multiple criminal indictments against him and whose authoritarian tendencies are evident. Within weeks of taking office for a second time, Trump had already endangered the separation of powers, rule of law, free speech, and academic freedom—critical norms on which liberal democracy rests. While there are many reasons for our recent political malfunction, the erosion of the middle class lies at the center of it. Growing regional, social, cultural, and political divides, racism and xenophobia, the decline of democratic values, and the corrosive tide of authoritarianism are all strongly linked to economic insecurity. Automation, deindustrialization, globalization, and fiscal austerity have each contributed to these trends, to varying extents, in different parts of North America and Europe. Since good jobs are the backbone of a middle-class society, addressing these problems will require a strategy for reversing the decline in their supply. Policies in the US and other advanced nations gesture in this direction, but they overlook a critical reality. The bulk of future jobs will be created in services rather than in manufacturing. A coherent approach that focuses on good jobs in services has yet to emerge.

On the global poverty front, experience in recent decades has been more encouraging. There was striking success after the 1980s, as economic growth took off and hundreds of millions were lifted out of extreme poverty in China and many other countries. But optimism has faded since the COVID pandemic, and even more so after Trump's attacks on the world economy and foreign aid. The global conversation has yet to face up to the reality that the nature of the development challenge today is quite different. What worked in the past is unlikely to do so in the future. The economic growth strategy that delivered earlier results—export-oriented industrialization—is no longer viable, not only because of the imperatives of the green transition or the challenges of protectionism but also because of new technologies, such as automation, which undercut the advantage of low-cost, unskilled labor in manufacturing. Developing countries need a new approach to promote growth and poverty reduction.

Democracy, prosperity, and sustainability are vast subjects, each with enormous bodies of literature of their own. It might seem foolhardy to attempt to tackle all of them in a single volume. I do not pretend to provide a comprehensive discussion of each, with detailed remedies. But these challenges are interrelated, and focusing on one challenge at a time risks creating blind spots on the other fronts. Each requires a critical ingredient, with implications and spillovers for the other two. Healthy democracies require *a strong middle class*. Poverty eradication requires rapid, inclusive *economic growth* in low-income countries. And environmental sustainability requires *greening our economies* to slow down and ultimately stop climate change. We need a policy agenda that spans all three arenas. Moreover, as we shall see, addressing these challenges requires a common policy mindset, an updated version of industrial policy that I call *productivism*. Seeing how this shared framework plays out in diverse arenas will allow us to make unexpected connections across them.

The policies we pursue in each domain can be mutually reinforcing. The green transition not only would help on the environment front; it would have a significant positive impact on economic growth and poverty reduction around the world, since poor countries are the ones most at risk from rising sea levels, extreme weather events, and loss of biodiversity. Greater prosperity in the developing world might in turn help strengthen middle classes in the advanced economies, by providing larger markets for other nations' exports and investments and easing pressures for climate-change-driven outmigration. A stronger middle class in the advanced economies would produce societies that are more open to the rest of the world and less prone to hostility to others. A key theme in this book is that these are achievable outcomes if we pursue the right approach.

But win-win outcomes are not assured. In fact, current policy thinking suggests our three goals are very much in conflict with each other. Addressing climate change and global poverty reduction requires, on the face of it, significant global cooperation. Yet most nations, led by the advanced economies themselves, are increasingly turning inward. Their strategies seem mutually incompatible. Developing countries that pursue conventional growth strategies emphasizing rapid industrialization make the climate crisis worse, without necessarily achieving their poverty reduction goals. Policies in the US and Europe that prioritize competitiveness in manufacturing end up discriminating against poor nations, even as they fall short on good jobs. On the other hand, a global agenda designed to maximize economic opportunities for the poorest people in the world by providing greater access to their goods and workers in the markets of advanced economies would clash with the imperative to shore up the middle class in rich nations. We might call this scenario global Rawlsianism, in reference to Rawls's principle that justice requires maximum attention to the needs of the least fortunate.[1] These tensions are illustrated in the accompanying diagram.

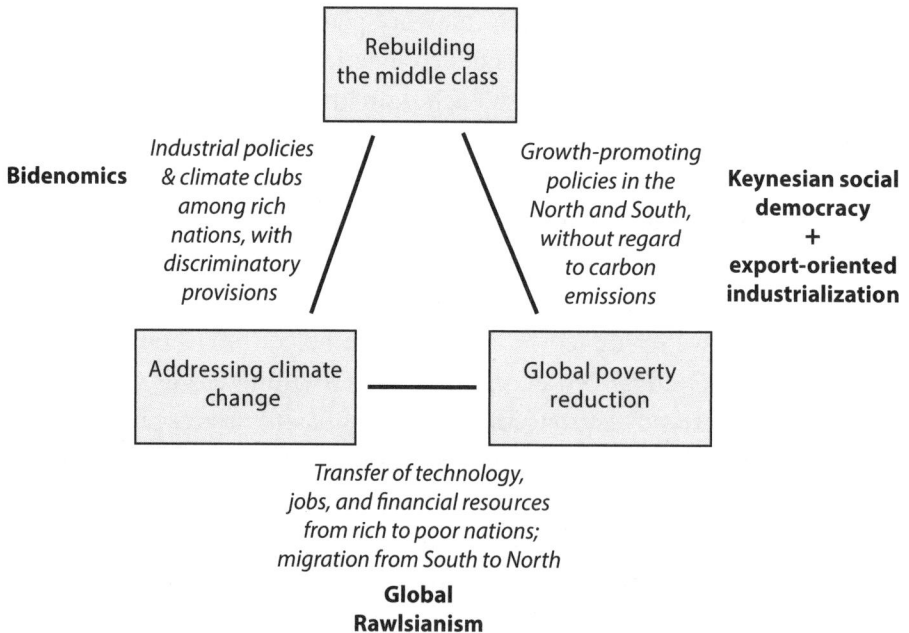

It is time for new ideas and fresh approaches that avoid these cruel trade-offs. The global economy is taking new shape in front of our eyes, but so far without a clear guiding direction. The pandemic, geopolitical tensions between China and the West, the uncertain future of low- and middle-income countries, rising inequality in most parts of the world, the increase in support for ethno-nationalist populism, and not least the climate change crisis have irrevocably altered the economic landscape. Conventional policy approaches and economic orthodoxies are being questioned everywhere. The old consensus, whether one calls it neoliberalism, market fundamentalism, or the rules-based international order, is gone.

This is in part because of the old order's shortcomings and the predictable backlash that has ensued. Neoliberal policies not only failed to lift all boats; they created damaging blind spots on the environment and public health. Past arrangements no longer fit new realities. A US-dominated international order is not suited to a world where the US is no longer a hegemon, China and other rising powers want to have a greater say in global rules, and the zero-sum logic of geopolitical competition among major powers has risen to the fore.

What will replace the old order is unclear. A return to the Keynesian social democratic model of the mid-twentieth century will not work, as management of aggregate demand, social insurance, and worker empowerment cannot on their own restore the middle class in the advanced economies without commensurate increases in most workers' productivity. In developing countries, the strategy of export-oriented industrialization has run out of steam. Greater international cooperation to strengthen global rules on trade, migration, technology, and climate might be desirable, but it cannot be our main hope in a world where national sovereignty rules with greater force than ever. The new industrial and green strategy adopted under the Biden administration was an important start insofar as it recognized the need for a new direction focused on the middle class and the climate. But its preoccupation with manufacturing and US-China geopolitical competition created new blind spots. It ignored the importance of services for the future of middle-class jobs. It also failed to heed the developmental concerns of poor nations.

Trump returned to office in 2025 on the back of the economic anxieties that President Biden had vowed to address, but his policies took a very different turn. Trump was determined to reverse policies on climate change, made his disdain for other nations clear, and did not have a coherent vision of industrial policy, relying on higher tariffs as his exclusive tool to revive manufacturing. But the speed and recklessness with which Trump took a wrecking ball to the world economy was nevertheless a surprise. His erratic trade policies, sky-high tariffs, and aggressive approach to foreign nations—geopolitical rivals and long-term allies alike—produced greater disruption and turmoil than most observers had predicted.

Trumpism moves us even further away from our goals. It offers no real remedy for workers and regions left behind, turns America's back on the global poor, and threatens to reverse recent gains on the climate change front. It fails to meet even a single one of our three challenges, let alone manage the trade-offs among them. But its failures make Trumpism also the perfect backdrop for the ideas advanced in the book. They starkly highlight the costs of manufacturing fetishism and of zero-sum thinking on international trade; the priority of developing good jobs strategies for services that generate the bulk of employment; the centrality of industrial and technological policies that help the climate as well as workers; the need for new growth strategies for poor nations that go beyond trade and foreign aid; the necessity of an alternative framework for the global economy that does not rely on the false hope of global cooperation; and the urgency of charting a healthier, more sustainable path between the extremes of neoliberalism and hyperglobalization on the one hand and destructive economic nationalism and protectionism on the other.

Trumpism is a cautionary tale of how things go wrong when we lack fresh ideas to address our challenges. It makes it clearer than ever that we need a new, coherent approach that fixes our problems and does not offer fake solutions. Authoritarian, ethno-nationalist leaders should not make us pessimistic about the possibilities of a better alternative. Nor should they leave us yearning for an old order that enriched many but left many others behind. We need to move forward instead of going back or faltering sideways.

But is there such an alternative, and what does it look like? I offer in these pages both a warning and some reason for hope. The caution is that our present policy menu is inadequate to the task and creates serious conflicts among the objectives. It falls short because it overlooks political realities, the trade-offs among our multiple objectives, and our altered technological or geopolitical landscape. To meet all three of these challenges simultaneously—rebuilding the middle class, reducing global poverty, and addressing climate change—we need to depart from established ways of thinking and consider new approaches. We must do things differently, relying often on unconventional remedies.

The good news is that it is neither infeasible nor too late to carve such a superior path. The seeds of these innovative approaches already exist within prevailing practices around the world. What we require is not a revolution; it is a reconfiguration of our priorities and policies. Domestic politics and lack of global cooperation often rule out what economists and other technocrats would consider preferred options. But they rule in other approaches that are often more effective in the real world.

1

Overcoming the Triple Challenge

What are the new ideas the world requires and how do we make sure they will work? In this chapter, I present a preview of the arguments in the book. The chapter outlines and synthesizes the main threads of my approach—though not so fully, I hope, that the reader will want to skip the rest of the book! I first discuss the three main challenges individually and then summarize the cross-cutting ideas that shape the common policy mindset behind my proposals.

Addressing climate change

In the technocrats' ideal world, climate change would be addressed through a three-pronged global agreement: a high enough global carbon price (or equivalent cap-and-trade system); global subsidies for innovation in green technologies; and a substantial flow of financial and technological assistance to developing nations. The real world has failed to deliver this trifecta. But there has been unexpected progress as a result of a variety of uncoordinated local and national actions. I argue that these unorthodox approaches potentially lay the groundwork for a more frontal assault on climate change.

Let us start by reviewing the rationales for the orthodox remedies. Raising the price of carbon (and other greenhouse gases) is needed so that the private and social costs of emissions are brought closer together and producers and users of energy internalize the environmental damage fossil fuel use generates. Subsidizing green innovation is required, because new technologies that foster renewables and green industries are a critical part of the climate transition and innovators' incentives need to be boosted in view of the positive spillovers they generate for the rest of the economy.[1] Financial and technological assistance to poorer nations is required for reasons of both expedience and fairness. These countries have the least resources to invest in the transition. And it is the rich nations that are responsible for the bulk of global emissions to date. Since climate change is already a reality, these mitigation efforts must be complemented with adaptation measures by individual countries—investments that enhance the resilience of our economies and built environments to hotter temperatures and extreme weather events.

The real world, organized around individual sovereign nations, is very unlikely to produce anything approaching this first-best solution. There has been no shortage of global climate summits, worldwide conferences, and promises to cooperate internationally. But the process has yielded little real fruit. The present global system revolves around voluntary national commitments to emission reductions and a patchwork of limited ad hoc arrangements of financial assistance to developing countries.

However, a confluence of considerations has pushed localities, nations, and regions to move independently and more forcefully to advance their own particular green agendas. Few had anticipated this, since global warming is the archetypal global commons problem: it does not matter where carbon is emitted or where such emissions are controlled. In a world where each jurisdiction minds only its own self-interest, none has the incentive to act to reduce emissions. Or so the logic goes. In reality, a mix of commercial motivations, green consciousness in public opinion, and a perceived necessity to adjust to the economic realities of the future has prevailed. And some of these efforts have produced significant results.

China's policies to promote its solar and wind industries have slashed the costs of renewable energy worldwide beyond what anyone thought was feasible not so long ago. The hundreds of billions of dollars of green subsidies provided under the 2022 Inflation Reduction Act (IRA) in the US are widely seen as a "game changer" for promoting renewables and de-carbonizing the US economy, Trump's attempted reversal notwithstanding. There has been widespread local experimentation with carbon pricing in Europe and beyond. California's cap-and-trade system in carbon has delivered large cuts in emissions from the power sector, along with more than $20 billion in revenues for the state government since 2013, and has been copied by thirteen other states in the US and many other local governments worldwide. The Canadian province of British Columbia's fuel tax is estimated to have reduced emissions by as much as 15 percent (relative to what would have happened in its absence).[2]

It is not surprising that local politics plays a big role in the shaping of such programs. This often yields outcomes that are far from the first best and impose some costs on other localities or nations. China's green industrial subsidies—first in solar and wind and lately in electric vehicles and batteries—have been much derided by commercial competitors and met by import barriers in the US and Europe despite their unquestionable benefits on the climate front. The IRA has been called protectionist because of the requirement that firms that receive subsidies under the program source some of their supplies locally. The EU's emissions trading system (ETS), which targets a significant increase in the European price of carbon, now comes with a mechanism that restricts imports from nations without emission controls. Pundits have begun warning about a "subsidy war" in world trade as countries ramp up subsidies on green industries of the future, ranging from electric batteries to green hydrogen.

Typically, nations have sought to bring domestic opponents and potential losers from green policies on board while prioritizing their own commercial considerations. From the perspective of the ideal approach, such local political bargains can leave a lot to be desired. Yet they are likely to do more for emission reduction than any attempt at a global carbon deal will probably achieve. We cannot afford to be first-best purists or focus excessively on the efficiency costs of such policies. In the fight against climate change, a global subsidy war would actually be a good thing, not a bad thing! Extremism in the defense of climate, to paraphrase Barry Goldwater, is no vice.

We should not be overly optimistic about what these local, national, and regional efforts will achieve. At least not yet. Global warming is still on path to exceed, possibly by a considerable margin, the 1.5°C–2°C target that most scientists regard as prudent. Much more will have to be done, including on adaptation. But we need to recognize the relative inefficacy of the global coordination approach and put more faith on the messy solutions generated by local and national politics. Overall, these unilateral efforts must be applauded and encouraged rather than denigrated. As I discuss in chapter 3, it is quite possible not only that their cumulative effect will be significant but also that they will alter the political landscape in a direction that makes more ambitious (and even more efficacious) actions possible. For example, political opposition from Republicans and regions dependent on fossil fuels has long prevented the US from adopting a more frontal approach on carbon emissions. As green industries and their political weight grow, these political difficulties may no longer look insurmountable, especially since many red states, such as Texas, offer natural locations for clean energy production.

The major downside of the current approach is that it leaves developing countries in the cold—or, phrased more accurately, in the heat! Low-income countries are strapped for resources, and most of the technology they need is proprietary to firms based in rich countries. Without concessional finance and access to Northern technology, they cannot decarbonize their economies and invest in the costly adaptation measures they need in agriculture, cities, and low-lying areas. This exacerbates poverty; it also makes it less likely that these countries will contribute significantly to global emission reductions.

The obvious solution lies in a quid pro quo: a transfer of financial resources and technology to developing economies in exchange for these countries committing to multiyear green transition programs. There are various ways such a deal can be designed and implemented, depending on country circumstances. For debt-stressed countries, it can be combined with the provision of liquidity and debt reprofiling. There is no shortage of potential revenue sources that could finance such a deal, including special drawing rights issued by the IMF, a global wealth tax, or a tax on short-term financial transactions. A bargain along these lines appears imperative if the climate and poverty reduction goals are both to be met. But the lack of global cooperation and coordination that has hampered global carbon control policies is likely to be a serious obstacle on this front as well. Perhaps the US and China will manage to set aside their other differences and lead the way here. Otherwise, low-income countries are likely to be forced to fend for themselves. They will then remain dependent on private financial markets and will have to find ways to increase access to such financing and reduce its costs.

Restoring the middle class

If climate change is the most severe threat to the physical environment, the erosion of the middle class is the most significant challenge to the social and political environment of the world's leading democracies. We might care for the middle class because we dislike large income gaps in society. But regardless of our individual preferences on inequality, the health of the middle class matters to us all. Put bluntly, the middle class is the backbone of a democracy. It is very difficult to maintain democratic governance without a large group of citizens who share reasonably similar living standards, neither too rich nor too poor, and, not unrelatedly, some common values and aspirations. Societies that are polarized in terms of income and values tend to either disintegrate into anarchy and conflict or end up with authoritarian rule.[3] Social scientists debate how to measure the size of the middle class and whether it has really declined over time. But there is little doubt that the sense of belonging to the middle class has weakened, and perception of economic insecurity has risen in the advanced economic world, especially among working people.

A solid middle class requires in turn the provision of an adequate number of "good jobs" to the preponderant number of workers who lack advanced or professional educational credentials. While there is no precise definition of what a good job is, we might think of it as a job that enables living standards that are not far below a country's average income level and offers prospects of career advancement and core labor rights, such as collective bargaining rights and regulations against arbitrary dismissal.[4] Social insurance, redistribution, and a strong welfare state may help reduce material inequality and economic insecurity. But without productive employment opportunities, it is impossible to establish a middle class. Jobs provide not only a source of income but also a sense of self, personal dignity, and social recognition.[5] Hence the syllogism: good jobs create a middle class, and the middle class sustains democracy.

Against this background, it should not be surprising that the disruptions wrought in labor markets by the neoliberal age played a critical role in fueling the rise of authoritarian populists and undermining liberal democracies. There is by now a large body of scholarship that finds local and regional job losses caused by globalization, automation, fiscal austerity, and weakening of labor market protections have been responsible for increased support at the polls for right-wing populist candidates and parties.[6] According to one influential study, had the spike in Chinese imports been half as big, three critical battleground states of the 2016 US election would have gone to Hillary Clinton instead of Donald Trump, resulting in a Clinton victory for the presidency. The swing of working-class, especially male, voters in even greater numbers toward Trump in the 2024 election shows these concerns are very much alive, despite a rise in real incomes for those with the lowest wages during the Biden administration. Interestingly, this literature shows that economic dislocation not only causes income losses but also amplifies polarization with regard to culture and values. In regions that experienced a larger China trade shock, there was an increase in authoritarian values in politics, a rise in conservatives' attachments to guns and religion, and a hardening of negative sentiments among Whites toward immigrants and minorities. Racial animosity, hostility to immigrants, and xenophobia may have deep cultural roots. But they are also fueled by economic insecurity and the disappearance of middle-class jobs.

The question all over the rich world is how the demand for relatively less educated workers will be boosted to repair the fissures in labor markets. None of the prevailing approaches is fully adequate to the task. Strengthening the social safety net, as I mentioned, does not go to the root of the problem. Stimulating aggregate demand helps, by creating more jobs at the low end of the skill distribution, but it risks igniting inflation, and in any case a cyclical remedy cannot solve a structural problem. Investing in education is always a good idea but does little for the present generation of workers. We need the greatest improvement in job quality in occupations such as long-term care or food services that do not require college degrees. Fostering labor rights and unionization strengthens workers' bargaining power but does not create what is needed: more productive jobs for workers with less than a college education. Finally, and critically, efforts to reshore manufacturing and invest in new manufacturing capacity miss the mark, because the jobs are and will remain in services, not in manufacturing. This last point requires some elaboration, as both the Trump and Biden administrations have focused so much on bringing manufacturing jobs back to the US.

On the face of it, the logic of reviving manufacturing seems clear and powerful. Unionized jobs in manufacturing have historically been the foundation of the middle class. But the world has moved on, and the nature of manufacturing technologies has changed irrevocably. As a consequence of automation and other kinds of innovations—which economists call *skill-biased technological change*—labor productivity in manufacturing has grown by leaps and bounds. In the US, it expanded nearly sixfold in the six decades since 1950, compared to a mere doubling in the rest of the economy. The result is a striking increase in the manufacturing sector's ability to produce goods, but an equally dramatic decline in its capacity to generate jobs. Despite shifts in consumer demand from goods to services, value added in manufacturing (at constant prices) has broadly kept pace with the rest of the economy. Yet the US economy has lost six million jobs in manufacturing as it created seventy-three million nonfarm jobs elsewhere (mainly in services) since 1980.[7]

The decline in manufacturing employment, as a share of total employment even if not in absolute terms, seems to be an inexorable trend in all advanced economies (as well as in most middle-income countries). Reversing it seems virtually impossible. Recent experience in the US illustrates the difficulty. The Trump I and Biden administrations both focused, in their own different ways, on manufacturing jobs. President Trump failed during his first term to raise the share of manufacturing in nonfarm employment, which remained flat at 8.5 percent. President Biden significantly upped the ante, by adding extensive subsidies for manufacturing on top of Trump's import tariffs on Chinese goods. By the time Biden left office in January 2025, the share of manufacturing employment had dropped further to an all-time low of 8.1 percent.[8]

A skeptic might object that Trump and Biden were going about it the wrong way, and there are far more effective strategies for boosting manufacturing jobs. But the reality is that even countries we consider as manufacturing successes have not fared better. Germany has a larger manufacturing sector than the US, relative to the size of its economy, but its share of manufacturing workers has dropped like a rock. South Korea achieved the remarkable feat of steadily increasing manufacturing's weight in the economy, but this has not prevented the shrinking of the sector's employment share in recent decades. Even in China, the world's manufacturing powerhouse, employment has been falling in manufacturing for more than a decade, both in absolute terms and as a share of total employment.[9]

Governments that focus on manufacturing to promote good jobs are chasing after a fast-receding target.[10] Even if government policy succeeds in boosting manufacturing investment, output, and value added, the decline in employment is irreversible. Whether we like it or not, services will remain the main job engine of the economy. Many service jobs are well paid and desirable. We do not have to worry about bad jobs for software developers or managers! But the bulk of service jobs are (and will remain) in retail, care, and other personal services. These occupations typically do not require college degrees and offer some of the worst jobs in economies such as that of the US. An inescapable conclusion follows: a good jobs economy hinges critically on our ability to increase the productivity and quality of jobs in such services.

How do we do that? Is it even possible? The unfortunate reality is that we do not have a tried-and-tested approach to enhance productivity in labor-absorbing services. We will have to innovate and experiment with different policies. But we don't have to start entirely from scratch. We can learn from our experience in promoting industrialization and adapt it to the new context. The result will be, effectively, a new set of "industrial policies" for services.

Consider what such an effort might look like for the US. Later in the book, I describe a program with both a local and a federal component. The local component would build on existing development and business assistance partnerships among local development agencies, firms, and other stakeholders aiming to revitalize local communities and create good jobs. We have a fair amount of experience with such local initiatives, and some lessons about what's required for success are beginning to emerge. The national initiative would be an Advanced Research Projects Agency (ARPA) focused on the promotion of a particular type of innovation: employment-friendly technologies. The direction of technological change need not be biased against labor, and governments can put their fingers on the scale to get innovation on a more socially desirable track. Importantly, neither of these components represents a sharp departure from industrial, innovation, and local development policies that already exist in the US. But unlike prevailing practices, their focus would be starkly on services and on good jobs. Examples from long-term care, health care, and retail (discussed in chapter 4) suggest that a mix of organizational and technological innovations can put us on the right track.

Extending the syllogism, then, good jobs in services will have to build the middle class that sustains democracy.

Reducing global poverty

The world today has 1.4 billion fewer people living in extreme poverty than in 1990, using the World Bank's poverty line (below $2.15/day in 2017 PPP).[11] This is a remarkable achievement, especially in light of the fact that the world's population has increased by 2.7 billion over the same period. Depending on where the poverty line is drawn, of course, we might reach different conclusions on whether the absolute number of poor people has come down or not. More-over, a proper evaluation of poverty trends has to take into account broader measures of well-being beyond material consumption lev-els, such as health status, access to education, and vulnerability to adverse shocks. But regardless of how one cuts the data, it is hard to avoid the conclusion that the last few decades have been good for the world's poor.

The pandemic briefly reversed these gains in poverty reduction and also left deep scars in developing economies that will require some time to heal. School closures of up to two years have pro-duced losses in education, especially for younger students, offsetting about a decade of learning gains for the poor.[12] A growth slowdown, which had begun prior to the pandemic, along with fiscal spending pressures during the health emergency, left many low- and lower-middle-income countries in debt distress, facing default or unable to borrow on global financial markets. The World Bank expects global poverty reduction to continue, albeit at a slower pace.

Moreover, the band of uncertainty around baseline projections is wider than it has been for some time. Even if global carbon emis-sions are curbed drastically, many low-income areas of the world will be hit badly by the consequences of the global warming that has already taken place. This includes losses in agricultural productivity, damages from sea level rising, and extreme weather events. Over the previous decade, developing countries were hit by nearly eight times the number of natural disasters as they had experienced over preceding decades.[13] Development strategies not only will have to be greener in the future but will also require a heavy dose of spend-ing on adaptation measures. There is a possibility that developing countries could turn adversity into opportunity by using the needed investments to give themselves an economic lift. But this will require substantial amounts of external finance.

The world economy is another area of risk. Mounting geopo-litical tensions and the rise of economic nationalism will possibly render the global economy a lot less hospitable to economic growth in poorer nations, especially for those pursuing export-oriented development strategies. Even more seriously, and regardless of the openness of markets in advanced economies, export-oriented industrialization strategies will be undercut by changes in manufacturing technologies and the requirements of international competition. Indeed, it will be virtually impossible for latecomers to replicate the experiences of the successful cases discussed previously.

But first let's step back and understand how this extraordinary poverty reduction became possible in the first place. Development economists have long debated whether poverty reduction is achieved more effectively through economy-wide economic growth or through programs that target directly the needs of the poor. In many ways this is a false distinction. Policies that enhance the productivity of poor households, by giving them access to education, health, technology, new markets, or better employment opportunities, will naturally enhance growth. And it is difficult to generate growth without doing at least some of those things. No matter what position one takes in this debate, however, history has repeatedly shown that sustained economic growth is the most powerful vehicle for poverty reduction. Countries with the fastest rates of economic growth were responsible for the stupendous poverty reduction experience post-1990, with China alone accounting for more than half of the decline.[14] Countries with little or no economic growth, on the other hand, didn't achieve much on the poverty front either.

Ever since the Industrial Revolution, industrialization has been the main instrument for delivering economic growth. The countries that engineered postwar economic miracles, such as Japan, Taiwan, South Korea, and most spectacularly China, combined industrialization at home with an export push on foreign markets to produce growth rates that were unprecedented in economic history. This recipe, export-oriented industrialization, worked best when governments relied on a judicious and pragmatic combination of market incentives and state direction, rejecting an ideological dichotomy between the two. "It doesn't matter whether a cat is black or white, as long as it catches the mice," as Deng Xiaoping said. Too much state intervention and the economy will be engulfed in inefficiency and corruption. Too much emphasis on free markets and the economy will be stuck producing primary products and other traditional commodities.

Hence a heavy dose of government support for new manufacturing economic activities played a key role in all these growth miracles. Government help for business took different forms: credit subsidies, tax incentives, special regulatory treatment, or customized infrastructure. Each country started with relatively simple manufactures (such as garments and toys), moved on to assembly of consumer electronics (TVs and PCs) and heavier industries (steel and shipbuilding), and eventually into more sophisticated high-tech products (such as semiconductors). The secret sauce that made these countries' industrial policies successful remains a subject of great debate. I dissect it in chapter 5, since so many of the lessons are crucial to the strategies of structural change at the heart of this book—the green transition, the creation of good jobs, and services-led economic development.

I discussed previously the importance of manufacturing jobs to the middle class. For developing countries, manufacturing also has been a growth engine. It has three ingredients that made it so. First, it exhibits productive dynamism: factory work not only is more productive relative to traditional agriculture but also tends to promote learning and technological catch-up.[15] Second, it is tradable: domestically produced manufactured goods can be exported, which removes the demand constraint that small home markets would otherwise pose to the expansion of successful firms. Third, traditionally manufacturing was intensive in relatively low-skill labor, meaning that it relied heavily on the one resource that was plentiful in poor countries: workers with little schooling, willing to work at low wages. These three factors combined made the manufacturing sector a powerful income escalator for poor countries—one that rose rapidly, kept going, and could accommodate a lot of people.

Of these three ingredients, the last is no more. Technological changes have rendered manufacturing increasingly skill- and capital-intensive, with the result that, just as in the advanced economies, factory work has ceased to be labor absorbing for the vast majority of poor nations. It may be feasible sometimes to use more labor-intensive production techniques in factories, using workers rather than robots to assemble parts, for example. But there are limits to how much unskilled labor can be substituted for modern equipment and technology. Competing successfully in a world of global value chains requires meeting quality standards that manual labor can no longer satisfy. As a result, many developing countries have been experiencing what I have called *premature deindustrialization*. They fail to reach levels of industrialization achieved by others before them and begin to shed manufacturing jobs at much lower levels of income. In countries where manufacturing employment continues to rise, it typically does so in informal, micro enterprises that are not globally competitive and do not exhibit the productive dynamism of larger, formal firms.[16]

The implication is that, in the future, developing countries will have to rely less on industrialization and more on creating productive employment in services, just like advanced economies. Labor-absorbing services in developing countries tend to be dominated by small, informal firms: self-proprietorships and micro enterprises, few of which have realistic prospects of growing and becoming significantly more productive. Moreover, even though remote work and tradable services are slated to expand, the bulk of these services are not exportable and depend on domestic demand and will remain so for the foreseeable future. Therefore, services-oriented development strategies will require a new orientation and often untested policies. Luckily, there is once again a range of experience around the world that points the way.

This experience suggests four lines of attack to foster services-led development. The first entails working with large and relatively productive incumbent firms to incentivize them to expand employment, either directly or through their local supply chains. These firms could be large retailers, ride-sharing services, or even manufacturing exporters with potential to generate upstream linkages with service providers. A second strategy focuses on the provision of specific public inputs to smaller firms to enhance their productive capabilities. These inputs range from management training, loans or grants, and customized worker skills to specific infrastructure and technology assistance. In view of the heterogeneity of the firms, policies here must be highly differentiated and customized to the needs of different segments of firm size and capabilities. They also require mechanisms to select the most promising and entrepreneurial entities.

A third strategy focuses on technology to provide workers directly or digital tools and other forms of new technologies to make labor more productive. The objective here is to enable less educated workers to do (some of) the jobs traditionally reserved for more skilled professionals and to increase the range of tasks they can perform. The final strategy combines vocational training for less educated workers with "wraparound" services to enhance job seekers' employability, retention, and eventual promotion. Such training programs typically work closely with employers, both to understand their training needs and to foster human resource practices that enhance employment potential.

I give concrete examples of each of these strategies in chapter 5. Where successful, they almost always involve collaborative partnerships between governments or NGOs on the one hand and service firms on the other, to deliver crucial inputs to enhance productivity, upgrade quality, and expand quality employment. They require a version of an "industrial policy for services" that is suitable for developing countries.

A downside of the services-based development strategy is that it cannot deliver the rates of economic growth that export-oriented industrialization has produced when successful. Exports enabled unbalanced but fast growth as some key sectors expanded much more rapidly than the rest, pulling the rest of the economy along. Services-based growth has to be balanced, and requires productivity increases across the board. Moreover, raising productivity in services is typically much more difficult to achieve. But there is a silver lining. Growth might be lower in a services-based strategy, but it will be broader based and less reliant on trickle down. The strategy has the virtue that, by design, it combines growth with social inclusion.

Trade-offs redux

This book provides a somewhat different perspective than the conventional understanding regarding the trade-offs I mentioned in the introduction among our three key objectives. In particular, my focus on services rather than manufacturing (in both advanced economies and poor nations) takes the edge off a potential conflict between rebuilding the middle class in the global North and fostering poverty reduction and economic growth in the global South. Promoting reindustrialization in the advanced economies would necessarily undercut poor nations' potential in manufactures. But, as I argued, it will do little for good jobs and the middle class. Services, and especially employment-absorbing services, on the other hand, are mostly nontradable. They do not create trade frictions on global markets. Creating good jobs in the US and Europe does not, and in fact will not, come at the expense of growth-promoting structural change in developing nations. Trade and industrial policies in manufacturing are really a side show when it comes to our core challenges.

Relatedly, I argue that a lack of global governance and cooperation poses fewer obstacles to a positive agenda than is commonly imagined. Effective forms of self-help at the national level—in climate, social inclusion, and economic growth—do not create significant problems for the world economy as a whole. In fact, they help other nations too. While countries still need to abide by some rules of the road, these need not be comprehensive or overly constraining, as I show later in this book.

Realism poses both a limit and an opportunity for policy making. In an ideal world, we would employ policies that target problems as directly as possible, are tried and tested, and are the result of global cooperation. But we cannot wish the world to be too different from how it is. Instead of wishful thinking, we need to operate close to the constraints we face. Policy makers must be inspired by, and build upon, what already exists and works. But they also must be bold and creative to push the frontier farther. I advocate in this book a particular policy mindset that orients us in this direction to help overcome what might otherwise appear to be insoluble challenges.

This mindset cuts across all of our areas. It has three ingredients that keep popping up all over the book. These are a preference for second-best over first-best approaches, policy experimentation over fixed remedies, and national solutions over global cooperation. I discuss each in turn.

Second best over first best

The first predilection is a preference for second-best over first-best thinking. In colloquial terms, second-best strategies are those that finesse complicated situations by adapting policies to circumstances, while first-best approaches try to maximize impact through head-on reforms, even if that implies wholesale transformation. The science of economics provides these terms with more precise meanings, alongside a theoretical apparatus that offers guidelines for selecting appropriate remedies under each.[17]

I illustrate the difference to my students by asking them to consider the following thought experiment. Suppose we are in 1978 and you are an economist who has been asked to help China's reformers carve a path toward a market economy. There is no shortage of problems to fix. Farmers do not own the land they work on and are required to deliver fixed quotas of grains to the state at low prices. There is no market for farm products (or anything else), and virtually all prices are fixed by the state. Private enterprises are not allowed, while state enterprises operate under a centrally planned system. Foreign trade and foreign investment are heavily restricted. There is no tax system: the government obtains its revenue by rationing food to urban workers at somewhat higher prices than it acquires it from farmers. Commercial law and contracts do not exist, and courts have no experience enforcing them.

A naive reformer might say, "Let's embark on reform by addressing one of the more important of these problems, and we can fix the others in due course." Since the bulk of poor people are in farming, we might want to start, for example, by removing state quotas for grains, liberalizing agricultural prices, and allowing farmers to sell on free markets. This sounds sensible enough. However, there is a problem. When an economy has multiple problems—"distortions" in economists' jargon—fixing only one or two at a time does not guarantee an improvement. It may even make things worse. This is the conundrum posed by the theory of second best. In this particular case, letting prices rise to market levels while land is still collectively owned by communes may not be enough to give farmers the incentive to work the land more efficiently. More damagingly, abolishing state quotas in grains undermines the government's revenues, requiring either a sharp cut in spending or inflationary finance.

An economist with a first-best mindset would say, "No problem, I can fix all of that for you. First, we need to privatize land alongside freeing up markets. We also need to implement a modern tax system. Since food prices will rise in the cities, we need state enterprises to be able to set their own wages and prices. To ensure competition, we will need to free up imports. Some state enterprises might then have to shut down, but we can establish unemployment insurance and a good financial system to provide credit for industrial upgrading. Alongside all this, of course, we need legal reform to ensure private contracts are enforced. In other words, wholesale reform can ensure that the process is not undercut by complications from the unreformed parts of the economic system."

An economist with a second-best mindset would find this answer impractical and unsatisfying. The first-best approach presumes not only the ability to undertake all these reforms simultaneously but also a certain degree of omniscience in foreseeing all possible complications beforehand. Instead, the second-best economist would look for pragmatic shortcuts that preserve the naive analyst's insight—start from big problems first and deal with others later—and that minimize adverse effects elsewhere. These often take the form of unorthodox policies that depart from conventional wisdom but have the virtue of being well adapted to context.

That is indeed what the Chinese reformers did to achieve their phenomenal success. They did start in agriculture, but with policies that would not be on any Western economist's list of recommendations. Instead of privatizing land, which would conflict with the Communist Party's ideology, they gave farmers long-term leases—which was just as good. And instead of abolishing state quotas, they instituted a dual-track regime that allowed farmers to sell any of their excess grain production, beyond the state quota, in free markets. Together, these reforms would mimic a market-based incentive system in agriculture, though without private ownership and without undercutting government revenues. It was a nearly perfect second-best solution, though of course it emerged not from economics textbooks but from practical experience and pragmatism. This was a recipe that would be followed in other domains of reform. Private investment outside agriculture was fostered through township and village enterprises (TVEs), which had the backing of local governments and hence did not need to rely on well-functioning courts to protect entrepreneurs from expropriation. Opening up to the world economy happened through special economic zones, which did not undercut employment in state enterprises serving the home market.

Dealing with the challenges at the heart of this book requires a similar frame of mind—less obsessed with ideal policies and more willing to look for pragmatic solutions that respect political realities and the world as is. We might wish for a global carbon tax, but in its absence, we will need to lean more heavily on green subsidies shaped by national logics. We might wish that free markets would generate a sufficient number of good jobs, but when they don't, governments need to engage in interventions that will often look messy. We might wish that investments in education and good governance would produce economic growth and poverty reduction, but since they are generally not adequate, developing countries need deliberate strategies to accelerate structural change. We might wish all governments find it in their interests to pursue free trade, but they don't, and we need a global order that recognizes (and accommodates) the tensions that result. "The world is second best, at best," as the Princeton economist Avinash Dixit once said.

Policy experimentation over fixed remedies

In the throes of the Great Depression in 1932, Franklin D. Roosevelt called for "bold, persistent experimentation." "It is common sense to take a method and try it: If it fails, admit it frankly and try another. But above all, try something."[18] It was an approach that would receive encouragement from the greatest economist at the time, John Maynard Keynes. Keynes praised FDR in an open letter for "feeling your way by trial and error." "You are the only one who sees the necessity of a profound change of methods and is attempting it without intolerance, tyranny or destruction."[19] Not all of FDR's experiments worked (or survived Supreme Court scrutiny), but the end product was the New Deal, a significant revamping of the American economy that enhanced economic security for ordinary Americans and helped end the Great Depression. Many years later, the great political economist Albert O. Hirschman advocated similar ideas for developing countries, emphasizing the importance of flexibility and tinkering over accepted doctrine in achieving progress.[20]

The experimental spirit clashes with orthodoxy, conventional wisdom, and established ways of doing things. In the same letter to FDR, Keynes mocked "the average City man" who "believes that you are engaged on a hare-brained expedition" and hopes "[you will] return to the old ways." It is not just financiers who abhor departures from convention. Economists, technocrats, and policy experts tend to be enamored of "best practices"—policy designs that supposedly are proven and work everywhere and at all times regardless of context.

"Stabilize, privatize, liberalize" were the universal policy commandments of the Washington Consensus, the guidebook that shaped policy reforms around the world after the 1980s.[21] Never mind that China (as we have just seen) and other East Asian miracle countries paid little heed to it and charted their own paths to growth. Many commentators try to fit these countries into the conventional mold, claiming that their success was rooted in the orthodoxy of their policies instead of the heterodoxy. They highlight their turn toward markets and denigrate their extensive and custom-made state interventions and industrial policies. But such arguments do not ring true as they do grave injustice to the evidence. Had these countries turned out to be abject failures instead of stupendous successes, one can be sure that these same experts would lay the fault at the feet of their departures from the Washington Consensus.

A predilection for policy experimentation does not mean anything goes. Along with a willingness to try new things, it requires recognition that some of the experiments will necessarily fail. If you want to increase your success rate, you must double your failure rate, as former IBM CEO Thomas J. Watson once said. A corollary is the need for feedback loops and policy flexibility: initiatives that do not seem to be working must be scaled back, while those that pay off must be expanded. In democracies, where failures are fodder for the political opposition, "experimentation" does not always have an appealing ring for politicians. It seems more suitable for authoritarian regimes, such as China, or during extraordinary times, such as the Great Depression. However, as Charles Sabel of Columbia University has pointed out, experimentalist practices are quite common in democracies. They are used in a variety of settings, from the promotion of frontier technologies in the US to the regulation of water quality in the European Union.[22] We see them at work in a variety of initiatives tackling good jobs, the green transition, and economic growth around the world. This is the productivist approach that I discuss at greater length in chapter 6.

Experimentalist governance is a response to the extreme uncertainty that prevails when rapidly changing circumstances make existing remedies unreliable or technological trajectories remain inherently unpredictable. In such circumstances, policy makers can articulate neither clear policies nor even specific policy targets ex ante ("reduce emissions by x percent by the year 2030"). Policy objectives and instruments must be developed iteratively and in cooperation with the principal stakeholders, such as firms, innovators, and labor unions. The quality of this process of strategic collaboration ultimately matters more than the constellation of specific policies or regulations at any point in time. Along with his coauthors,

Charles Sabel has developed a useful framework for thinking about such experimentation. I draw on it in later chapters as I discuss green industrial policies, promotion of good jobs, and fostering services-led economic development.[23]

The primacy of the national over the international

A cartoon I saw once depicts a large international gathering preparing to get started, with delegates from all around the world. At the back of the hall are a long line of translators' booths, labeled "English to French," "Spanish to English," "English to Arabic," and so on. One of the delegates is asking another, "What's holding up the meeting?" "We are missing one translator" comes the answer. Indeed, one of the booths remains empty. The sign on it reads: "Promise to Action."

It is a common refrain. In our interconnected world, what one country does affects everybody else. And if our problems are global, so necessarily are their solutions. "Virtually every problem destabilizing the world in this plastic moment is global in nature and can be confronted only with a coalition that is global," wrote Thomas Friedman in 2019. "Global cooperation is our only hope to recover from the COVID-19 pandemic," wrote Erna Solberg and Hugh Evans in 2021.[24] Climate change, pandemics, financial crises, global poverty—all of these seem to require individual nations to come together to reach agreement. But as the cartoon pithily captures, the real world has thrown out one disappointment over another for those who look for global cooperation to address such problems.

It is virtually impossible to read a book on economics that does not bemoan the lack of international cooperation and call for more of it. This book is a bit different. My predilection is for action at the local and national levels. I do not deny the world would be a better place if we had stronger global governance that tackled common problems in a fair manner. But the search for global cooperation often distracts us from the real problems, which are failures of domestic governance and not failures of global governance. It also blinds us to the advantages of second-best arrangements that fall short of global agreements that are nonetheless often better suited to a world that is politically divided. Those arrangements typically entail local and national arrangements instead of international coordination. This book looks for solutions in the world we have, rather than the one we wished we had.

First, a dose of realism. It is safe to say that the missing translator will not show up soon. Nations rarely prioritize international agreements over their own domestic social, economic, and security agendas. The pandemic, rising geopolitical tensions, and the legacy of hyperglobalization itself have shifted the pendulum further in the same direction. The Biden administration expressed its commitment to a "foreign policy for the middle class," which signaled its explicit intention to put national economic interests ahead of international cooperation. President Donald Trump has been openly hostile to international rules and norms and will likely make the US more isolationist. China plays a greater role today in international institutions. But its global efforts focus on bringing these institutions' practices closer to China's preferences, in areas ranging from international debt to human rights, while preserving its own ability to act autonomously. Don't expect the US, China, or any other nation for that matter to set aside their own interests to shoulder the burden of global cooperation.

In a sense, this is perhaps how it should be. All policies are an outcome of politics, and international governance is neither democratic nor accountable in the conventional sense of these terms. The institutions of well-ordered polities that we are familiar with in democracies—citizenship, elections, legislative bodies, political parties, constitutions, enforceable legal orders—are conspicuous by their absence at the international level. These are replaced by a long chain of delegation that connects national deliberative institutions to their international representatives. Even the European Union, with its elected parliament, has not managed to create a true European politics that competes in any meaningful way with national politics. Policy is made in Brussels, but politics mostly plays out in national capitals.[25]

This creates two disadvantages for global governance. The first is lack of legitimacy, as decisions that are made in international forums can seem remote from ordinary people's preoccupations and preferences. That is the reason why the slogan "Take back control" resonated so strongly with the British electorate that voted in favor of Brexit in 2016. It is also the reason why the World Trade Organization receives little public support in rich countries despite strong support for international trade in general.[26] In practice, this distance from national capitals has enabled a small number of powerful lobbies from the advanced economies, such as international banks and large corporations, to exert outsized influence on the agenda of the international trade regime and the trade agreements that have emerged.[27]

The second problem is power politics. The absence of anything resembling democracy and accountability to the broader public in the global arena implies that any enforceable international agreement reflects the interests of the powerful countries—or their lobbies—and overlooks the interests of the weaker, poorer nations. Global institutions that matter, such as the World Bank, the IMF, and the UN Security Council, are those where rich countries exercise disproportionate power, while institutions where poor nations have an equal vote, such as most UN specialized agencies, carry little weight in world affairs. The only meaningful exception to this generalization is the WTO, which has been undone by its legitimacy deficit.[28] The consequence is that, when we do get global agreement, the terms tend to be heavily biased to favor major powers. A recent example is the multilateral treaty that establishes a global minimum tax rate of 15 percent on large corporations. It provides limited gains to developing countries while restricting their ability to tax digital services.[29]

All of this would be quite depressing if global cooperation were in fact the only way we could achieve our goals. Luckily, this is not the case in most instances. Open trade, macroeconomic stability, financial prudence, technological innovation, supply chain resilience, sound public health, social cohesion, and clean air are all objectives that national governments should pursue for their own narrow self-interest. And in so doing, they contribute to a healthy global economy as well. Economics teaches that the purpose of freeing up trade is to enlarge the economic pie *at home*, by allowing the forces of comparative advantage to shift domestic resources to more productive uses. The goal is not to help other nations, though they too benefit. In economic policy, virtue is generally its own reward.

There are areas where countries can push for their national advantage at the expense of other nations. These are called "beggar-thy-neighbor" policies. But as I discuss in chapter 7, such instances are much less common than conventional wisdom allows. Most trade disputes concern different types of polices. For example, trade partners may object to the industrial policies of a nation, complaining about their loss of market share. But if these industrial policies are appropriately targeted on learning spillovers and other economically sensible rationales, the world benefits as a whole from their use. China's trade and industrial policies have been much derided by Western nations. But to the extent that these policies contributed to the growth of the Chinese economy, they did the rest of the world a service by offering a larger market for their exporters and investors. Even in the case of global public goods, such as fighting climate change, it is possible to see a role for national action that benefits the world, as I have discussed previously.

To be clear, I am not saying that countries always do the right things for themselves. Democracies do not always serve their electorates well, and authoritarian systems have many other problems on top. Policy is too often captured by special interests, overwhelmed by short-termism, and inadequately informed by technical expertise. But these are all failures of domestic governance rather than global governance. There is no reliable way in which they can be fixed by transferring policy-making powers to international arrangements, which have their own capture problems and lack democratic legitimacy, as discussed earlier. The solution lies in fixing our political malfunction at home, where democracy provides—at least in principle—the mechanisms of self-correction.[30]

A new global order

A focus on the national does not imply global anarchy and disorder. In fact, one of my theses is that a better and more sustainable international order becomes more likely when we rein in our ambitions for global governance and leave national authorities more room to pursue their economic, social, and environmental agendas.

The model of globalization that emerged in the 1990s—what I have called *hyperglobalization*—was unsustainable.[31] It was eventually undermined by distributional struggles, the new emphasis on resilience, and the rise of geopolitical competition between the US and China. Inevitably, we are in the midst of a rebalancing between the demands of the global economy and competing economic, social, and political obligations at home. While many worry about a new era of rising protectionism and the prospects of an inhospitable global environment, the outcome need not be all bad. During the Bretton Woods period, national economic management was significantly less restrained by global rules and the demands of global markets. Yet international trade and long-term investment rose significantly, and those countries that pursued appropriate economic strategies, such as the East Asian tigers, did exceptionally well despite higher levels of protection in advanced-country markets.

A similar outcome is possible today, too, provided the major powers do not prioritize geopolitics to such an extent that they start to view the global economy from a purely zero-sum lens. Economics has been tarred by the excesses of neoliberalism, but it does have a constructive role to play. Instead of expressing nostalgia for a bygone era that produced mixed results and was never sustainable in the first place, we can use economic principles to design a new set of rules for the global economy that assist in the rebalancing. As I show in chapter 7, these principles can help develop new arrangements that clarify the distinction between domains where global cooperation is necessary and domains where national action should take priority. In particular, we can help craft policies for governments to attend to their domestic economic, social, and environmental agendas while avoiding explicitly beggar-thy-neighbor policies. A useful starting point is the trade-off between the gains from trade and the gains from national institutional diversity. Maximizing one undermines the other. In economics, corner solutions are rarely optimal. How these contending objectives should be balanced in trade, finance, or the digital economy is a challenging question on which economics has much to say.

Beyond economic principles, much depends on the future evolution of geopolitical competition between the US and China, which will be the primary force shaping the world economy. If the US and China are to make a positive contribution to addressing the triple challenge, they will have to devise new rules to govern their relationship. A first step is for each side to recognize that their conflict arises as much from their increasing similarity as from their differences. America's relative power decline has made it feel more insecure, prompting economic and national security policies that are reminiscent of China's own decades-long strategy of prioritizing national economic strength and renewal ahead of the requirements of an open, "liberal" global economy. Paradoxically, as the US emulates strategies that served China quite well, the strains in the bilateral relationship multiply. Neither side seems to be aware of the irony: the US has taken a page from the Chinese playbook, while US departures from the "liberal order" should be readily recognizable to Chinese policy makers from their own practices.

A second important step is to engage in greater transparency and better communication about the objectives of policies. In an interdependent global economy, it is inevitable that many policies that target national economic well-being and domestic social/environmental priorities will have some undesirable side effects on other nations. When nations engage in industrial policies to fix important market failures, their trade partners must be permissive and understanding. Such policies have to be distinguished from those that are explicitly beggar-thy-neighbor—that is, those that generate benefits at home *because* of the harms they produce for other nations.

Third, it is important to ensure that restrictive national security policies are well targeted. The Biden administration characterized its trade and investment sanctions against China as "carefully tailored" measures on "a narrow slice" of advanced technologies that raise "straightforward" national security concerns.[32] These self-professed limitations are praiseworthy. But there remain the questions of whether the actual policy on semiconductors and elsewhere fits this description, and what new policies in other advanced technologies will look like. President Trump has thrown any semblance of self-restraint to the wind. The US has a tendency to define its national security in overly expansive terms, with nothing short of continued global primacy sufficing.

In future years, the US is set to engage in policies that look out for its own economic, social, environmental, and national security concerns first. China will not give up on its own state-driven economic model and will try to adapt to the new constraints it faces. Neither will be predisposed to abide by external rules that are perceived not to serve their interests well. Cooperation will not be the order of the day. But it may become just a tad easier if both countries recognize that their respective pursuit of domestic economic, environmental, and security goals need not be harmful to each other. The passing of hyperglobalization should not be resisted or mourned.

The road ahead

We have a unique opportunity to right the wrongs of hyperglobalization and establish a better international order based on a vision of shared prosperity. The future of the world economy will depend on how we respond to three distinct, but interlinked challenges. First, how do we mitigate and manage climate change? Second, how do we rebuild the middle class? Third, how do we reduce global poverty? I hope to show in greater detail in the pages ahead that it is possible to make progress on these problems, but only if we reorient our mental frames and are willing to experiment with new policies. The germs of these new policies already exist. We do not need to go far to find initiatives that work, though such examples remain limited in scope and acceptance thus far.

In the next chapter, I review why the economic policies that prevailed since the late 1980s—known variously as the Washington Consensus, neoliberalism, hyperglobalization, and market fundamentalism—were unsustainable, contributed to widening economic, social, cultural, and political cleavages within societies, and created blind spots (with respect to climate change and public health in particular). While this period experienced significant poverty reduction, I argue that the countries that had the best economic growth record (such as China) were in fact the ones that violated the rules of neoliberalism and marched to their own drummers.

In chapter 3, I focus on the climate change challenge. In contrast to conventional accounts that stress global cooperation around carbon pricing or cap-and-trade, this chapter argues that a collection of local, national, and regional policies, driven by domestic political bargains, is more likely to achieve a rapid green transition. Chief among these are green industrial policies, where China has led the way. I discuss how these policies help, why they can be the foundation for more ambitious programs of decarbonization, and what needs to be done to ensure poor countries are not left out in the cold.

In chapter 4, I turn to the challenge of restoring the middle class. The traditional approach to creating inclusive economies combines full employment policies, investment in education, and social insurance. I argue that this approach is inadequate when there is a "structural" shortage of good jobs as a result of new technologies and new modes of market competition. This necessitates government policies directly targeting the demand side of labor markets, incentivizing firms to create more good jobs, and reorienting innovation in a direction that augments and complements the existing skills of the workforce instead of replacing them.

Chapter 5 focuses on developing economies. As the experience of China and East Asia more broadly has shown, economic growth is the most potent engine for poverty reduction, and export-oriented industrialization has been the most effective strategy for delivering it. In this chapter, I argue that this strategy no longer works, in large part because of technological changes that have reduced the importance of labor costs. Services will have to be at the core of poor countries' growth strategies, requiring governments to provide a range of productivity-enhancing inputs to their service firms, such as management and workforce training, technology and market assistance, specialized infrastructure, and coordination.

A common thread running through the policy agenda of chapters 2–5 is an emphasis on "productivist" policies, or industrial policies, to use the traditional but increasingly outmoded label: explicit government programs designed to alter the structure of economies, by orienting firms' investment, innovation, and employment decisions. In chapter 6, I focus on the question of whether these types of policies can actually work. There is considerable skepticism among economists about their efficacy. I argue that recent (and better) evidence points to a more positive evaluation. However, the practice of these policies must change in light of new imperatives—the focus on green sectors and on services, in particular—and what we have learned from the rich experience with industrial policies around the world.

Chapter 7 discusses new rules for a thinner, but more sustainable form of globalization. The debate on globalization has become stuck on the unproductive question of whether we should have more or less globalization. The more important question is what kind of globalization we want. I show that it is possible to construct a thinner globalization (less ambitious than what hyperglobalization aimed to achieve) that still preserves the bulk of the gains from trade, while also allowing individual nations the policy space they need to achieve the goals discussed previously. Such a globalization has to be designed and implemented against the background of what could be intense geopolitical competition between the US and China. If these two powers approach the world economy as a zero-sum game of weaponized interdependence, the climate, middle-class, and development goals discussed in this book will become harder to achieve—and neither nation will be more secure. I offer a framework that might moderate conflict between the major powers, provide them with the space to pursue their distinct national security and economic imperatives, and encourage cooperation for mutual benefit.

If the ideas in this book are successful, they will also serve to forestall the dangerous rise of the far right around the world. I conclude in chapter 8 by pulling together the main themes of the book and sketching the implications for a renewed progressive agenda.

2

The Failures of Hyperglobalization

"I hear people say we have to stop and debate globalization," exclaimed an irritated Tony Blair, the British prime minister. "You might as well debate whether autumn should follow summer."[1]

It was September 2005 and it had been another year of militant protests against the global economic order. As international trade, investment, and finance picked up speed, the antiglobalization movement seemed to follow suit. The World Trade Organization's ministerial meetings in Seattle in 1999 had been met by combative demonstrators ranging from labor and environmental advocates to anarchists. Similar protests were now commonplace whenever leaders of the rich economies got together. The movement seemed to reach a new peak in 2005, when thousands of activists gathered in Gleneagles, Scotland, during the G8 meetings in July to demonstrate against what they called "corporate globalization."

Blair's response to the antiglobalizers was to tell them, essentially, that they were tilting at windmills. Globalization was not up for debate. It was an unstoppable force, out of anyone's control. You either went along or were doomed to be left behind. This sense of inevitability and powerlessness was a common thread running through statesmen's views on globalization at the time. "Globalization," US president Bill Clinton would say, "is the economic equiva-

lent of a force of nature, like wind or water."[2] Note again the physical metaphor signaling the futility, indeed folly, of human efforts to
redirect the phenomenon. Lionel Jospin, France's socialist prime
minister between 1997 and 2002, sounded similarly resigned: "The
question is no longer whether we want or do not want globalization.
It is a fact."[3]

These statements sound remarkably naive in hindsight. What had
emerged after the 1990s was a particular variant of globalization. It
rested on shaky foundations and was unsustainable, as its unraveling
in recent years has amply shown. It deserves its own name, and I
have called it *hyperglobalization* to distinguish it from historical pre-
cedents and future variants.[4] In this chapter, I discuss the peculiari-
ties of hyperglobalization and the reasons for its fragility, viewing it
in the historical context of alternative economic policy paradigms.

But first let's note another striking point about these quotes: they
all come from political leaders who were left of center. When Blair
mocked antiglobalization protestors for defying the laws of nature,
he was addressing not a group of businesspeople or investors but
trade union delegates and the Labour Party's own rank and file. We
normally think of the left as speaking for workers, the environment,
and other causes overlooked by unfettered capitalism, while holding large international firms and financiers to account. Blair, Clinton, and Jospin (or for that matter the social democrat Gerhard
Schröder, who pursued a similar line in Germany) were certainly
not right-wing libertarians who worshipped markets. Yet far from
challenging the prevailing globalization regime, they came to fully
embrace it, along with most other left-of-center leaders in the Western world. These leaders had apparently all drunk the Kool-Aid on
globalization's immutability and irreversibility.

As the historian Gary Gerstle points out, we know an economic
paradigm has become truly hegemonic when its putative opponents fully buy into it.[5] Milton Friedman famously said, "We are all
Keynesians now" in the mid-1960s, and the sentiment was echoed
by Richard Nixon in 1971.[6] Just like the Keynesian consensus of the
1960s, the hyperglobalization consensus of the 2000s set the terms
of the debate for both sides of the political aisle.

Policy paradigms and economics

Hyperglobalization is a close cousin of what has come to be called neoliberalism or market fundamentalism. Neoliberalism itself is a contested term, and it is used mostly by its critics rather than supporters.[7] But the predispositions it captures are real and have shaped the policy landscape of our era: a preference for free markets over government intervention, economic incentives over social or cultural norms, and private entrepreneurship over collective or community action. The term is often used as a shortcut for deregulation, liberalization, privatization, or fiscal austerity. Hyperglobalization is the logical extension of neoliberalism onto the global stage.

No matter what label we put on them, paradigms are an indispensable element of economic policy making. They are "meta frameworks" that are rarely articulated or tested explicitly yet provide a general orientation for policy, by shaping how we think about the economy and its relation to society and the polity. In the language of contemporary economics, paradigms rely on a set of "maintained assumptions" about the nature and prevalence of market failures, governments' capabilities and intentions, possibilities of collective action, and binding constraints on economic prosperity. They also embody an implicit prioritization among values that may be in tension with each other, such as efficiency versus equity, risk taking versus stability, personal freedom versus social cohesion. A short list of economic policy paradigms that have ruled elites' minds since the eighteenth century would include mercantilism, classical liberalism, Keynesianism, the welfare state, market socialism, developmentalism, and of course neoliberalism.

Economic policy needs paradigms because economics itself rarely ever provides clear and universal guidance on what to do. This may seem a surprising statement in our day since economists often seem united in their policy prescriptions—in favor of freer markets, freer trade, and less government intervention. Indeed, many prominent economists played a role in laying down the policy anchors of the neoliberal age. But this was despite, rather than because of, their profession's teachings.[8] In reality, and as anyone who has progressed beyond Economics 101 knows, economic "science" is remarkably open ended. Depending on how the analyst specifies the goals of policy, the structure of the economy, and the real-world constraints that determine feasible remedies, policy prescriptions in economics can vary from laissez-faire to state planning and anything in between. The only universal answer in economics is, "It depends"!

What makes economics different from the natural sciences is that its raw material, economic relations, is entirely human-made and hence malleable to a degree that our natural environment is not. What works in one setting will not work in another. Economists' main tools of the trade are models, which are highly simplified, typically mathematical frameworks that clarify cause-and-effect relations in particular contexts. ("Economists do it with models" goes the old and politically incorrect joke.) Different assumptions about the setting will produce different, often diametrically opposite conclusions.

For example, in a model where employers behave perfectly competitively—meaning they have no power individually to determine wages—a government-set minimum wage will reduce employment. This is typically what students learn in an introductory economics course. But in a model where employers have some market power in determining wages, a minimum wage will *raise* employment (as long as it is not set too high).

Or consider another question that readers may think is well settled: Does freer trade enlarge a nation's economic pie? Leaving aside complications having to do with income distribution or noneconomic consequences of trade, it seems like an economist's answer would be straightforward (and affirmative). Not so fast. Graduate students in economics are exposed to a variety of models, with wrinkles such as increasing returns to scale or technological spillovers, where in fact the answer could well be negative. Again, different models, different results.

As usual, Keynes put it best when he defined economics as the "science of thinking in terms of models joined to the art of choosing models which are relevant to the contemporary world."[9] Economists tend to be quite good at the science part, but not so good with the art part. They will often focus on models that are appealing because of their mathematical properties or consistency with a priori reasoning, even when these models miss critical aspects of reality and risk being misleading. Or they will stick with old models for far too long even when their usefulness has been thrown in doubt. But for all its faults, economics is never short of new, creative answers to policy questions. As another economist ruefully remarked more than fifty years ago, "By now any bright graduate student, by choosing his assumptions . . . carefully, can produce a consistent model yielding just about any policy recommendation he favored at the start."[10]

In the presence of such an embarrassment of riches, paradigms are like cognitive maps for policy makers. They convert rough, uncharted terrain into a well-labeled street map. Some possible pathways are closed off, others are circuitous or full of potholes, while yet others appear as inviting five-lane highways. Each paradigm offers a different map, with old roads crossed out and a multitude of new roads added in. Once policy makers adopt one of these maps—internalize the rules of a paradigm—their behavior is shaped by the constraints of the cognitive map as much as the realities of the world. Indeed, hyperglobalization was sustained less by international rules or treaties, which have little enforcement power in any case, than by policy makers' views about the necessity to act in particular ways. (Recall the quotes at the beginning of this chapter.)

Policy paradigms in history

New economic ideas ("models") play a role in the emergence of policy paradigms. But so do shifts in the balance of political power. Probably the most radical shift in economic thought in history came with the publication of Adam Smith's 1776 book, *Wealth of Nations*. Smith presented a compelling argument in favor of free markets and competition, and his ideas ushered in the age of classical liberalism. But the book's hold on the public imagination cannot be ascribed solely to the power of Smith's ideas. It helped that the new free market paradigm was aligned with the interests of an emerging commercial and industrial elite that wanted to break the power of landlords and established monopolists. Smith's ideas had less impact where it conflicted with those interests, as in his criticisms of the East India Company (a state-chartered monopoly) or his arguments against colonial expansion and imperialism.

Smith took aim at the dominant economic paradigm of his time: mercantilism. Under mercantilism, the purpose of economic policy was to maximize the amount of gold in the sovereign's coffers. This required as large a trade surplus as possible, with imports limited only to essential commodities not produced at home. Economic life was regimented and heavily regulated by crafts, guilds, and state-sanctioned monopolies. In the Smithian vision, by contrast, the purpose of economic policy was to maximize the consumption possibilities of the population, and the best instrument for achieving this was unchecked competition among firms. Free markets and private entrepreneurship comprised the engine that drove prosperity; monopoly power was the enemy. While the state had a role, it was limited to national defense, protection of private property rights, and the administration of justice. Smith's views on markets and the government were considerably more nuanced than subsequent renditions. But they inspired the classical liberal paradigm that became victorious in Britain and other front-runners of the Industrial Revolution, where free trade helped reinforce their head start. The liberal paradigm is less dominant today but survives in contemporary libertarianism and its aversion to government regulations and intervention in markets.

Elsewhere, skepticism about markets and competition survived. Especially in peripheral regions that were being left behind, classical liberalism was often perceived to reinforce economic backwardness rather than alleviate it. Accordingly, the Smithian vision has always coexisted in economics with an alternative paradigm that emphasizes the role of the state in fostering economic and technological catch-up with the leaders of the day. This paradigm, which we might call developmentalism, was a descendant of mercantilism as it was suspicious of free markets and often promoted import barriers. But it came in different variants. America's first secretary of the treasury, Alexander Hamilton, and the German-born Friedrich List were among the earliest to stress the importance of protecting "infant industries" to close the gap with Britain and other advanced economies. Their ideas were picked up by Latin American economic theorists in the twentieth century to formulate the economic development strategy of import-substituting industrialization (ISI). East Asian policy makers put their own twist on developmentalism after the late 1950s, by combining a heavy dose of industrial promotion policies with export orientation.

Paradigm shifts are often also the result of major shocks in economic circumstances that reveal significant shortcomings in the prevailing vision. The momentous event that ultimately undid classical liberalism in the advanced economies was the Great Depression. Skyrocketing unemployment and social unrest during the 1930s, unleashing radical political reactions in the form of fascism and communism, showed that markets left to their own devices could wreak great havoc. Furthermore, it appeared obvious that the massive challenge of economic reconstruction following World War II needed a strong government hand to mobilize and guide investment. Markets could not be trusted to self-regulate and self-stabilize. They needed to be embedded in a wide range of nonmarket institutions maintained by the state. The ensuing reforms reflected the emergence of a new Keynesian-welfare-state paradigm, which would orient the practice of economic policy until the late 1970s.

Keynes of course was the intellectual father of the idea that governments had to manage aggregate demand through fiscal spending to ensure full employment and full capacity utilization. His views helped shape Franklin D. Roosevelt's New Deal during the mid-1930s, which launched large-scale public investments in infrastructure as well as new government programs to provide safety nets and social insurance. In Europe, government initiatives went further, especially in the immediate aftermath of World War II, with the creation of what came to be called the welfare state. The state was now charged with ensuring access to adequate health and education for all, as well as providing social insurance against unemployment, old age, disability, and poverty. Public ownership of basic industries went hand in hand with the expansion of the welfare state in many countries, including Britain, Italy, and Sweden.[11]

Bretton Woods: A different globalization

The Keynesian-welfare-state paradigm's extension to the global stage took the form of the Bretton Woods regime, named after the New Hampshire resort where the delegates from the victorious powers established the basic rules of the postwar international economic order. The regime sought economic recovery and the revival of international trade and long-term investment, which had been badly scarred by the war and the crises of the interwar period.

Keynes, who represented Britain, once again put his mark on the arrangements. He was keen to ensure that governments had ample space to resort to monetary and fiscal policies to regulate the macro-economy and achieve full employment, without being overwhelmed by short-term capital flows that could be fickle and destabilizing. He recognized that domestic publics were much less likely to put up with the demands of financial markets in an age where they had acquired a stronger voice through labor unions, democratic franchise, political parties, and the mass media. Therefore, a key decision taken at Bretton Woods was the enshrinement of capital controls as a central feature of the postwar architecture. Moreover, while exchange rates were to remain fixed during ordinary times, countries were given the flexibility to adjust them in case of "fundamental disequilibrium." The principle was clear: when the demands of the domestic economy clashed with the requirements of external openness, the latter would have to give way.

This was in sharp contrast with the gold standard, the global regime that had prevailed through the interwar period. The gold standard was based on the classical liberalism model, presuming a self-adjusting economy that performs best when the government does the least. Countries on the gold standard allowed money and finance to move freely in and out of the country, which meant that their interest rates and credit conditions were determined by global financiers' and speculators' decisions. The value of their currencies was fixed irrevocably against gold, depriving them of a valuable means of adjustment to internal or external shocks. By the assumptions of the classical liberal model, this ought not have been costly.

Wage and price flexibility—the forces of market competition—should have ensured a quick return to equilibrium.

Time and again, though, things would turn out differently. Countries losing gold would experience tight credit, bankruptcies, job losses, and often a political backlash against the global economy. It was one of those episodes that gave rise in the late nineteenth century to the first self-consciously populist movement in the Western world, the People's Party in the US. "You shall not crucify mankind upon a cross of gold" were the immortal words of its leading spokesman, William Jennings Bryan. It remains a stirring cri de coeur against the tyranny of the world economy over the social order. Keynes was determined to avoid this conflict by prioritizing domestic economic management and providing policy makers with a shield, in the form of capital controls, to conduct it in unencumbered fashion.

The specific rules governing international trade during the early postwar decades were equally permissive. These emerged more gradually under the auspices of the General Agreement on Tariffs and Trade (GATT), whereby countries engaged in a series of multilateral negotiations to eliminate quantitative restrictions and reduce import tariffs. There was considerable trade liberalization in the advanced nations over the next four decades, with quotas largely removed on manufactured goods and average tariffs slashed to less than a third of their wartime levels.[12] However, from the standpoint of the subsequent hyperglobalization regime, the early postwar liberalization experience stands out more for its lack of ambition than for its reach. The text of the GATT in 1947 made it clear that the goal of the trade regime was mainly to support domestic economic objectives, such as raising living standards and ensuring full employment. Increasing the volume of trade itself ("exchange of goods") is mentioned in the preamble at the very end of a long list of desiderata, almost as an afterthought. In the hyperglobalization era, by contrast, trade agreements would put the elimination of barriers to free trade front and center.

Accordingly, economic integration among nations remained limited during the Bretton Woods–GATT era. Trade restrictions in agricultural products and services were largely untouched. Developing countries benefited from loopholes that permitted them to pursue whatever trade policies they wished. Domestic policies, such as subsidies or investment regulations, were similarly left outside of the negotiations, which covered only explicit import barriers at the border. The GATT's dispute settlement mechanism was very weak, unlike the subsequent version in the WTO, allowing any single country to veto decisions.

Moreover, when imports surged, the system allowed countries to easily reimpose barriers, either using antidumping or safeguard measures or through informal arrangements with exporter nations. Such arrangements were used in advanced economies in the 1970s to moderate the labor market effects of the boom in textiles and garments from newly industrializing countries. They were also prominent during the 1980s when the US and European nations negotiated so-called voluntary export restrictions (VERs) with Japan in autos and steel. Many economists at the time considered these restrictions as derogations from the free trade spirit of the GATT and lamented the rise of what they called "the new protectionism." Yet this was a misreading of the nature of the Bretton Woods–GATT system. As in the case of the international monetary regime, the trade regime was built on the idea that the world economy was to serve national economic goals, not the other way around.[13]

This leaves us with an apparent paradox. The Bretton Woods regime put few fetters on domestic policy makers' ability to manage cross-border economic flows, yet it produced a phenomenal increase in the volume of international trade and long-term foreign investment. The world economy not only recovered, it expanded more rapidly than it ever had. The best way to unravel the paradox is to invert a statement made by Christine Lagarde, then managing director of the IMF, on the seventy-fifth anniversary of the Bretton Woods meeting. "Bretton Woods launched a new era of global economic cooperation," she wrote, "in which countries helped themselves by helping each other."[14] The reality was closer to the opposite. Countries helped each other by helping themselves first. The best gift that a country can give to other nations' well-being is to have a prosperous economy and cohesive society. The Bretton Woods regime provided the space in which the Keynesian-welfare-state paradigm, as long as it worked, helped governments do just that.

We cannot return to the postwar paradigm, despite its success, because technologies and global markets are no longer the same, and we are confronted with different challenges today. Nevertheless, the experience with the Keynesian-welfare-state paradigm and the accompanying Bretton Woods regime holds important lessons for the design of a new global order, which I pick up later in the book.

Hyperglobalization follies

No policy paradigm lasts forever. New ideas, new vested interests, and new problems overtake prevailing economic narratives. By the 1980s, the Keynesian consensus had unraveled, due to a confluence of developments. The 1970s hike in oil prices presented a different kind of challenge to policy makers—a supply-side shock that produced both inflation and unemployment—which Keynesian aggregate-demand management could not address. Many developing countries handled the oil price shocks poorly as well, and their growth was derailed. The 1980s debt crises in Latin America and elsewhere convinced many policy makers that the prevailing development strategy—inward-looking and based on import substitution—needed an overhaul. Meanwhile, economists had become an influential intellectual lobby for freer markets. They had been documenting since the 1970s the inefficiencies of high marginal tax rates, excessive levels of trade protection, and overextended states.

The postwar paradigm was a victim of its own success as well. The boom in world trade and finance created a new set of powerful interests—exporting firms, international banks, multinational companies—pushing for global rules that favored them and provided them with greater access to foreign markets. Since trade liberalization had been so beneficial to date, would it not be better to go several steps further and push for even deeper trade integration and unrestricted capital flows?

By the 1990s, these groups' political influence, complemented by economists' arguments, would produce neoliberalism and its global expression, hyperglobalization. The GATT was replaced by the much more expansive World Trade Organization, with universal rules covering domestic policies as well as border restrictions. An ever-expanding network of trade agreements—bilateral, regional, multilateral—would ensure governments would tie their hands and live up to their "free trade" commitments. Multilateral institutions, such as the IMF and the OECD, would play a similar role for financial globalization by turning the free flow of finance into a global norm. They pushed for openness to capital flows in poor and rich countries alike.[15]

What mattered more than international rules and institutions, however, was the new vision of economic policy internalized by policy makers. The free flows of goods, firms, money, and capital across national borders would produce greater economic prosperity. Globalization was not just unstoppable; it was a powerful economic wave that would lift all nations' economic fortunes. Advances in technology and communication were pushing the world inexorably toward greater economic interdependence. Instead of resisting these forces, governments should boost them. They had to remove impediments to global commerce and finance, not only by reducing import taxes or financial restrictions at the border but ensuring their domestic regulations did not impose burdens on foreign companies or investors. "Integration into the world economy is the best way for countries to grow," noted the distinguished economist and (at the time) deputy managing director of the IMF, Stanley Fischer.[16] Deep integration, which stood in sharp contrast with the shallow integration of the Bretton Woods regime, came to be seen both as inevitable and as an overriding objective of economic policy. Hyperglobalization transformed globalization from a means for shared prosperity into an end in itself.

As the quotes at the start of this chapter reveal, leaders on the left of the political spectrum agreed with those on the right that integrating into the world economy was imperative. To the extent that there was any disagreement, it was on what needed to be done to ensure desired results. The right wanted tax reductions, deregulation, and cutting the government down to size. The left emphasized investments in education and infrastructure while strengthening social safety nets. The means might differ, but the goal was the same: to position their economy and society to become more competitive internationally.

The economists and technocrats who promoted hyperglobalization were aware of some of the potential downsides. But they maintained that these were arguments in favor of additional policies that would ameliorate the downsides rather than arguments against hyperglobalization per se. Yes, some workers who lost their jobs to imports or outsourcing would end up worse off. But the labor market disruptions would be temporary, and the workers who got displaced could be trained or compensated. Yes, openness to volatile short-term capital flows could unleash financial instability and crises. To ward off such risks, governments had to adopt disciplined macro-economic policies and adequate prudential regulation of banks and other financial intermediaries. Yes, governments may find it harder to raise taxes since large corporations are now footloose and can book their revenues in tax havens. But governments can respond by making their countries more attractive to international firms. Yes, some global trade rules might clash with domestic environmental, health and safety, or consumer regulations. But social, public health, and environmental goals were always better pursued through policy instruments that did not interfere with global commerce. In all cases, there were alternative, first-best domestic policies that did not require throwing sand in the wheels of international trade and finance.

One of the convenient consequences of this first-best mindset was that it shielded hyperglobalization and its boosters from direct criticism. When the regime produced unwanted side effects, the smug response was ready: the fault lies not with globalization but with the governments who did not do their job and failed to deliver the requisite complementary policies. Meanwhile, in the real world, hyperglobalization continued to erode the nation-state and its capacity to be responsive to the citizenry.[17]

Alternative globalizations

Even though the Keynesian paradigm and the Bretton Woods regime had become unsustainable by the late 1970s, the turn toward hyperglobalization was not preordained. The world did stand to benefit from greater international cooperation and coordination. But the political capital governments spent on negotiating trade and financial rules and pursuing international competitiveness might have been better deployed toward more critical and genuine global public goods. Human-made climate change was a growing threat that required urgent global action yet remained largely unaddressed. Warnings on the need to enact preemptive measures with regard to global pandemics and other public health challenges also went unheeded. And even if the focus remained on economics, there were other domains where market-liberalizing rules would have yielded significantly greater benefits. The barriers to the international mobility of workers were much higher and therefore much more costly to the world economy than barriers to goods or finance.[18] International arrangements that increased the number of short-term work visas for foreign workers even modestly would have yielded economic gains that were much larger than what was in store for trade or financial liberalization.[19] A global agreement could have set a floor on corporate tax rates to all nations' benefit, preventing multinational corporations from playing governments off against each other. These alternative possibilities received very little attention, while trade negotiators hammered out deals that would generate huge windfalls to large corporations at considerable cost to other segments of society.

The gold standard, the Bretton Woods regime, and hyperglobalization were each different models for the world economy. In a world where markets strive to be global while politics is national, tensions are inherent in any global economic order.[20] When policy makers went for hyperglobalization, they leaned on market integration much more heavily than the Bretton Woods regime had done, effectively mimicking aspects of the gold standard. A predictable consequence was that the tensions deepened considerably. We need to understand these contradictions so that we learn to manage them better in the future. I discuss them in the remainder of the chapter.

David Ricardo versus Alexander Hamilton

Free trade has a beautiful logic, articulated by Adam Smith and more fully four decades later by David Ricardo in his principle of comparative advantage. It says that opening an economy to international competition allocates its resources—labor, capital, entrepreneurship—to their most productive uses, maximizing overall consumption. Yet the historical reality is that no country has ever developed through free trade. Rapid and sustained economic growth is always the result of a combination of policies that leverage the world economy while intervening in markets to promote new industries. The world economy is a source of technology, capital, and markets. It would be foolhardy for countries not to take advantage of the opportunities they offer. But while markets are good at making the best of a nation's resources at any point in time, they are not very good at ensuring the development of new productive capabilities over time.[21] That was Alexander Hamilton's argument for the young American republic—hence the need for government policies that complement and, often, moderate international competition.

In brief, economic success requires a judicious mix of liberalism and developmentalism. By ignoring this lesson, hyperglobalization raised false hopes where it was applied. It also sowed the seeds of conflict with the developmentalism of successful countries.

China was both the greatest success of the hyperglobalization era and its greatest contradiction. A common misconception in the West is that China's phenomenal economic success can be chalked up to economic liberalism and hyperglobalization. After 1978, the argument goes, Chinese policy makers turned to markets and opened their economy to trade, reaping a bucketful of rewards. In any debate on globalization, you can reliably expect to hear from hyperglobalization's defenders something along the following lines: hyperglobalization may have fallen short in some respects, but it enabled hundreds of millions of poor people to lift themselves from poverty!

Yet this take on China is at best half the story. No country in fact better illustrates that markets need to be combined with developmentalism.

Consider how well the Chinese experience fits the hyperglobalization guidebook. According to hyperglobalization's rules, China was supposed to open its economy to imports and capital flows. Instead, the country continued to protect its state enterprises from import competition, allowing imports freely only in special designated zones. It also restricted capital flows in and out of the country. It was supposed to privatize its economy. Instead, it maintained significant state ownership and relied on hybrid township and village enterprises (TVEs) that were owned by local governments. It was supposed to stay away from industrial policy. Instead, its national and provincial governments engaged in a wide variety of industrial policies, channeling cheap credit to foster new firms and industries. It was supposed to allow foreign firms to operate freely, without discrimination. Instead, it imposed significant restrictions on them, requiring that they form joint ventures with Chinese firms as a condition for entry. It was supposed to respect the intellectual property rights of foreign firms. Instead, it flagrantly violated them. It was supposed to either fix its exchange rate or let it float freely. Instead, it actively managed its currency to ensure a high level of external competitiveness for its products.[22]

Chinese policy makers describe this strategy as opening the window but placing a screen on it. This way the Chinese economy would get fresh air—foreign technologies, access to global markets, critical inputs—but it would keep out harmful elements, such as destabilizing short-term capital flows, excessive competition that might harm its nascent industrial capabilities, or restrictions on the government's ability to conduct industrial policy. Effectively, China applied a mix of mercantilist and Bretton Woods rules to its management of the economy.[23] I have often joked that, had the country been a dismal underperformer instead of the remarkable success it turned out to be, hyperglobalization's boosters would have had an equally compelling explanation. Look at the heavy hand of the state! Look at all the restrictions on trade and capital flows! What do you expect with all these industrial policies?

Many other developing countries also grew rapidly in the two decades prior to the pandemic. Once again, little of this performance had to do with comparative advantage or hyperglobalization policies. Some of it was the direct by-product of China's growth, which led to a boom in commodity prices and pulled resource-producing countries along. Some of it had to do with declining interest rates in Western financial markets, which pushed cheap finance to "emerging" and "frontier" markets. In typical fashion, the result was faster consumption growth in the developing economies, followed by debt distress in subsequent years. Remarkably, none of the growth outside of East Asia was the product of export-oriented industrialization. As in India, it was led by services and largely unrelated to trade liberalization at home or in the advanced economies.[24] We return to this experience in chapter 5.

What about countries that lived by the rulebook? Perhaps they did well too? Consider Mexico. No other country embraced the agenda as wholeheartedly or was better positioned to reap its rewards. Successive governments in Mexico decided that the best way to extricate the economy from the macroeconomic crises of the 1980s and secure economic growth was to ditch policies of import substitution—which had delivered decades of high economic growth prior to the debt debacle of 1982—and open the economy to international trade and investment. The country's location on the southern border of the US was a great opportunity to join North American supply chains. The country liberalized its trade regime and capital account in the late 1980s, signed the North American Free Trade Agreement in 1992, and joined the WTO in 1995. Free trade and openness to foreign capital became its explicit and sole growth strategy. The theory was that getting rid of industrial policies would remove costly inefficiencies while a rise in exports and inward foreign investment would fuel the takeoff.

In some ways, the strategy worked as it was supposed to. Trade and investment, particularly with the US, boomed. Mexico received more than a half trillion dollars of foreign direct investment over the subsequent two decades, the export share of GDP more than tripled, and the country became one of the most open economies in the world.[25] The northern parts of the country became manufacturing hubs for the North American economy. Yet where it mattered, in terms of overall economic performance, the outcome was a big disappointment. Economic growth was one of the slowest among peer countries, income levels fell further behind its large northern neighbor, and overall productivity actually fell![26] The strategy essentially created two Mexicos: a relatively thriving one in the border regions of the north and a stagnant one elsewhere.[27] Of course, regional divergence is not uncommon in developing countries. In China, too, the coastal regions did a lot better than the interior areas. The difference in Mexico was that growth in the north was not enough to propel the rest of the economy forward and was more than offset by the poor performance everywhere else.

Where Mexico went wrong is a continuing source of debate. To some, the problem is that Mexico is still too heavily regulated and did not globalize nearly enough.[28] But the experience of China and other successful countries before it (such as Japan, Taiwan, and South Korea) suggests a different lesson. Mexico relied too much on the world economy and too little on the developmentalism that had paid good dividends in earlier decades.

Winners versus losers

"Trade benefits most, if not all people." "Even if trade creates losses for some groups, those losses are transitory and are eventually undone." "People whose jobs are adversely affected by trade will still gain because of lower prices for imported goods." Chances are you have heard some version of these arguments during debates on globalization. In fact, none of them is supported by economic analysis.[29] Serious economists would not be caught making such statements. Nevertheless, they have entered our public conversation, contributing to the complacency of hyperglobalization's winners and the lack of empathy for the losers.

Let's be clear about what economic theory says. One of the most robust predictions of economics is that openness to trade generates sharp distributional consequences. As resources reallocate across the economy in response to trade, those workers, investors, and entrepreneurs whose fortunes are linked with exporting activities gain, while those linked with import-competing sectors lose out. The identities of gainers and losers are determined by how the change in competition affects each group as well as by the contours of social stratification in society (along the lines of class, occupation, skills, education, gender, region, etc.). While consumer price declines can compensate for some workers' losses, other groups are still guaranteed to lose. Essentially, it is theoretically inconsistent to argue for significant gains from trade without recognizing that there will be both losers and winners. Distributional effects are the flip side of the gains from trade. No pain, no gain!

There is more. The magnitude of redistribution can be quite large relative to the overall increase in the size of the economic pie, especially when the prevailing trade barriers are relatively low. For example, when import tariffs are in single digits, as they have been in recent decades, our benchmark economic models—the ones we use to teach students about the benefits of comparative advantage and free trade—suggest that further trade liberalization would shuffle $5–$6 of income around society per $1 of overall expansion of the economic pie.[30] Consider what that means: it is as if we took away $5 from one person, gave $6 to another, and called the result a great advance for society!

In principle, it may be possible to compensate the losers and leave everyone better off. Imagine we tax the winner in the previous example $5.50 and transfer it to the loser. They both come out 50 cents ahead. But under hyperglobalization it is difficult to contemplate such compensation, on account of both economics and politics. The economic reason is that tax transfer schemes create their own inefficiencies. When the distributional effects are so stark, the economic costs of redistribution would likely eat away the full gains from trade, and then some![31] The political reason has to do with the relative power of the winners and losers. If the losers—less-than-college-educated workers in lagging regions—were in a position to demand and receive the requisite transfers, they likely could have blocked the trade opening in the first place. And the winners—skilled professionals and large corporations—have the political power to resist the redistribution and keep the entirety of the gains for themselves. It is not surprising that trade adjustment assistance programs (TAA) in the US have typically been underfunded and ineffective in shielding affected workers from income losses.[32]

On income distribution, the real world behaved pretty much as economic theory predicted. Hyperglobalization's distributional consequences were clearest across regions within countries. A cottage industry of empirical studies has documented the negative shocks to workers in areas particularly badly hit by NAFTA in the US and by the increase in imports from China (in both the US and Europe). One study, for example, found that a high school dropout in heavily NAFTA-impacted zones had eight percentage points slower wage growth over 1990–2000 compared with a similar worker not affected by NAFTA trade. Similarly, wage growth in the most protected industries that lost their protection after NAFTA fell seventeen percentage points relative to industries that were unprotected initially. Another study found substantial adverse effects on employment and labor force participation rates (along with wage losses) in US commuting zones hardest hit by Chinese exports.[33] These losses were far from transitory, with wage and employment effects persisting for at least a decade following the initial trade shocks.

Beyond income losses, communities that experienced factory closures in response to trade and outsourcing suffered significant psychological and social costs. Unemployment is among the worst things that can happen in one's lifetime. When workers become unemployed, they can lose self-respect, social recognition, and their mental health. Scholars estimate that the monetary equivalent of the decline in subjective well-being following a job loss is a *multiple* of the direct income loss.[34] When factories shut down, marriages break down, crime rises, addiction spreads, and suicides increase. In his groundbreaking book, *When Work Disappears*, sociologist William Julius Wilson documented the social consequences of the decline in manufacturing and blue-collar jobs for racial minorities in urban areas, including divorce, addiction, and crime.[35] Wilson's pioneering work focused on the 1960s and 1970s, but recent research has shown that the China trade shock produced similar effects. The costs of these psychological and social scars may be immeasurable in dollar terms but are substantial. They are an important additional reason why providing financial compensation to the losers from trade, even if it were feasible, wouldn't address the problem.

Wage and employment declines also had political consequences. Wherever imports hit hard, there was a turn away from centrist politicians and parties and a rise in support for nonmainstream political groups, typically right-wing populists.[36] Identity polarization was aggravated as well, deepening ethnic, racial, and cultural cleavages. In the US, the counties most adversely affected by NAFTA and Chinese imports deserted the Democratic Party in 2016 and voted for Donald Trump. It was the same in Europe, where populist parties of the right were the greatest beneficiaries of rising levels of import penetration. (Automation and fiscal austerity had similar consequences in boosting support for populists, while the effects of immigration were more mixed.) Hyperglobalization did not just exacerbate inequality; it also damaged democracy.

Institutional convergence versus diversity

Shortly after Brexit, I was speaking at a panel along with a *Financial Times* journalist. It was silly for Brexiteers to have resorted to the motto "Take back control," the journalist complained. Politicians in London had as much control as they could possibly want. The idea that Brussels imposed any constraints on Westminster was a mirage. Later the discussion turned to Britain's post-Brexit industrial strategy. The journalist was pessimistic. Nothing will stop the country from going back to its bad old ways now that Britain is out of the EU, he bemoaned— oblivious to the contradiction with his earlier affirmation of Britain's freedom to choose its own policies as an EU member.

The Keynesian–Bretton Woods regime provided a degree of insulation for national economies so that each could maintain its own distinct institutional arrangements without being impinged on by others'. That meant countries could choose their own industrial promotion systems, labor market arrangements, banking regulations, consumer protection, health, safety, and environmental rules, and so on, and not worry that they would be overwhelmed by dis-similar practices elsewhere. "Live and let live" might have been the motto.

Hyperglobalization turned this understanding on its head. Institutional convergence and harmonization became an implicit, and often explicit, imperative. Pressure was exerted in this direction from several sources. First, institutional divergence was often portrayed as a trade barrier and, therefore, as requiring removal. Nations that had strict consumer safety rules—a ban on genetically modified organisms, for example—were prima facie protectionist since they closed their markets to food exporters from nations that had less restrictive rules. Nations with patent and copyright laws that were less friendly to corporations discriminated against firms from countries with stronger "intellectual property" rules and had to reform their policies. Government subsidies had to be brought under international discipline regardless of whether they were justified by domestic market conditions. The EU, the most hyperglobalist arrangement of all, went the furthest: even having a money of one's own was an impediment to trade. A common currency was the obvious solution.

Even when institutional harmonization was not an explicit goal, international arbitrage could accomplish the same purpose. No policy maker of note ever suggested that countries ought to have similar labor market institutions—minimum wages, hiring and firing regulations, collective bargaining arrangements, and so on. But there is little doubt that trade competition penalized those countries that were more generous to their workers and amplified their voices. The same was true for countries with stricter environmental regulations or higher taxes on corporations. Hyperglobalization generally forced a downward adjustment in taxes and regulations toward the lowest common denominator. The effect on corporate taxation was visible to the naked eye: between 1985 and 2018, average corporate tax rates halved, going from 49 percent to 24 percent.[37] The primary motive behind this downward cascade was tax competition: governments felt they had to reduce their taxes to prevent corporations from leaving for lower-tax jurisdictions.

The third source of pressure for institutional harmonization was the neoliberal playbook itself. Governments all over the world internalized identical rules of good behavior on how the economy was to be managed. Deregulation, stabilization, liberalization were the mantra of the day. In macroeconomics, floating currencies, inflation targeting, open capital accounts, and (where possible) fiscal rules were the way to go. In regulation, governments had to have a light hand and rely on market incentives. As US vice president Al Gore, another Democrat, noted: "In this fast-moving, fast-changing global economy—when the free flow of dollars and data are [a] source of economic and political strength, and whole new industries are born every day—governments must be lean, nimble, and creative, or they will surely be left behind."[38]

In light of these pressures, it is not difficult to understand why electorates generally felt their political leaders were becoming less responsive to them. Mainstream politicians appeared distant and less accountable. Governments seemed to be responding primarily to the demands of the global economy instead of the needs of their voters. The real decisions were apparently taken somewhere out there where ordinary people had little say. When voters complained or asked for change, the response was (as in the quotes at the start of the chapter): not possible; get on with it. Those who wanted a different relationship with the world economy either did not know what they were talking about or were blatant protectionists pleading for their special interests. It is also not difficult to see how the political space left vacant by absconding mainstream politicians could be filled by populists. Populists, who pride themselves on speaking for the people, were ready to pick up the torch for groups who felt abandoned by elites.

Economics versus geopolitics

The belief in the inevitability of institutional convergence under hyperglobalization led to disappointment on the international stage as well. It spawned the false hope that China would eventually look more like a Western country, with little interest in asserting itself as a geopolitical rival to the US.

China was an authoritarian, socialist country with a distinctive mix of state direction and free markets. A common expectation among leaders in the West was that China's integration into the world economy would ultimately enhance transparency, the rule of law, and attachment to liberal principles. "Supporting China's entry into the WTO," noted Bill Clinton in 2000, "represents the most significant opportunity that we have had to create positive change in China since the 1970s." "Membership in the WTO," he cautioned, "will not create a free society in China overnight. . . . But over time, I believe it will move China faster and further in the right direction."[39] Even earlier, in 1996, the US national security and intelligence expert Henry S. Rowen boldly predicted that China would become a democracy by 2015, thanks to "the demands of a market economy," among other forces.[40] Others were more circumspect about China's transition to liberal democracy. But most Western elites believed that China's (and Russia's) integration into the world economy would speed up convergence to Western institutional norms.[41]

As we have already seen, in reality China had integrated into the world economy under its own rules, marching to a rather different drummer—violating the tenets of financial globalization and the spirit, even if not the formal strictures, of the WTO. Since China's peculiar economic and political practices had paid off so well, there was little reason for the country's leader to want to abandon them. It fell to Henry Kissinger, on his ninety-ninth birthday in 2023, to state a truth that was already clear to everyone: waiting for China to become Western was no longer plausible.[42]

China's rise as a major player in the world economy was supposed to reduce international tensions and contribute to global peace. A country that relied so much on trade and foreign investment, as China did, could not turn into a potentially hostile geopolitical rival for the US or Europe. That idea, however, was a "great delusion," in the words of John Mearsheimer.[43] China brought its own distinctive values and institutions, and most importantly its own national interests, to the global arena. It wanted a greater say in global governance arrangements and expected greater compliance from others, especially smaller or waning powers. It felt entitled to act freely in its immediate neighborhood—in Hong Kong, Taiwan, and the South China Sea. In other words, just like any other major power, it wanted to throw its weight around. One does not have to believe, as Mearsheimer does, that great powers are always destined to come into conflict with each other. But it seems clear that a rising power would challenge the prerogatives of an established power long accustomed to others falling in line, and that the result would be greater tension rather than harmony.

International economic relations among sovereign entities tend to be positive sum. You and I both win when we trade or engage in financial transactions with each other. The world of geopolitics is different. Since political power is relative, whatever makes you stronger makes me weaker. Geopolitics is a zero-sum relationship. When geopolitical considerations begin to trump economic ones, the world order starts to look radically different. Retreating into self-sufficiency begins to make sense, no matter what the economic costs, if my trade partners lose more as a result than I do. The purpose of economic interdependence becomes not to enhance our mutual prosperity but to "weaponize" it so I can weaken or extract concessions out of you.[44] Economics turns into an instrument of coercion or one-sided advantage.

Hyperglobalization was built for a world where geopolitics played little role or was consigned to the sidelines. It presumed that national security and military interests could be subsumed under economic motives. It could not be sustained in a world where the US and China conceived of each other as strategic rivals, offering contrasting visions for the economy and world order. Instead, we require a global order that meets the economic, social, and environmental challenges of the day while respecting our new geopolitical realities. I discuss how we can erect such an order later in the book.

3

Making the Green Transition Happen

Pakistan is accustomed to heavy rainfall during the summer months when the monsoon hits. But what happened in July and August of 2022 was unprecedented. It had been an unusually hot spring during the preceding months, with temperatures rising to more than 50°C across many parts of the country. Then, during the summer months, the rains that came down broke all records. Sindh and Baluchistan experienced six to seven times their usual rainfall totals, and much of the country was left under water. The Indus River overflowed across thousands of square kilometers. The floods and landslides displaced thirty million people, killing nearly fifteen hundred and destroying 1.7 million homes. This was the worst flood Pakistan had experienced in its recorded history. It was, scientists concluded, most likely the result of climate change.[1]

Sadly, such calamities are no longer rare. Scientists have documented around 400 extreme weather events over the last decade where the anomalous weather patterns can be linked directly to human-made climate change.[2] In 2015, warmer equatorial waters in the Pacific Ocean produced a stronger-than-usual El Niño and contributed to Ethiopia's worst drought in decades, leaving hundreds of thousands of farmers with failed crops.[3] Warmer temperatures have been linked to the most destructive wildfires on record experienced in California in recent years.[4] In October 2019, the typhoon Hagibis that hit Tokyo caused large-scale flooding and $4 billion in damage attributable to human-made climate change.[5] Climate change was likewise responsible for the extreme heat wave that hit the Sahel in the spring of 2024.[6]

Climate change is a reality. Temperatures have increased by more than 1°C since the late nineteenth century, sea levels have risen by an average of 20 centimeters, and extreme weather events—heat waves, heavy rains, droughts, and cyclones—have become increasingly frequent. Climate change has produced irreversible losses in ecosystems on land and water, and hundreds of species have disappeared. Even though some regions and crops have benefited, food security and overall agricultural productivity have taken a hit. The incidence of climate-related water- and food-borne diseases has risen. Mass displacements from severely affected regions have ensued. Low-lying areas, including urban centers in which around a tenth of the global population resides, are increasingly at risk.

Carbon removal technologies and geoengineering may someday play an important role, but the key to mitigate climate change and its destructive consequences for now is to decarbonize our planet. We need "deep, rapid, and sustained" cuts in emissions, in the words of the Intergovernmental Panel on Climate Change (IPCC).[7] Even if all countries live up to their present net-zero commitments, the IPCC believes global warming will exceed 1.5°C, and it will be "very difficult" to stay below 2°C. The challenge remains enormous. Our best bet at present for winning the race against catastrophic climate change lies in the large-scale deployment of low-carbon technologies.

We have made some progress along the technological dimension in recent years, with drastic reductions in the cost of renewables. But existing policies not only need to be scaled up; they also need to be combined with more forceful action on two other fronts: raising the price of carbon and other greenhouse gas emissions, on the one hand, and financial and technological assistance to developing nations, on the other. This chapter sketches a path toward these outcomes.

Reasons for optimism

The IPCC issued its first assessment report in 1990. At the time, the IPCC's scientists put together a kind of worst-case projection, in which the world takes few or no steps to reduce emissions. According to that scenario, the global average atmospheric CO_2 concentration level would rise to 437 parts per million (ppm) by 2025,[8] an increase of more than 50 percent since the Industrial Revolution. In the meantime, any reasonable doubts one might have had about global warming, its human-made nature, and its catastrophic consequences have dissipated. Yet as I write these words, average concentrations stand above 420 ppm, not too far below what the IPCC's scientists thought was an unacceptable outcome three and a half decades ago. Emissions of methane, another greenhouse gas, are also at an all-time high and rising more rapidly than ever.

But there is cause for some optimism. There have been remarkable gains in renewables in recent years, including solar and wind power and electric batteries. If decarbonizing is not to come at the expense of economic prosperity, renewable sources of energy will have to replace the fossil fuels that currently power our economies. The good news is that the cost of renewable energy has fallen dramatically over the last decade, by 80 percent in solar, 73 percent in offshore wind, 57 percent in onshore wind, and 80 percent in electric batteries.[9] Today in many parts of the world solar and wind energy are effectively cheaper to deploy than fossil fuels like oil and coal, and the cost advantage of renewables is likely to increase further in the future.

The renewables transition has been far more rapid than experts expected. Cost declines have resulted in nearly exponential rates of installment of new renewable energy capacity. Solar capacity, for example, has consistently exceeded, by a wide margin, the projections made by the International Energy Agency since the early 2010s. At present, the bulk of new investments in energy is in renewables.

Each day more than $1 billion is being spent on solar deployment.[10] Greenhouse gas emissions, which include methane and nitrous oxide in addition to carbon dioxide, have already been on a downward path (in absolute terms) in the leading economies. These advances could play a significant role in further curbing global demand for fossil fuels.

Three things lie behind the renewables story: China, industrial policy, and the learning curve. On the one hand, China is a big part of the problem. China's total emissions continue to grow, and the country remains the world's largest emitter of carbon, accounting for nearly a third of annual global emissions. At the same time, China is currently the global leader in renewable energy. In 2023, the country on its own contributed 59 percent of the global additions to renewable power generation capacity, including solar, wind, and hydro. China added more solar power capacity in that same year than the entire installed capacity in the US.[11]

It was a combination of government push, private investment, and technological innovation that enabled the costs of renewables to come down as sharply as they did. China is the paradigmatic case of this mix, as I discuss below, but there are other examples. Denmark stands out in wind power, where government subsidies along with strategic foresight by management propelled a fossil fuel energy company into the world's leading offshore wind power producer, Ørsted.[12] More than half of Denmark's energy needs are supplied today by offshore wind farms. The US embarked on its version of the same approach in 2022 with its misnamed Inflation Reduction Act (IRA). The IRA is the US government's most ambitious effort to date to speed up the green transition and has been called a "game changer," though its future under a Trump administration remains unclear. It encompasses a vast array of subsidies in the form of production and investment tax credits as well as direct government investment expenditures on renewables, green manufacturing, decarbonization, and conversion. If implemented in full, the IRA is expected to cost the government over its ten-year life anywhere between $800 billion and $1.2 trillion.[13]

Developments in green technologies have emboldened governments to be more proactive on the climate front. Various other decarbonization experiments, including more than seventy unilateral carbon pricing schemes, have proliferated all over the world. More governments have made net-zero pledges, with 90 percent of global emissions of greenhouse gases currently covered by net-zero emissions pledges. This is up from virtually none a decade earlier.[14] These initiatives give us some hope that climate change will be brought under control. Yet they often depart significantly from what economists and climate scientists would consider to be the first-best approach, as we examine in greater detail below. They are also not enough on their own.

A realistic climate change mitigation strategy must build on existing initiatives without losing sight of the full range of policy essentials. Following an overview of China's green industrial policies, I turn to the three key requirements of the climate transition and discuss how we can chart a realistic path toward meeting them.

China's green industrial policies

The municipal Communist Party leader of Hefei City was speaking on a TV interview program. The anchorman cautiously raised a complaint he said he had seen on the internet. Some people were worried that the city government was paying too much attention to investments in companies and losing focus on its real job. The party boss conceded that "some people think that [it is a risk if] the government in Hefei jumps into the water and swims [with the companies]." But helping firms, he argued, was the government's job. "It is precisely because of this action of the government that many companies have fewer worries. If you only watch and do not pull them out even if the company is drowning, what do we need a government for?"[15]

The interview took place in June 2021. Two years earlier, the fledgling electric vehicle (EV) company Nio stood at the edge of bankruptcy. A series of battery failures had forced the company into a large recall and its share price had collapsed. Then the Hefei municipal government stepped in. Following a due diligence analysis typical of venture capital firms, it pumped $1 billion into Nio through a holding company. State lenders came up with an additional $1.6 billion. In return, the city received not only a 24 percent stake in the company but also an agreement for Nio to relocate its headquarters to Hefei. The company's share price recovered, and its presence turned the city into an important hub for a thriving EV and electric batteries industry.[16] The concern about its financial entanglement with private firms notwithstanding, the city government could be proud that it not only had achieved a hefty financial return but had also become a leading player in the green transition.[17]

China introduced a national cap-and-trade program in 2021 for emissions from the power sector—currently the largest in the world in terms of coverage. But what stands out in China's approach are the industrial policies promoting green industries. While these policies have not always worked, thanks to them China is a global powerhouse today in EVs, producing 60 percent of the world's EV supply.[18] China's leading EV manufacturer, BYD, a vertically integrated firm that produces everything from electric batteries and microchips to plastic components and whose name stands for "build your dream," surpassed Tesla in total sales in 2023. More all-electric vehicles are sold in China than in the rest of the world combined.

The industry is an example of what Elizabeth Thurbon and her coauthors call "developmental environmentalism," a modern-day developmentalism adapted to the challenge of the climate transition. Chinese leaders realized around the time of the global financial crisis in 2009 that their traditional growth model was unsustainable economically, environmentally, and politically, and they made the green transition a key pillar of their economic strategy.[19] Like developmentalism in general, developmental environmentalism emphasizes public-private collaboration to advance economic growth, national autonomy, structural change (in the direction of green industries in this case), and geopolitical objectives all at once.

The Hefei-Nio partnership illustrates the model. However, public venture capital is only one form of Chinese industrial policy, and the set of policy instruments used has been much broader. On top of venture capital and directed credit, the government has resorted to direct subsidies, procurement, state-owned enterprises, spending on R&D, customized infrastructure, preferential access to raw materials, demonstration projects, specialized training, and regulatory and administrative privileges.[20] Incentives are fine-tuned when needed, to tailor them more closely to desired outcomes or to consolidate excess capacity.[21] These policies have spanned the national government, provinces, and municipalities, in mutually supportive but also occasionally competing fashion. The hallmark of Chinese developmentalism is an experimental approach. The national government sets broad objectives. Then a variety of industrial policies are deployed in different industries and locations, followed by close monitoring, iteration, and revision when called for.

Government promotion of renewables followed this playbook, also to great effect. Europe and the US were technologically ahead early on. After the financial crisis of 2009, as European countries were removing many of their subsidies on renewables, China made a decisive shift in the opposite direction. Solar, wind, and electric batteries were provided hefty subsidies by both the national and local governments, along with other supports. These policies essentially produced a virtuous cycle of capacity expansion and declining costs. Government assistance crowded in private investment and expanded installed capacity, which in turn allowed firms to travel rapidly down their learning curve. In solar photovoltaic (PV) cells, for example, the learning rate was at least 20 percent, which meant that each doubling of capacity reduced production costs by 20 percent or more.[22] Lower costs meant lower prices and higher sales, which in turn led to more investment and greater capacity, producing further reduction of costs and prices, and so on.

Industrial policy is often pictured as a process whereby the government implements its directives in top-down fashion, with firms given little chance to shape the goals or the outcomes. Authoritarian states like China are supposed to hold an advantage insofar as they are "hard states" that can prevent firms from gaming the system to their benefit. But as Thurbon and her coauthors emphasize, the

Chinese government acted more like a "collaborative catalyst." In solar, senior government officials periodically solicited feedback from industry leaders, which in turn helped shape their diagnoses of bottlenecks and possible solutions.[23] In EVs, the government set up China EV100 in 2014, a think tank to facilitate dialogue and coordination with the industry. This association included not only representatives from domestic and foreign firms but also prominent politicians and academicians. Among other things, it produced a report in 2019 on the full electrification of vehicles in China.[24] Public-private collaboration is an important feature of industrial policies, which I return to in chapter 6.

In China, collaboration between the national and local governments also played a significant role. One model for this was the establishment of demonstration programs in selected cities or regions, which then received financial incentives (for EVs, for example) from the central government. The localities were then expected to pursue complementary policies to advance the national government's priorities. The city governments in turn cooperated extensively with private firms, as in the Nio-Hefei case. The city of Liuzhou, for example, achieved a very rapid increase in EV penetration thanks to a partnership between the municipal government and the local EV manufacturer, SAIC-GM-Wuling. The city introduced subsidies for the purchase of EVs, provided free and reserved parking, and invested in charging infrastructure. The company and the municipality engaged in an extensive campaign to raise awareness on EVs and invited recommendations from the public about features that would increase ease of use. The company ended up developing popular models specifically designed for transportation in the city.[25]

There have also been costly mistakes; some industries have failed to get off the ground despite sustained government support.[26] There is some evidence that public venture capital is financially less profitable than the private kind.[27] Competition among provinces and municipalities to attract investment has tended to result in excess capacity, with the national government periodically having to step in to consolidate particular industries. Inefficiencies in wind power and turbine manufacture have been widely reported.[28] Skeptical outsiders have faulted the Chinese government for putting too much emphasis on industrial policy. But in green industries, so critical to the climate transition, the far more expensive mistake would have been not doing enough.

This is a crucial point, especially against the background of ongoing trade tensions between China and Western countries in key green industries, such as PV panels, EVs, and electric batteries. The US and the EU have complained bitterly and persistently about Chinese subsidies and have responded with trade barriers. On a visit to China, then US treasury secretary Janet Yellen warned her hosts that the US government would not sit idly by while "large-scale government support" by the Chinese government undermined US green industries, as it had previously in steel.[29] China has in turn taken the US to the World Trade Organization for provisions in the US Inflation Reduction Act that discriminate against imports. How global trade rules should handle subsidies and other kinds of industrial policies is a question I pick up in chapter 7. Suffice it to note here that there is a key difference between green industries, such as solar PV cells, electric vehicles, and batteries, and traditional industries, such as steel and gas-powered autos. Green technologies are a crucial component of fighting climate change. Governments that are promoting renewables and green industries are contributing to a global public good. They deserve praise, not condemnation.

To understand green industrial policies' proper role, it is useful to step back and consider what an ideal climate policy might look like.

The three planks of climate policy

Economists like to imagine themselves as "social planners." A social planner's job is to design a solution that leaves everyone as well off as possible, unencumbered by politics, pressure from special interests, or administrative constraints. In the case of climate change, the social planner's starting point would be that the problem is a global one, and hence the solution must also be global. Indeed, climate change is the archetypal global commons problem. Carbon and other greenhouse gases accumulate in the atmosphere with no regard to national borders. Irrespective of where the carbon is emitted, the entire world suffers the consequences. And on the flip side, every other country gains from one country's emission reductions. No country can keep the benefits to itself.

The social planner would first focus on fixing the immediate behavioral source of the problem: distorted incentives. In a market economy, consumers' and producers' incentives are aligned with desirable social outcomes only to the extent that they face the true social costs of their actions. This is far from the case with greenhouse gases. When fossil fuels are burned to generate energy, carbon dioxide is released into the air. When the adverse environmental and climate effects are all figured in, the social cost of carbon emissions can be as high as $200 per ton.[30] Yet the user of fossil fuels pays nothing for these external damages (beyond the cost of extracting, processing, and transporting the fuel itself).

Basic economics suggests that emitters of carbon should bear this cost, to bring their production, consumption, and investment decisions in line with socially optimal outcomes. Hence the first leg of the solution would be a global tax on carbon and other greenhouse gases, ideally set equal to the social cost of emissions. Alternatively, the social planner would institute a global cap-and-trade or emissions trading system, under which producers around the world would be allotted quotas on their emissions but would also be allowed to buy or sell "emission permits" from other nations or producers. The trading of permits would ensure that emission cuts would occur where the costs of doing so are the lowest. The carbon tax and cap-and-trade regimes are close cousins and would produce identical results under certain conditions.[31]

Next, the social planner would turn to technology and innovation. Since new technologies are crucial to decarbonizing our world, it is essential that markets provide adequate encouragement for investing in green innovation. Raising the price of carbon would go some distance to ensure this, but not the full way. Green innovation, like any other form of R&D, generates learning spillovers—or what economists call *positive externalities*. Learning by doing that benefits other firms (say, in the case of solar panels) is a typical example of this. Latecomers can benefit from the innovations of pioneers, either by copying their practices or by poaching their workers and managers. Cost declines also spill over across national boundaries, spurring adoption of clean technologies by other countries. Such spillovers provide a generic case for subsidizing R&D in general and green innovation in particular. Hence the second prong of the social planner's attack on climate change would be global subsidies and a range of other government programs—i.e., green industrial policies—to incentivize the development and dissemination of green technologies.[32]

The case for green subsidies is even stronger when carbon taxes (or cap-and-trade systems) fall short of raising the global or national price of carbon to its full social cost. Carbon taxes and green industrial policies can reinforce each other and substitute for each other to some extent. This is important to bear in mind in our second-best world, where carbon taxes are politically difficult. The more constrained the social planner is on the first prong of the strategy (carbon pricing), the greater weight she would place on the second (green industrial policies).

The instruments our social planner has so far deployed address efficiency but not fairness. Climate change is a function of the *stock* of accumulated emissions. And it is the advanced countries that have done the bulk of the damage to the carbon budget of our world. The US alone accounts for a quarter of total global emissions since 1850, and member states of the European Union have contributed an additional 17 percent. China's share already amounts to 15 percent, while India has contributed a mere 3 percent.[33] With the major exception of China, today's developing countries have played to date a minor role in climate change. Yet they would be expected to shoulder a burden equivalent to that of advanced economies under a global arrangement that yields a significant increase in the price of carbon and demands generous subsidies for green innovation. (Of course, there could be fairness considerations within countries as well. Climate change and its remedies can have stark distributional implications across different regions and income groups. I leave those aside for the moment but return to them when I discuss the political economy of climate transition policies in the next section.)

Our enlightened social planner would find this unfair, on two counts. First, since it is predominantly the rich countries that have exhausted the world's carbon budget, they should be the ones paying for most of the costs of putting climate back on track.[34] And second, developing countries, being poor, are those with the least ability to pay for the short-term costs of the green transition. It is estimated that developing countries (leaving China aside) need up to $1 trillion per year in external finance by 2030 to prepare for the climate transition.[35] For both reasons, the social planner would prescribe large transfers from the rich nations to the poor nations. These transfers would take the form of both financial and technological assistance. Financial assistance would compensate for the higher costs of carbon and help pay for decarbonizing existing economic structures and adaptation investments in the developing world. Technology transfer for renewables and for green manufacturing and agricultural production, without strings attached in the form of intellectual property restrictions, would facilitate poor nations' transition to cleaner production.

Hence the social planner's three-pronged attack on climate change would consist of (1) raising the global price of carbon, (2) green industrial policies, and (3) financial and technology transfers from the North to the South.

How do our existing arrangements stack up against these criteria? The short answer is not so well. A global agreement on taxing carbon or instituting an emissions trading system (ETS) has never been more than a distant hope. When carbon prices have been pushed up, it has been the result of unilateral regional, national, and subnational initiatives, such as those in the EU, New Zealand, California, and Quebec. Today nearly a quarter of global greenhouse emissions are covered by some kind of carbon pricing or emissions trading scheme, with varying degrees of effectiveness.[36] But the World Bank estimates that less than 5 percent of global greenhouse emissions are covered by a carbon price that can be regarded as adequate for the climate transition.[37]

The main global agreement on climate, the Paris treaty signed in 2015, obligates individual countries only to submit their own voluntary commitments to cutting emissions—so-called nationally determined contributions (NDCs). As previously mentioned, around 90 percent of global greenhouse emissions are at present covered by some kind of net-zero commitment. The US (2050), European Union (2050), and China (2060) have all made such pledges, along with more than a hundred countries. The bulk of these commitments, however, are rated "poor" or "average" by Climate Action Tracker.[38] Even if fulfilled, they still leave us considerably behind mitigation aspirations articulated at global convenings.

There has also been failure on the financial assistance front. Rich nations did not live up to their promise to deliver climate finance on the order of $100 billion per year by 2020. Even though they eventually exceeded this amount, it is hard to see how significantly more ambitious requirements, estimated at $1 trillion per year by 2030, could be met under current arrangements.

The most encouraging developments, as we have seen, have been on the industrial policy front. China, the US, and many other nations are engaged in extensive subsidization of renewables and green industries, to good effect. These efforts are not globally coordinated and indeed are the source of considerable trade friction. On their own, they are clearly not adequate. But they could well provide the most effective path forward. Green industrial policies cannot only be extended and rendered more effective, in ways I discuss later, but, equally important, they can be a catalyst for progress on the other two planks of climate policy: carbon pricing and assistance to developing nations. This would complete the social planner's trifecta, albeit in quite different form, and put us in a far better position to address the climate challenge.

To assess the likelihood of this optimistic outcome, we need to understand better the political realities behind climate transition policies and, in particular, the reasons for resistance to carbon pricing.

The political economy of the green transition

On paper, Carbon County, Wyoming (population 14,537), should be a success story in the green transition. The county is named for its rich coal deposits, which were first mined in 1868. But as reserves and the demand for coal declined, Carbon County's economic fortunes sank. Its last two mines were finally closed in 2005. Unlike many other communities dependent on fossil fuels, however, the county made a transition to renewables. County officials courted wind companies and managed to attract what would become one of the largest wind farms in the US.

But wind industries create few jobs and tax revenues. Despite steady declines, Wyoming's fossil fuel industry employs around 15,000 people, while wind farms generate jobs in the hundreds, most of which are in construction and eventually disappear. More than half of the state's tax revenues still come from fossil fuels. "The great thing about coal and minerals is that they funded Wyoming, helped people raise their families and building our schools," a state senator says. "Wind is never going to do that." The state's voters heavily support climate-denialist Republicans. Donald Trump, who won Wyoming handily in all three of the presidential elections in which he ran, campaigned there in 2020 with signs that read, "Trump digs coal." A local official warned visitors that they should mention global warming only "if they want to be punched in the face."[39]

It is easy to attribute the political resistance to phasing out fossil fuels to short-sighted, vested interests. But when jobs disappear, communities decay too. Losing a job is one of the most scarring things that can happen to people. The consequences are felt beyond the affected individuals as families break down, crime and addiction rates rise, mental health deteriorates, and mortality increases. Governments can promise to provide compensation in the form of social assistance and job retraining. But such promises typically ring hollow, because they lack credibility for a variety of reasons. Trust in government is low, the taxes needed to pay for the compensation can be blocked by other voters, and circumstances can change, leading to promises being revoked.[40] In any case, compensation cannot fully offset the psychological and social traumas of joblessness. Investments in renewables and green industries can help too, but their net job benefits remain unclear and are often far off in the future. It is difficult to exchange economic security for an uncertain economic future.

Fossil fuel companies have their own financial reasons to oppose decarbonization and can be relied on to take the lead against measures to decarbonize. Their tactics have included spreading misinformation about climate change—so-called greenwashing—in addition to lobbying and campaign contributions.[41] Combined opposition from corporations and local communities has prevented the US federal government from mounting an effective carbon phaseout strategy until recently, notwithstanding the well-recognized environmental and economic benefits. The US failed to pass economy-wide cap-and-trade legislation in 2010, despite having a Democratic president and a Democratic Senate and House of Representatives.

Since raising the price of carbon is equivalent to imposing a tax on its use, political opposition to carbon pricing also comes from consumers. That is why consumer subsidies on oil, gas, and fuel-based electricity are more common than taxes, especially in low- and middle-income countries. Removing such subsidies, let alone taxing fossil fuels, has proved very difficult. There were mass protests against proposed cuts in gasoline subsidies, such as the *gilets jaunes* movement in France, in at least twenty-four countries between 2006 and 2019.[42] Governments are more prone to increase subsidies than to lower them, especially when oil prices rise on world markets. In the aftermath of the spike in oil prices following the Ukraine war, fossil fuel subsidies more than tripled globally, reaching above $1 trillion.[43]

It is not difficult to appreciate the fundamental political problem carbon pricing faces: it creates an immediate and typically concentrated set of losers, while its benefits are diffuse, come largely in the future, are harder to attribute directly to the policy, and are often perceived as uncertain. These features are a climate-friendly politician's nightmare. They make it exceedingly difficult to mobilize a sufficiently large coalition in support of raising the price of fossil fuels and other sources of greenhouse gases. And this is true in authoritarian regimes as well as democracies. Autocrats pay a price, too, when they step on the toes of important groups in their society.

The political advantages of green industrial policies

There is an alternate strategy, based on carrots rather than sticks. It focuses on creating immediate winners instead of losers, which is what subsidizing investments in renewables and decarbonization accomplishes. As Alexander Gazmararian and Dustin Tingley note in their book *Uncertain Futures*, the political impasse over climate change can be overcome in one of two ways: by reducing the opposition and by strengthening support. The political appeal of green subsidies over carbon pricing rests precisely on this distinction. When reducing opposition proves difficult, carrots help by increasing support. Nobody likes being taxed, but everyone loves subsidies.[44] This explains why industrial policies allowed the Biden administration to progress on its climate agenda where previous Democratic administrations failed, by relying on carbon pricing.[45]

From a purely economic standpoint, the distinction between taxes and subsidies is often immaterial. Suppose we can split the economy into two sets of activities, one green and the other dirty (i.e., emitting GHGs). In this context, subsidizing clean activities is equivalent to taxing the dirty ones. This might seem counterintuitive, but it derives from two economic considerations. First, the economy has a fixed amount of resources at any time, such as labor, capital, and entrepreneurship. If resources are to flow toward green activities, they can only come from emitting activities. Whether that is accomplished by subsidizing the former or taxing the latter is of secondary importance. Second, governments have to balance their books over time. Subsidies have to be financed by taxing the rest of society. Taxes generate fiscal revenues, which can be returned to taxpayers in the form of tax rebates or public goods. The economic outcomes are similar in either case.

The real world works differently, however, because of both cognitive limitations and pervasive uncertainty. Consumers, communities, and corporations do not necessarily see through the full economy-wide implications of different policies. The consequences of policies and the future path of government actions are inherently unpredictable. Understandably, in politics immediate, visible impacts greatly outweigh indirect and future consequences. This renders subsidies and other forms of government supports a much more politically attractive path for the green transition than carbon pricing or other approaches that directly harm fossil fuel interests.

Moreover, green subsidies can make it easier to mount a more frontal attack on fossil fuels eventually. This can happen in three ways. First, they can make the benefits of the green transition more concrete by creating early wins. Companies and communities that are beneficiaries of government supports for renewables can see firsthand the profits, jobs, tax revenues, and cleaner air that green industries bring. This may not overcome resistance in areas where fossil fuels have become deeply entrenched in the social life of a community, as in Carbon County, Wyoming. But it may diminish opposition and mobilize support in others.

Second, and relatedly, green industrial policies can bring new political allies to climate advocates. As Gazmararian and Tingley note, "If new allies can be created, then the opponents of energy transition, such as fossil fuel companies, could be outflanked or even converted into supporters."[46] Or as another observer puts it, "American politics must have a powerful, durable, and flexible pro-decarbonization coalition if the U.S. is to succeed in reaching net zero."[47] How this might work can be observed in the political activities of different types of companies. In the US, oil and gas companies are among the most influential special interests, spending annually more than $125 million on political lobbying. But renewable energy companies have steadily increased their footprint in Washington, DC, and now contribute nearly half that amount ($60 million) to political lobbying, up from less than $5 million in 2000.[48] Similarly, the shift toward renewables can prompt localities that have traditionally resisted curbs on fossil fuels to rethink their economic interests. The state of Texas now generates more electricity from solar than from coal.[49] As green subsidies help renewable energy companies grow, their increased political influence in turn reinforces climate-friendly policies, including controls on fossil fuels.

The geographical distribution of green subsidies can play a similar role in broadening the proclimate coalition. Biden's Inflation Reduction Act (IRA) subsidies appear to have disproportionately favored Republican states.[50] The motive may have been to woo voters in advance of the 2024 presidential election as much as it was to reduce resistance to the green transition. Nevertheless, the effect is likely to strengthen the climate coalition and weaken fossil fuel interests that often dominate red states.

There is also a more subtle way in which green industrial policies facilitate eventual restrictions on fossil fuels. These policies spur new technologies that reduce the costs of carbon abatement and transitioning to renewables, which in turn can help overcome opposition from fossil fuel companies. An example of this can be seen in rules promulgated by the US EPA in April 2024 on power plant emissions. These rules gave coal-fired power plant operators a choice: they had to either close down by 2039 or reduce carbon emissions by 90 percent until 2032 through carbon capture or other means.[51] This was just about as tough a regulation against coal plants as the prevailing regulatory and legal regime allowed. It was rendered politically feasible, at least in part, by the additional subsidies introduced in the IRA, passed two years earlier, for carbon capture and sequestration (CCS). These subsidies helped nullify coal plant operators' objections that carbon abatement is too costly. The carrots made it easier to deploy the sticks down the road.

The experience in East Asia is also instructive. The region generally remains much more dependent on fossil fuels than the US and Europe, and has not made much progress in reducing their consumption. Elizabeth Thurbon and her coauthors note that in these countries the government first focused on creating new green industries, leaving the phasing out of fossil fuels until later. As I described earlier, China was a pioneer in green industrial policies, deploying a wide range of incentives for renewables and other green industries. South Korea pursued a similar path. In the words of Thurbon et al., "The state is encouraging the destruction of the fossil fuel economic order not by seeking to harm incumbent firms but by heavily supporting them to switch their investments towards 'green' projects."[52] Indeed, by assisting firms in making the transition away from fossil fuels, governments are trying to turn a threat to their profitability into an economic opportunity. These efforts have in turn facilitated more ambitious efforts down the line to curb emissions directly and phase out fossil fuels. By 2015, several years after the ramping up of green subsidies, the Chinese government had begun to promote an exit from coal and the greening of state utilities. China rolled out an emissions trading system that became fully operational in 2021. Even though carbon prices remain low, the system covers 2,000 power plants and is already the largest in the world.[53] Carbon reduction was articulated as an explicit goal for the first time in the Chinese Communist Party's third plenum in 2024.[54]

In short, green industrial policies are helpful not only in their own right but as a critical tool to overcome political obstacles faced by carbon pricing and other direct restrictions on fossil fuels.

Global problems, local remedies

Recall that our social planner would formulate globally coordinated policies since fighting climate change is a global public good. Climate change is the result of cumulative global emissions, and individual nations contribute at most a small part. None has the incentive to invest in decarbonization when the benefits are shared equally by all others. And each has the incentive to free ride on others' decarbonization efforts.

Viewed this way, the initiatives described in this chapter pose a puzzle. Green industrial policies in China, the US, and elsewhere are helping the entire world decarbonize by promoting renewables, speeding up the green transition, and ultimately reducing emissions everywhere. These countries are effectively paying for a global public good with their own taxpayers' money. It is a similar situation with carbon pricing schemes. When the EU or New Zealand raises the price of emissions, they impose a cost on their industries and consumers, while the benefits go to the entire world. Even more puzzling are subnational carbon pricing schemes, such as those in California or Quebec, given the minute share of benefits these jurisdictions capture.

The proliferation of unilateral, decentralized efforts is an unexpected (and welcome!) surprise in climate policy. It suggests that economists may have overstated the need for global cooperation and underestimated the degree to which climate concerns might eventually drive local, national, and regional politics.

The European case is instructive for unraveling the puzzle. Europe set up the world's first cap-and-trade regime, the emissions trading system (ETS). The European Commission initially proposed a carbon tax during the 1990s but failed to receive support from all the nation-states. Paradoxically, it was the failure of international cooperation that gave the commission's efforts a boost. The US decision not to ratify the 1997 Kyoto proposal laid the groundwork for the commission's push in the early 2000s for the ETS. The ETS was eventually adopted in 2003, and the EU market for trading carbon allowances became operational in 2005.[55] Carbon prices were low at the beginning but have increased significantly in more recent years.

It is tempting to attribute Europe's pioneer role to the relatively greater climate consciousness of the continent's citizens. Germans, for example, have been significantly more concerned about global warming than Americans.[56] Today European citizens rank climate change as the third most serious problem, after poverty and war.[57] The Green movement and Green political parties have featured as important players in European politics since the 1980s. But industrial lobbies have always been better organized and more powerful in Brussels than citizens' groups. Green groups were in any case traditionally not in favor of the ETS, denigrating it as "trading in pollution."[58] And the German government opposed a mandatory ETS during the early years, preferring a voluntary system. Bottom-up politics does not go far in explaining how the EU moved forward with the ETS.

Policy leadership provides a more convincing explanation. EU leaders came to view, and present, climate policy as a way of killing multiple birds with one stone: in addition to responding to public demands, it would address regulatory challenges created by unco-ordinated national policies, promote further European integration, and position the EU as a global leader in climate. The European Commission, in particular, played the role of "epistemic leader."[59] It built up and disseminated technical expertise on the ETS and mobilized support from both state and nonstate actors across different decision-making levels. To national political leaders, it framed the ETS as a vehicle for exercising global leadership. To businesses, it framed the system as a cost-effective mechanism for a necessary transition that would also enhance their competitive position on global markets. Opposition from the biggest emitters was overcome by ensuring they were given large allowances based on their historical emissions. The commission thus marketed emissions trading as a "magic formula" that would achieve economic and strategic goals in addition to environmental protection.[60]

The European story illustrates how leaders can transform conceptions of national self-interest by redefining it in ways that incorporate climate goals. Doing this turns climate action into a self-sustaining norm, internalized in governments' principles of good behavior without regard to national boundaries. It was no different in China and the US (under Biden), where climate action predominantly took the form of green industrial policies.[61]

China's developmental environmentalism was a reframing of national goals that combined the green transition with other environmental, commercial, geopolitical, and national aggrandizement projects. It was meant to achieve multiple ends: reduce pollution in urban areas, upgrade the technological capacity of domestic firms while positioning them for global leadership in a future climate-conscious global marketplace, achieve energy security and self-reliance, and secure a large role for China on the global stage, while bringing emissions under control at the same time.

In the US, the IRA's broad framing is evident from its name ("Inflation Reduction Act"). The legislation incorporated social, industrial, distributional, and place-based objectives on top of climate goals.[62] On its first-year anniversary, President Joe Biden lauded it for "delivering on promises that have long been made to the American people to lower costs for families, especially health care costs, increase America's energy security, restore fairness to a tax code, create good-paying jobs here in America, and to address the existential threat of climate crisis." He added: "It's part of a much broader vision for our country: growing the economy from the middle out and the bottom up, not the top down."[63] (The EU responded to the

IRA with its own green subsidies, concerned more by the potential loss of manufacturing capacity than the climate impact.)[64]

In all these cases, since climate action was marketed as part of a wider agenda that benefits local interests, political compromises necessarily had to be made. Such compromises explain some of the blemishes of these unilateral initiatives, especially their adverse commercial consequences for trade partners. Europe is in the process of phasing in a carbon border adjustment mechanism (CBAM) that will impose import duties on dirty products from outside the EU, such as steel and aluminum. The rationale is to ensure a level playing field for European producers, which pay a price for their carbon emissions. Developing country exporters see this as a form of protectionism and as an instance of the EU forcing its own rules on them. China's focus on global competitiveness in renewables and green industries has created considerable consternation in the US and Europe, as discussed earlier. The IRA has raised the ire of the rest of the world for discriminatory provisions that favor domestic sourcing and local suppliers in the US. In each case, governments are privileging the competitive position of their firms while they compromise on a pure climate agenda and harm trade interests of other nations. This is a legitimate concern. On the other hand, a pragmatist might respond, when countries unilaterally pay for global public goods, it is not surprising (or even objectionable) that they may want to keep some of the benefits at home.[65] The world is second best, at best.

What about developing countries?

This brings us to developing nations. There is no reason that the virtuous cycle of investments in renewables and green industries followed by carbon phaseouts cannot work in these countries too. Moreover, since many of them are rich in natural resources that are critical to electric batteries, such as lithium, nickel, cobalt, and graphite, the green transition presents developing countries with new industrialization opportunities. Indeed, many middle-income countries have latched on enthusiastically to green industrial policies. Brazil is channeling concessional loans to solar and wind farms

through its development bank, coupled with local content requirements, and promoting domestic production of EVs with tax incentives. Chile's plans center on green hydrogen and lithium and include
public cofinancing of hydrogen production and the creation of a
national lithium company to hold a majority stake in all lithium projects. India has a wide range of programs and incentives for EVs, PVs,
batteries, and green oxygen. Indonesia is keen on building an entire
EV supply chain, including batteries, and has banned the export of
unprocessed nickel to help its nascent battery industry. Such initiatives could make a significant contribution to developing nations'
growth strategies, as I discuss in chapter 5.

Since developing countries will be hit severely with the consequences of climate change, their mitigation efforts will have to be
complemented by adaptation measures, such as investments in
climate-resilient urban infrastructure and ecosystem restoration. All
these investments will cost money—a lot of money—perhaps on the
order of $2 trillion a year for developing nations as a whole (excluding
China). Developing countries are short on resources, by definition.
The projection is that half of this amount ($1 trillion) will come from
external financing.[66] But developing countries have limited access to
external financial markets too, and foreign borrowing at commercial
rates comes with its own risks of overindebtedness and debt crises. In
the aftermath of COVID-19 and the Ukraine war price shocks, many
of them are already having difficulty servicing their external debts.
Nor do developing countries have the same capacity to innovate in
renewables and green industries as rich nations do. Green industrial
technologies would have to be globalized to enable developing countries to embrace renewables and green industries with the effectiveness that China and the advanced economies have.[67]

Hence the third plank of climate policy discussed previously:
assistance to low-income countries. Of all the challenges I discuss
in this book, this is the one that is perhaps the toughest to overcome.
The difficulty arises not from technical or administrative feasibility
but from political realities. Redistributing the burden of decarbonizing the world from poor to rich nations is a political problem. Within
nations, political leaders can sometimes fashion bargains between

winners and losers to move us toward more efficient policies, as we have just seen. Engineering similar bargains among nation-states is much harder, because global governance arrangements do not rest on a sense of shared political community and are therefore quite weak. One of the themes of this book is that we cannot count on global governance to solve our problems. Yet a large-scale transfer of financial resources and technology from the advanced economies to poor nations on a scale of $1 trillion a year requires a significant degree of global cooperation. In 2009, developed countries committed to providing $100 billion of climate finance for developing countries annually by 2020. This target was missed and eventually met with two years' delay in 2022. In 2024, they agreed to triple this target to $300 billion annually by 2035. The actual requirements are several times greater than this number.

The best model we have in operation at present is the Just Energy Transition Partnerships (JETPs). These are partnerships between individual developing countries and groups of donors, in which bilateral and multilateral donors, along with philanthropies, finance long-term programs of decarbonization formulated by the countries. South Africa (2021), Indonesia (2022), and Vietnam (2023) have been the inaugural cases, with packages of $8.5 billion, $20 billion, and $8 billion, respectively.[68] JETPs focus on the more limited goal of phasing out fossil fuels rather than the economy-wide promotion and dissemination of green technologies. They provide a mix of commercial loans (at market rates), concessional finance, and grants. The premise of the partnerships is that they will mobilize private financing at a much greater scale, but so far this has not happened.[69] Moreover, the dozens of countries that are in debt distress—either insolvent or illiquid—are unable to take advantage of this approach. They are shut out of private finance, and the loans they receive from official sources risk "leaking out" to private creditors, leaving with them with zero net transfers.[70]

There is no shortage of good ideas on how significant amounts of resources could be raised, only if major nations were to agree. Multilateral development banks, such as the World Bank, could scale up their climate loans if advanced economies pledged more capital.

They could also use their existing capital more effectively. Greater leveraging of the World Bank's capital base would raise its lending capacity by more than $100 billion while keeping credit risk at moderate levels.[71] More ambitiously, the IMF could generate as much as $300 billion a year by issuing special drawing rights (SDRs)—an international currency—and rechanneling them to developing countries.[72] Even critics of the idea concede that this would make an important contribution to the gap in climate finance.[73] This idea has been around for quite some time but has never gathered enough support in advanced-country capitals, as it would primarily benefit poorer nations.

A newer proposal is a global wealth tax, either on large corporations or on billionaires, or both. A global wealth tax, championed by economists Emmanuel Saez and Gabriel Zucman, would have been outside the realm of political feasibility not so long ago. But the 2023 international agreement on a 15 percent global corporate minimum tax suggests times may be changing. In early 2024, finance ministers for France and Brazil, along with the IMF chief, endorsed a global wealth tax on billionaires. Such a tax set at 2 percent would raise an estimated $250 billion a year to use for global public goods, including climate change mitigation and adaptation in the developing world. A 0.2 percent wealth tax on listed corporations in the Group of 20 would in turn raise $180 billion annually.[74]

So much for financial transfers. If the green transition is to turn from a pure cost to a growth opportunity, poor nations will also have to develop their own industrial ecosystems around renewables and green manufactures. This will require much greater access to technologies being developed in Europe, the US, and China. Some of this will happen naturally. The knowledge developed by firms in advanced economies will eventually be absorbed by poor nations, as in earlier stages of industrial development. But more may need to be done. As Bradlow and Kentikelenis note, some of the new technologies are currently closely guarded in the advanced economies through both intellectual property restrictions and domestic sourcing and procurement requirements.[75] Since so much of the R&D in China and advanced nations is publicly funded, these authors note that it might be possible to mandate making green innovations available in the global South. Similarly, Guzman and Stiglitz have suggested extending the compulsory licensing provisions of the WTO to green technologies or using a "green waiver" to facilitate technology transfer.[76] Needless to say, these solutions would face opposition from corporations, and they would also raise some practical difficulties (such as how to avoid leakage to commercial competitors in the North). But the moral and environmental case for providing developing nations access to green innovations is strong, akin to the public health argument for relaxing patent restrictions on HIV/AIDS drugs.[77]

All of this suggests that there are possible fixes on both the financial and technological fronts, awaiting global cooperation on the part of major nations. Our best hope for such cooperation is that advanced economies, including China in this instance, come to see transfers to poor nations to be in their immediate self-interest. Not enlightened self-interest, but selfish self-interest!

There are two avenues to that happy outcome. One is the realization that without assistance at scale it will be infeasible for developing countries to play their part in meeting any reasonable climate goal. Developing countries today produce a major share of global emissions; their contribution (excluding China) will soon exceed 50 percent of the total.[78] Historically, they may not have contributed much to emissions, but the current picture is very different. While emissions from the US and Europe have been declining, developing country emissions are still rising, and in many cases quite rapidly. Regardless of how rapidly the rest of the world curbs emissions, it will be virtually impossible to keep global warming within reasonable limits in the absence of strong action from poor nations as well. This is where the self-interest of major nations comes in. They need to ensure that developing countries have the capability to take on the challenge. To paraphrase Bradlow and Kentikelenis, the developed world's efforts to mitigate greenhouse gas emissions will simply be ineffective unless poor nations are enabled to undertake a similar industrial transformation.[79]

The second avenue is geopolitical. The rise of China as a major power and the geopolitical tensions that have arisen as a result may provide developing countries greater leverage in their dealings with both the West and China. As long as the US was the only sheriff in town, smaller nations had little power. The new global context may enable individual countries to extract greater financial and technological commitments for the green transition from major powers that woo them for strategic advantage. Paradoxically, geopolitical competition can be a friend of the climate. The result is unlikely to be pretty, and vastly different from what a truly global cooperative effort might look like. But, once again, a messy way forward could be better than stasis.

Final words

It was not how economists and technocrats thought it would come, but there has been good news on the climate front. Thanks in large part to uncoordinated, unilateral policies that depart significantly from the guidebook, especially green industrial policies in China and other major nations, the world has seen considerable technological progress in renewables. President Trump's climate denialism notwithstanding, these may eventually pave the way for more ambitious controls on fossil fuels and a better balance between the sticks and the carrots—i.e., more reliance on carbon pricing and less emphasis on government subsidies. A creeping, cautious optimism is emerging in climate circles on the feasibility of keeping global warming within reasonable bounds.[80] The greatest risk is that the developing countries will fail to get the support they need from the major economies. If advanced economies and China step up to the plate, it will be because they recognize it is in their immediate self-interest to do so. If they fail to do so, the cost will be borne by the entire planet, not just the developing nations.

4

Building a Good Jobs Economy

Joe Shrodek, a retired steelworker, stares ruefully at the empty lot where the steel mill that once employed him stood. Now closed, the Warren, Ohio, plant provided jobs to thousands of local workers. Shrodek has been a lifelong Democrat, but 2016 is different. Donald Trump is his choice now. "If he accomplishes 10 percent of what he says he's going to do," he says, "then that's 10 percent more than anybody else is gonna do."

Brittany Bucholz, a twenty-six-year-old nursing assistant from Dallas, Pennsylvania, has never voted before. This time around, she feels too strongly about what is happening around her not to go to the polls. "There's no more middle class," she points out. "There's poor or there's rich and there's nothing in between." Donald Trump is "the one who's speaking to us," she says.

Thomas and Erica McTague are a couple living in Plymouth, Pennsylvania. He is a police officer and she is a hairstylist. Their top concern is that so many people in their community are without a secure job that pays enough to support a family. "Go back sixty, seventy years and this area had industry and people had good jobs," he says. Their choice for president: Donald Trump.[1]

Good jobs, the middle class, and democracy

Since the presidential election of 2016, US media outlets have been full of stories like these. In the towns and communities where factories had closed and good jobs had disappeared, blue-collar and middle-class voters felt abandoned by mainstream politicians. They were turning toward Donald Trump, who promised to reverse the tide. The stories presaged an electoral upset that sent shockwaves through coastal liberal elites and threatened to take America down a dangerous path toward authoritarian populism. They also became fodder for a burgeoning academic literature on the political realignment that followed the China trade shock, automation, and other labor market dislocations.[2] In early 2021, one intrepid researcher visited employee parking lots of still-operating unionized steel plants in western Pennsylvania to examine the bumper stickers on the cars and trucks. She discovered there were more than ten times as many vehicles with pro-Trump, gun rights, or other conservative signs than vehicles with prounion or Democratic bumper stickers.[3] A similar transformation was taking place in other advanced democracies as well. Far-right nationalist parties succeeded in severing the UK from the European Union in 2016 and gained significant ground in all the other leading countries of Europe (France, Germany, Italy, Sweden, and the Netherlands, among others). Trump lost narrowly to Joe Biden in 2020, but he would come back with a decisive victory in 2024. The support he received from his working-class base was, if anything, stronger the second time around. Trump "has a handle on making it about the American economy first and the American worker first," said a thirty-eight-year-old truck driver from the crucial swing state of Pennsylvania.[4]

Economic shocks were not the only forces feeding far-right populism. In the US, racial animus grounded in the historical legacies of slavery as well as cultural divides between large urban centers and smaller rural communities certainly played a role as well. In Europe, nationalist parties stoked fears of immigrants and Muslim minorities. Whatever the strength of these latent forces, however, they were magnified by job insecurity. When societies come under stress and their traditional ways of life are threatened, resentment toward racial, ethnic, and cultural "outsiders" increases. Hence economic dislocation stoked political extremism both directly and indirectly. First, it diminished trust in centrist political elites and spurred demand for nonmainstream economic policies. Second, it rendered prevailing racial and cultural cleavages more salient and facilitated their exploitation by political demagogues, such as Donald Trump.

Populism has a long history. As we saw in chapter 2, it has its American roots in the economic insecurities fostered by the gold standard during the late nineteenth century. It is typically fueled by a backlash against the elites and the established economic order. It is often the source of reformist policy ideas that later become mainstream. The rejection of the gold standard by the US People's Party and its support for a progressive income tax system, for example, eventually became thoroughly conventional components of modern economic management.

As a form of politics, though, populism is deeply corrosive of democracy. A healthy democracy requires more than free elections and constitutional checks and balances. As Steven Levitsky and Daniel Ziblatt have emphasized, it also rests on adherence by political leaders to unwritten norms that provide guardrails against a decline into authoritarianism. These include respect for the rule of law and a free press, tolerance for diverse viewpoints and identities, acceptance of political rivals as legitimate, and restraint in the use of the institutional machinery of the state against the opposition.[5] These are all necessary conditions for what is sometimes called *liberal democracy*, to distinguish it from pure majority rule. Populist leaders explicitly reject these norms, which they regard as roadblocks to the expression of the popular will. They claim to represent the people as a whole and to defend its interests against the enemies of the people, be they foreigners, racial or ethnic minorities, immigrants, or wealthy capitalists. Under populism, the "will of the people" easily mutates into dictatorial powers.

A broad, thriving middle class comes as close as anything we have to a guarantor of democracy. The idea goes as far back as Aristotle, who famously argued that a free society is possible only in the presence of a large middle class. The poor "do not know how to govern but know how to submit to government of a servile kind," he wrote, while the rich "do not know how to submit to any government, and only know how to govern in the manner of a master." So, unless the middle class hold the reins of power, "the result is a state consisting of slaves and masters, not of free men, and of one class envious and another contemptuous of their fellows."[6] One may quibble with Aristotle's low opinion of the poor and their ability to govern. There are other reasons why a society with huge gaps between the rich and the poor is unlikely to remain democratic for long.[7] Regardless of the underlying mechanism, Aristotle's insight has been validated in innumerable scholarly studies over the years. One comprehensive cross-national study finds that the middle-class share of a country's income is associated not only with better economic policies and higher economic growth but also with greater political freedom, lower political instability, and less discrimination against minorities.[8] An empirical study focusing on democratic backsliding in twenty-two countries in recent decades, including the US, Brazil, Hungary, Poland, Turkey, and India, finds that income inequality is the strongest predictor of which democracies will experience erosion.[9]

These considerations put the quotes with which this chapter opened in their proper context. As good jobs became scarce in the regions worst hit by hyperglobalization, technological change, and deregulation of markets, the middle class grew weak and insecure, and support for extremist politicians rose. Lack of good jobs leads to middle-class erosion, which leads to democratic erosion in turn. Our task for the immediate future is to make the syllogism work in reverse: to build a good jobs economy to strengthen the foundations of the middle class and restore faith in democracy.

The need to confront this challenge is well understood today by politicians of the center right and center left alike. The backlash against hyperglobalization and populists' gains at the polls have awakened them to the need to change economic course. Especially in the US, we have seen a dramatic transformation in the economic narrative of the Democratic Party, which now places good jobs and the middle class at the center of its policy agenda. "Building up the middle class will be a defining goal of my presidency," promised presidential candidate Kamala Harris on the campaign trail.[10] The resignation toward both the consequences and the inevitability of globalization, which the leaders of the party exhibited until recently, would be unthinkable today. Many mainstream Republicans have also grown skeptical of free markets and supportive of government interventions in markets to assist left-behind communities. Marco Rubio, former Republican senator from Florida and future Secretary of State under Trump, exemplifies the shift. "For much of my adult life," he said in 2021 on the floor of the Senate, "'industrial policy' was . . . a dirty phrase for me." But this is no longer the case: "In those instances where the market outcome is bad for our country . . . what we need is targeted industrial policy to further the common good and to protect our people, our country, and our future."[11]

This convergence in the positions of the moderate right and moderate left is welcome. It augurs a potentially significant paradigm shift, from neoliberalism to a more beneficial mix of market incentives and state intervention in pursuit of good jobs. Place-based policies that aim to revitalize left-behind regions and industrial policies that strengthen the productive and innovative backbone of the economy lie at the core of this nascent paradigm, along with the green industrial policies discussed in the previous chapter. If implemented well, it could go far to restore the middle class and ward off the threat of authoritarian populism.

But the new paradigm also comes with two birth defects that could derail it: an excessive focus on manufacturing and an unhealthy obsession with China. Manufacturing is important to an economy for a variety of reasons, but today it plays a very small role in job creation. A good jobs strategy that does not put services—retail, education, care, and other personal services—front and center of the agenda is unlikely to move the needle on good jobs. And the preoccupation with geopolitical competition with China distorts the economic agenda and distracts policy makers from genuine domestic priorities. In this chapter, I sketch out a good jobs policy that provides a corrective to these biases and keeps the focus squarely on productive employment opportunities for the vast majority of workers, who do not have advanced degrees or professional skills.

Good jobs and manufacturing

Good jobs are easier to recognize than to define. In general terms, we can say they are jobs that are secure and pay sufficiently well to enable a middle-class standard of living or provide a career ladder that leads up to it. They come with key labor rights, such as safe working conditions, collective bargaining rights, safeguards against arbitrary dismissal, and possibilities of self-advancement. What constitutes a good job necessarily depends on the broader economic and social context. It carries a different connotation in countries where productivity is low and most people are very poor than it does in advanced economies. Its meaning is also altered as workers' expectations change and the demographics of employment shift, as when women participate in the labor force in greater numbers and men are no longer the sole bread earners.

There have been many attempts at measuring job quality in recent years. Some of these measures are based on objective statistical indicators. For example, the Organisation for Economic Co-operation and Development (OECD) maintains a cross-national database in which job quality is assessed using data on earnings, labor market security (proxied by statistics on unemployment risk and unemployment benefits), and the quality of the working environment (proxied by the incidence of job strain).[12] Other measures are based on self-reports, or subjective assessments. A particularly interesting 2019 US survey measured job quality by taking a weighted average of respondents' satisfaction on ten dimensions of work, including "having a sense of purpose and dignity at work" and "having the power to change things that are unsatisfying at work," in addition to more standard aspects, such as "level of pay" and "job security."[13] The authors of the study defined a good job as one with a weighted-average score of 4 or higher on a scale of 1–5, with each indicator weighted by the importance workers placed on it. By this definition, 60 percent of Americans did not have a good job.

While the importance of good jobs seems self-evident, economists typically have exhibited a blind spot toward jobs and their quality. This is a consequence of the paradigm shift Adam Smith and his followers engineered in economics away from mercantilism. The liberal paradigm, subsequently codified in neoclassical economics, views individuals primarily as consumers. Well-being—what economists call *utility*—is determined by their consumption of goods and services. Jobs matter only indirectly, as a source of income that enables consumers to afford their purchases. This of course fails to capture the full importance of jobs in society. For most workers, jobs are also part of their identity and their main source of social recognition. When people are asked what gives meaning to their lives, their job and occupation typically come second only after family.[14] When workers lose jobs or move from a good job to a mediocre one, they lose not only income but part of their dignity and social identity.[15] In economists' jargon, jobs enter the utility function directly.

It is the manufacturing sector that has traditionally served as the good jobs engine of modern economies. The Industrial Revolution, as its name indicates, unfolded primarily in textile mills and other types of manufacturing activities. The application of new technologies and the use of inanimate sources of energy in these factories enabled, for the first time in human history, sustained growth in the productivity of labor.

It took a while, however, for workers themselves to benefit from this. Real wages in Britain remained stagnant on the whole until the 1830s, well into the Industrial Revolution, though workers in the more rapidly industrializing northern parts of the country did experience some gains.[16] Factory work hardly seemed a path to good jobs at the time. Workers, many of them children, toiled for long hours in hazardous conditions, with little protection against harsh treatment from their boss and under threat of dismissal at a moment's notice. Charles Dickens was sent off to work at one of these factories at age twelve, to help pay for his family's debts after his father was sent to debtors' prison in 1824. He stuck labels on bottles of boot paint blacking for ten hours a day. He would recall years later "its rotten floors and staircase, and the old grey rats swarming down in the cellars, and the sound of their squeaking and scuffling coming up the stairs at all times, and the dirt and decay of the place."[17]

Conditions of work improved over time. Workers began to organize and act collectively to press for their rights. Labor unions were illegal in Britain until the 1870s, but this did not prevent workers from setting them up and joining them. Strikes and other forms of industrial action were common. The Chartists (1838–1857) were the first organized working-class movement pushing for political reform. They demanded in particular the expansion of the suffrage to all male workers, something that would not become a full reality until 1918. As the voices of workers began to be heard in factories and in Parliament, legislation was passed to prevent some of the worst excesses in employment practices. The first act restricting the use of child labor was passed in 1833 and labor unions were legalized in 1871. Pension benefits and unemployment insurance were introduced in 1908 and 1911, respectively. The Labour Party, which had its origins in Britain's labor union movement, was established in 1900. It would eventually surpass the Liberal Party to become the main opposition to the Conservative Party.

These organizational and political changes enabled workers to demand and receive a greater share of the productivity gains made possible by technological innovation. They augured an age in which factory work would be relatively well remunerated, providing a path for many blue-collar workers to join a middle class that had previously been dominated by professionals and small business owners. In the words of a French observer, the "democracy of small property owners" was replaced by a "democracy of wage-earners."[18] The trend reached its peak during the three decades following the end of World War II. This was a period during which the policy makers' worldview was shaped by the Keynesian–Bretton Woods paradigm. In the US and Western Europe alike, the early postwar decades experienced rapid, stable, and *shared* economic growth, with an expanding welfare state (though the US lagged behind Europe), full employment, low inequality, and mass consumption. In Europe, this golden age came to be known as *les trentes glorieuses* ("the glorious thirty years") in France and the *Wirtschaftswunder* ("economic miracle") in Germany. In the US, it was marked by the "Treaty of Detroit," in reference to the 1950 agreement between the United Auto Workers (UAW) and General Motors, which set the framework for subsequent labor negotiations, guaranteeing secure employment, rising wages, and pension benefits.[19] Unionized workers, including for the first time many Black workers, came to enjoy a middle-class quality of life, which they attributed in part to the labor movement.[20]

Thanks to technological progress, labor productivity in manufacturing grew very fast after World War II, much more rapidly than in the rest of the economy, as we saw in chapter 1. This meant that fewer workers were required to produce an identical quantity of autos, steel, or garments. Yet employment in manufacturing continued to grow in most advanced economies through the early postwar decades. Workers' pay also improved. What explains this apparent paradox is the increase in incomes that the productivity growth enabled. As the middle class grew richer, it demanded more consumer goods and services, more than offsetting innovation's immediate negative impact on labor demand.

This happy situation did not last very long. By the 1970s, the manufacturing share of employment was in decline pretty much in all developed economies—a process that came to be called deindustrialization. Part of the reason was that overall productivity growth declined, slowing down the expansion of aggregate demand. A shift in consumer demand from goods to services also played a role. But the more important factor was the transformation in manufacturing technologies. After the 1970s, technological progress increasingly favored machines and automation—and, among workers, the more skilled ones. Manufacturing firms invested heavily in capital equipment. They continued to hire skilled workers, but less educated workers, who had formed the backbone of manufacturing factories, began to have a harder time. In the US, the total number of jobs in goods-producing sectors actually fell by four million between 1979 and 2022, while jobs in services increased by fifty-nine million.[21] At its height, manufacturing employed around a third (or more) of all workers in the advanced economies. Today this share is down to below 9 percent in the US and around 18 percent in Germany.

This was not the first time the structure of employment shifted dramatically in today's advanced economies. A similar transformation had occurred earlier in agriculture. As agricultural productivity rose, thanks to mechanization and other new technologies, societies could be fed with far fewer farmers. People flocked from the countryside to urban areas. It was manufacturing (and related services) that absorbed the workers released from farms. Since manufacturing offered productive, high-paying jobs, this was good for both equity and economic growth. But when manufacturing employment too began to shrink, there was no comparable bonus. Most blue-collar workers either ended up in low-paying services or withdrew from the labor market, discouraged by the lack of good jobs. The result was what economists call *labor market polarization.* College-educated and other highly skilled workers did well, while production workers (along with those in sales, clerical, and other occupations adversely affected by automation) generally did poorly.[22]

The middle class took a big hit from these changes in labor markets. In the US, the share of adults living in middle-class households shrank from 61 percent in 1971 to 50 percent in 2021, according to one study.[23] As male earnings fell and employment became less stable, families needed two or more incomes to have a chance of reaching middle-class living standards. In Europe, the collapse of the middle class was not as marked, but economic insecurity and vulnerability rose throughout the continent as more middle-class workers faced unemployment and the risk of falling into poverty along with their families.[24]

Where will the good jobs come from?

Disappointingly, since the 1980s advanced economies have failed to generate adequate numbers of good jobs to sustain a prosperous and growing middle class. Against that background, political leaders' rediscovery of manufacturing is not surprising. In their different ways, Donald Trump and Joe Biden both embraced revitalizing manufacturing as an avenue for good jobs. In August 2020, then president Trump stood before a Westinghouse plant to tout his accomplishments: "We're building factories now. We're building plants." "You'll see what's going to be happening with the job numbers very soon," he promised.[25] Four years later, in March 2024, President Biden was on the campus of Intel's semiconductor facility, the recipient of billions of dollars of grants from the federal government. He hailed the jobs the investment had created. "Where the hell is it written saying that we're not going to be the manufacturing capital of the world again?" he declared.[26]

Manufacturing is everywhere these days, except for where it counts for the middle class: in the job numbers. Manufacturing employment did rise during Trump's presidency until the pandemic struck in early 2020, by about 400,000 workers. But this increase has to be viewed in the context of the overall labor force, which expanded by seven million workers in the same period. As a share of nonfarm employment, the manufacturing sector remained flat at 8.5 percent under Trump. Biden adopted ambitious industrial policies in green industries and semiconductors and can take credit for the significant boost in manufacturing investment that ensued. Construction spending in manufacturing actually doubled in real terms during Biden's term in office. Yet manufacturing employment resumed its decline (relative to total nonfarm employment), dropping from 8.5 percent to an all-time low of 8.1 percent (in December 2024).

At first sight, it may seem puzzling that the revival in investment has not boosted employment in manufacturing. But a factory today is very different from what it was in the 1950s or 1960s. Consider one of the Biden administration's signature achievements under the CHIPS Act, the Taiwan Semiconductor Manufacturing Company's investment in Arizona to make some of the world's most advanced chips. TSMC was awarded $6.6 billion in grants and up to $5 billion in loans by the federal government to build a third state-of-the art facility in the state. Once the facility is completed, TSMC's investment in Arizona will total $65 billion.[27] The number of workers that will be employed in these plants: 6,000. That's a whopping $10 million investment per job. No doubt, there will be additional jobs in construction and in supplier industries as well.[28] Nevertheless, these are not numbers large enough to move the needle and reverse employment deindustrialization.

As today's manufacturing typically requires significant capital outlays and a relatively skilled, but small workforce, it exhibits an output-employment disconnect. Look at the countries with the world's most successful manufacturing industries and you will find they have been no better at avoiding job loss in their factories. Since the 1990s, Taiwan, South Korea, Malaysia, Japan, and Turkey have all experienced a rise in the real share of manufacturing value added in GDP. Yet in all of them the sector's share in employment has fallen, sometimes drastically (as in Japan and South Korea).[29] Germany has a larger manufacturing sector than the US, relative to the size of its economy, but its share of manufacturing workers has dropped like a rock. China, the world's factory, registers a growing export surplus in manufactures nearly every year. Yet the country's manufacturing employment has been in decline since 2011.

None of this is to downplay the importance of manufacturing along other dimensions. Manufacturing plays an outsized role in driving innovation, and it is key to national security. It will play a critical role in the green transition, as we saw in the previous chapter. Governments have legitimate reasons to ensure they have a solid manufacturing base. But where good jobs and the middle class are concerned, manufacturing is no longer the answer. With the employment picture so bleak in the world's manufacturing powerhouses, it is extremely unlikely that the US or advanced economies in Europe can turn manufacturing into a job engine, even if they are successful in revitalizing investment and output in the sector. We cannot run history in reverse.

The green transition does present new employment opportunities. There will be good jobs in construction of solar and wind facilities, green manufacturing, and renewables. One study estimates that five new jobs will be created for each $1 million shift from brown to green sources of energy.[30] But the main impact of the green transition will be to shuffle jobs across economic activities and regions, which will in fact complicate existing labor market imbalances.[31] Evidence from Europe suggests that green jobs are typically more skill intensive than the brown jobs they replace.[32] Even if addressed successfully, the climate transition will not provide a huge boost to labor demand. The solution to the good jobs problem will have to be found elsewhere.

Services are by far the largest employer today in all advanced economies. In the US, the top five occupations are retail sales, home health and personal care, general management, fast-food and counter work, and cashier. Only general management requires a college degree. According to Bureau of Labor Statistics projections, the number of jobs in retail sales and cashiering will decline by 2033, though both occupations will remain significant sources of employment. Jobs in home health and personal care will explode, registering the largest increase among all occupations (a net increase of 805,000 jobs). This is nearly twice the size of the increase in the next most rapidly expanding occupation, software developers (410,000). Other occupations with the most significant increases are cooks (278,000), stockers and order fillers (179,000), and registered nurses (177,000). Three of these top five expanding occupations (home health and personal care, restaurant cooks, and stockers and order fillers) do not require college degrees and are low wage, paying at present significantly below the US median wage. Of the top ten largest occupations projected for 2033, only two require a college education.[33]

So where will the good jobs come from? The answer is services. Whether we like it or not, services will remain the primary labor-absorbing segment of the economy. If we want to shore up the middle class, we have no choice but to turn bad jobs in services into good ones. A second important conclusion is that greater investment in education will not help much here, as important as it may be for other reasons: most of the top occupations of the future do not require college or advanced degrees.

Turning bad jobs into good ones

Adelle Waldman's 2024 novel, *Help Wanted*, revolves around the lives of a group of workers at a fictional big-box store, similar to Target, called Town Square. The store is located in a community that has fallen on hard times after the departure of IBM and the Great Recession. The town has become a popular summer destination for wealthy visitors from nearby New York City, which is a mixed blessing as housing has become more expensive and less affordable. Even though the workers at Town Square try to make the best of it, they are caught in a typical bad job trap. Among other inequities, the company meticulously manages the hours of its workers to make sure they do not qualify for health benefits. Coupled with low pay, this leaves the store's employees with little choice but to take up second jobs.

Little Will, a high school graduate, is manager of "Team Movement," a group of workers who unpack and shelve the materials from delivery trucks overnight, before the store opens in the morning. He ruminates about his job as he throws boxes onto a truck in the early hours of the morning:

> He had nothing against retail in principle. Just Town Square. He despised its ethos of corner-cutting . . . , its willingness to cheat employees in any way that was technically not illegal (and call it "performing its fiduciary duty to stockholders"), its arbitrary rules, such as its insistence that the unload take no more than an hour, regardless of the size of the truck and no matter how little difference it made to finish at 5:01 rather than 5:00. Corporate didn't trust its own workers, was what it came down to—the big shots thought that without a hard deadline, its employees wouldn't work efficiently, which showed just how little corporate understood the people it employed.

Little Will thought he might have gone to college, but he failed to get a hockey scholarship. He would have preferred working in his father's carpet-and-tile store, as the next best thing, but the store had gone under during the financial crisis.

> Little Will's own ideas about business had been absorbed from his father, who never would have dreamed of, say, cutting an employee's hours to avoid paying for their health insurance. His father had felt an obligation to the people who worked for him, many of

whom had been with him for decades. . . . For decades—through recessions, gas shortages, periods of inflation, real estate depreciation, the departure of IBM—the store had survived, supporting their family and its ten or so employees. It would have continued to do so if the housing and lending markets hadn't collapsed simultaneously in 2008. That was the rub, both things happening at once. If Saunders & Son had gotten a loan to tide it over until home sales picked up, it would not only have regained its footing quickly but would be doing better than ever. All those second-home buyers from the city who had recently bid up prices around here, making it hard for Little Will to afford a house, would have been excellent customers for a high-quality, service-oriented carpet-and-tile store.[34]

Now he was stuck at a job with low pay, limited advancement opportunities, and a corporate culture that discouraged initiative and looked at workers as disposable and easily replaceable cogs in a machine.

What would make Little Will and his coworkers' jobs better? For starters, we might imagine the employees having a greater voice in the workplace. The company, like so many others in the US, is vehemently antiunion and is known to penalize workers trying to organize. "The year before, someone in Harvest—the team responsible for fresh produce and perishables—was fired for 'time theft' after he'd been spotted talking briefly to a union organizer during his shift."[35] As we saw during the Industrial Revolution, labor organization is critical for workers to obtain a fair share of the fruits of their labor. Unions were important in ensuring that the postwar period was one of shared prosperity in the US and Western Europe. Unions play at least three beneficial roles. They help equalize bargaining power between workers and their employers. They enhance productivity by giving workers voice and motivating them to work better. And they act as a counterweight to monopsony power, reducing the ability of local employers to repress wages (and levels of employment) by exercising market power. Note that the latter two effects go beyond equity and relate to productive efficiency. Economies in which labor has a significant voice are fairer; they can also be more productive.[36]

But more recently unions have fallen on hard times. In the US, union membership has been on the decline for five decades and currently stands at 10 percent, half its level in the early 1980s.[37] Union density tends to be higher in Europe but has generally fallen there as well.[38] Note that collective bargaining coverage can be significantly higher than what unionization rates indicate. In most countries outside the US, terms agreed with unions are extended to workers in the same sector that are not members of the union. In France, for example, the unionization rate is not higher than that of the US, but almost all workers are covered by collective bargaining.

Part of the decline in unionization can be attributed to government policies, which in the neoliberal era have been more hostile to labor unions. In the US, labor laws give employers considerable leeway in blocking unionization, and the penalties for violating the laws are minor. Given structural changes in the economy and deindustrialization in particular, however, it is not clear that unions can regain their past strength. Personal services and the gig economy are not as conducive to labor organization as mass production in factories. When workers do not share a workplace or toil in close contact with each other, they are less likely to develop a common identity (a "class consciousness") and articulate shared grievances and aspirations.

An alternative to union representation is government-mandated wage and employment standards. Governments already set minimum wages and basic workplace regulations on health and safety. The generosity of these rules has a direct bearing on job quality. The economist Arin Dube has proposed instituting wage boards to set minimum wages that differ by sector, occupation, and location. Such a system would provide greater flexibility than a national minimum wage, which can at best set a floor on workers' standard of living.[39] As Dube explains, wage boards might involve participation by diverse stakeholders, including businesses, workers, citizen groups, and politicians. Importantly, wage boards could be a vehicle for the articulation of the social value of work. The COVID pandemic exposed the huge chasm that currently exists between the societal importance of "essential work" in health, education, and food services on the one hand and its market remuneration on the other. A more participatory and deliberative approach to wage setting in such occupations might help close some of this gap.

Wage and employment regulations ensure that workers receive a fair share of the social surplus that their work generates. They can also contribute to greater productivity, by incentivizing workers to be more engaged in what they do and reducing costly labor turnover. Good jobs can sometimes pay for themselves. Hence improving job quality can be in the self-interest of the employers as well. Zeynep Ton has made a forceful case for this approach, arguing that retailers and other service companies can help their own bottom line by treating their workers better.[40] Workers with higher pay and better benefits are less likely to quit. This lowers hiring and training costs, which are often quite significant.

Workers who are given greater autonomy and decision-making power are more likely to come up with ideas to increase operational efficiency. An example is provided in the novel *Help Wanted*. One of the workers at the store, Raymond, is bothered by the unpacking process in the warehouse, which he finds inefficient and disorganized. He suggests a different method that would reduce the time it would take to do the same work. But he meets resistance from others. One of his coworkers, Ruby, doesn't "see why she should go out of her way for an employer that never went out of its way for her." His supervisor, Meredith, is also dismissive. If the change made sense, she retorts, "don't you think it would be part of our regular process?" Raymond understands what Meredith is implying: "If this were a such good idea, someone smarter than Raymond—someone in corporate—would have thought of it."[41] Eventually, Raymond wins out, to the store's benefit.

This is fiction, of course, but Ton's work with retailers, described in her book *The Case for Good Jobs*, makes a compelling case that corporations can benefit by taking the "high road" with their workers. A change in corporate culture in that direction would certainly be an improvement. But there are limits to how far we can push

BUILDING A GOOD JOBS ECONOMY 107

the high-road strategy. For one thing, it would not reach the vast numbers of low-paid workers who are in smaller enterprises or are self-employed. For another, employers' goodwill can take us only so far. Taking care of workers only to the extent that it benefits corporate profits leaves room for a host of undesirable outcomes. Employers would still have a bias toward practices that come at the expense of job quality as long as they increase overall productivity (no matter by how little).[42] Think, for example, of employee tracking technologies that monitor workers' actions (movements, speech, keystrokes) in detail. Such technologies may optimize workplace efficiency, but they conflict with worker privacy and autonomy. Furthermore, employers with a "high-road" corporate culture often tend to be among the most allergic to labor unions (or any other form of collective labor voice) and to government regulation of labor practices.

Collective bargaining and government-mandated standards have an important downside too. They can privilege more senior workers and those that already have job security while making it harder for younger and less educated job seekers to find employment. In France, for example, a high minimum wage ensures lower inequality than in the US and better jobs for employees at the lower end of the scale. But it also has a negative effect on job creation for young, unskilled workers and keeps many youth unemployed or out of the labor market. Youth unemployment stood as high as 25 percent before the introduction of an apprenticeship scheme in 2018 that lowered the cost to employers of hiring young workers. Holding the productivity of workers constant, there is an inescapable trade-off between the quantity and quality of jobs. Mandating higher wages and better working conditions comes at the cost of reducing the availability of jobs.

The only way to get around this cruel constraint is to increase the productivity of workers in low-pay, low-quality jobs. As we saw in the aftermath of the Industrial Revolution, labor productivity is a necessary, if by no means sufficient, condition for good jobs. We now need a corresponding revolution in services. This requires a strategy that relies neither on the paternalism of employers nor solely on collective bargaining or government regulations, and that directly targets productivity growth in a broad range of services.

Policies to enhance labor productivity in services

Labor productivity is the physical quantity of output produced per unit of labor—number of cars or tons of steel, say, per hour of work. To be meaningful, the measure has to keep track of the attributes of what is being produced. A high-performance luxury car is not the same as a family sedan. We can increase labor productivity either by producing more of the same good or service, by producing an identical quantity but with improved features, or by a combination of the two, for the same amount of labor. Since quantifying quality is difficult, measuring labor productivity can be tricky. The difficulty is magnified in the case of services such as home care, retail, education, or food preparation. The number of people served is the most direct measure, but it is obviously not enough. We would also want to know how effectively the service was delivered, whether the intended effects (such as improved health or learning) were accomplished, how satisfied the customers were, and so on.

These are tough issues that economists and statisticians spend a lot of time on, but they need not detain us here. In practice, we recognize an increase in services productivity when a salesperson is well informed and provides genuinely helpful purchasing advice, a cook delivers tastier food or serves more customers, a home health aide improves the health status of the elderly while making them feel better, a driver carries more packages to the correct destination, or a software engineer writes cleaner code with fewer bugs. When such improvements are made, they are reflected in a greater willingness of customers to pay for the service (or in reduced costs). A similar principle applies to nonmarketed services, such as public health or education, which do not have a market price. Improvements in the productivity of public services are reflected in a greater willingness on the part of the public to pay the taxes that support such services or in reduced administrative costs.

Historically, it has proved difficult to increase productivity in many services, which is why manufacturing productivity has generally outstripped services productivity.[43] The nature of the challenge is illustrated by economists' favorite example of stagnant labor productivity in services: the orchestra conductor. It takes as long to conduct a Beethoven symphony today as it did back in the nineteenth century, and while some conductors are better than others, we can presume the listening experience to have been just as enjoyable in Beethoven's day. Or consider barbers. Hairstyles may have changed over time, but the technology of providing haircuts has barely altered, requiring the same thirty minutes or so of sitting in the barber's chair.

But raising services productivity is not impossible either. Progress happens in part through the creation of entirely new occupations, such as DJ, software programmer, or airplane pilot. It also occurs through new knowledge and new technologies that enable traditional occupations to be performed more effectively. A teacher can deliver much better education by virtue of having access to a greater stock of knowledge. A health worker can perform tasks unimaginable in earlier times thanks to medical technology. An Uber driver can get her customer to her destination a lot faster than the horse-drawn carriage of old. Leaving live performance aside, even a musician or artist can now serve much larger audiences because the internet and recording technology provide access to a truly global market. We do not have to presume that progress in services should be as rapid as in manufacturing to be still hopeful about the possibility that technological and organizational changes in service occupations will deliver increases in labor productivity. Moreover, traditional service industries, such as personal services, education, and public services, are highly labor intensive. That means that the impact of services productivity growth on workers is more direct and larger in magnitude.

The task of government policy is to facilitate these changes. It consists of providing the public inputs, including financial incentives, that make higher productivity—and hence good jobs—possible for the less-than-college-educated segment of the labor force. To see what this might mean in a specific case, recall Little Will and his dream of joining his father's carpet-and-tile company. In its time, this small business had enabled a middle-class standard of living for two generations of Little Will's family, along with good jobs for ten or so workers. But it was driven to bankruptcy by the financial crisis of 2008–2009 as credit rates soared and loans for small businesses dried up. Little Will rues the missed opportunity: with many wealthy families having moved nearby, he could have been a supplier, had the store survived, of high-end, high-quality carpet and tiling services for a growing local market. Instead, Little Will works at a low-paying job he hates.

Imagine there were public agencies that provided a suite of support services for small businesses and entrepreneurs-to-be. These services would range widely from customized training for workforce and management to assistance with marketing and technology. In this instance, the most critical input would be credit. Had Little Will's father been able to secure a line of credit for his business, it might have weathered the storm, allowing the business to survive and Little Will to pursue his preferred career plan. Private financial markets are typically procyclical, meaning they are generous in good times but become stingy in bad times, just when a loan may be most needed. Most governments do maintain programs of credit for small businesses, but they do not always work well. In the US, Small Business Administration (SBA) loans generally go to areas well served by private banks and are not targeted to the neediest customers or regions.[44]

Other types of public assistance may have helped as well. Long before his store ran into trouble, Little Will's father would have benefited from management and financial training, enabling him to run his business better and perhaps be more prepared for an eventual market downturn. Market research would have helped him expand his customer base. Technology and machinery would have allowed him to supply higher-quality products. The workers he hired could have come trained in the relevant skills. And as he became more successful and looked to expand, thanks to these inputs, he could have used help to find a more suitable site for his growing business. These kinds of public inputs are broadly known as *extension services*. They have a long history in the US and other countries. Typically, however, extension services focus on agriculture and manufacturing. They have never had a services focus.

Sometimes what is needed is a financial carrot. Grants or subsidies can help small businesses get off the ground, take risks and experiment with new products or processes, and establish clusters of related firms. Tax incentives are of course a common tool to attract investment and create jobs. Even before Biden's ramping up of industrial policies in semiconductors and green industries, state and local governments spent tens of billions of dollars in tax incentives and other subsidies to woo firms.[45] Similar programs are common all over the world. Once again, though, subsidies have typically focused on manufacturing or large service firms in the belief that it is those firms that bring good jobs and economic dynamism. Amazon has been a prime beneficiary of such largesse in recent years, receiving nearly $7 billion in tax breaks by playing local governments off against each other. In 2019, the state of Virginia provided Amazon with a package of $750 million in incentives, including a whopping $22,000 grant per employee in return for Amazon creating tens of thousands of jobs with an average pay of at least $150,000 a year.[46] (Average pay is calculated by dividing the total wage bill by the number of employees, so the condition can be met by employing highly paid professionals along with low-wage workers.)

At the federal level, President Biden's CHIPS and IRA initiatives are massive subsidy programs targeted primarily at manufacturing investments. The CHIPS Act unleashed $53 billion in federal grants and subsidies for semiconductor facilities and research. The IRA encompassed around $1 trillion of tax incentives for renewables and green investments, as discussed in the previous chapter. Many of the incentives are conditioned on good labor practices by recipients, such as paying the "prevailing wage" and investing in workforce development.

Tax incentives have a poor track record in the US. Even when they create new jobs, they do so at high cost (compared to many of the extension services mentioned earlier) and tend to be poorly targeted on good jobs specifically.[47] They are most successful when they combine rigorous selection of recipients based on clear criteria with discretion and close monitoring to ensure firms live up to their employment and investment promises.[48] There is also some evidence, from other countries, that they are more effective when they are provided to smaller and medium-sized firms.[49] Perhaps the greatest shortcoming of subsidies is that, unless they are specifically designed for that purpose, they do nothing to directly encourage increased productivity alongside job creation.

Traditionally, government programs targeting workers' transition to good jobs have focused on training. Training provides workers with what economists call "human capital" and thereby increases their productivity and pay. Training programs do not always work well, however. Multiple reviews of the evidence on vocational training find that the benefits are often very small or nil.[50] One reason is that the programs do not consistently target the relevant binding constraints that render good jobs scarce. Low-wage workers or first-time entrants in the labor market might be unable to access better jobs for a variety of reasons. They may lack the vocational skills that the training helps provide. But they may also lack, say, access to transportation or the soft skills needed to interview well. There may be too few firms in the area looking for workers. Or the available training may be in occupations that firms are not trying to fill.

A coordinated, cross-sectoral approach at the local level

The training programs that work best in the US are local, community-based initiatives that work closely with particular employers. Exemplified by Project Quest, Per Scholas, and the Wisconsin Regional Training Program (WRTP), these are "sectoral training programs" that target specific industries or occupations—health care, information technology, construction—with the potential of local employment creation. Training courses are designed in close association with prospective employers. Trainees also receive wraparound services customized to their needs, including soft skills, child care, transportation, remedial education, and follow-up assistance after job placement. An important element of these programs' success is the relationship of trust that develops between the training organization and the employers it serves. This results in a high level of cooperation, and even the adjustment of hiring practices by employers to serve the local community better.[51] At the same time, community engagement ensures programs are not captured by business interests. There have been some experiments in Europe as well around this model of job placement and training services closely integrated with employers.[52]

Sectoral training programs remain small and have yet to leave a large footprint on labor markets.[53] But their success holds broader lessons. It points to three critical ingredients that good jobs programs require. First, there needs to be local leadership in providing a vision of the future economic landscape. Sectoral training programs do this by identifying segments of the labor market where intervention would be most effective. In other contexts, leadership can be provided by a variety of people or organizations, ranging from the local chamber of commerce to a community organization to an economic development agency. Second, they must coordinate across both the private and public sectors and different types of public inputs beyond vocational training. Tax incentives, for example, may be most effective when they are packaged with the provision of customized technology, training, infrastructure, and other inputs that enable productive upgrading.[54] And third, they must work on both sides of the labor market, with workers and firms together. This is important because workforce development and business development have often moved on separate tracks, serving different clients and priorities. In practice, good jobs require good firms and vice versa. Good jobs programs that work best are those where these three conditions are satisfied.[55]

The Right Place, a public-private partnership based in western Michigan, provides an example from the business development side. Set up by a group of local businesspeople in the mid-1980s to reverse the region's economic slide, it provides comprehensive, one-stop assistance to businesses. This includes development of strategic plans for the region, guidance through a maze of tax incentives, site location services, connections to local suppliers, and recruiting and training of the local workforce. While The Right Place is better known for its work on attracting investment from outside, the bulk of its work actually focuses on understanding and responding to the needs of local, family-owned businesses. These firms rely on The Right Place for everything from workplace layout assistance to help with immigration authorities. The organization provides a vital coordination and bridging function in an institutional and funding landscape that is divided into distinct policy silos. Birgit Klohs was president of The Right Place for over three decades after its founding. "We are at the center of everything, but control nothing," she says.[56]

In the aftermath of the China trade shock and the global financial crisis, the husband-and-wife team of James and Deborah Fallows hopped around the country in their single-engine prop airplane. They were hoping to learn why some communities were better able to pull themselves together. They found similar collaborations at work all over: A family-owned scrap-recycling company in little Holland, Michigan, had joined forces with the state correctional system to employ former convicts who would otherwise have trouble reentering the workforce. A partnership among the city, county, and state governments, the local colleges and universities, and tech start-up firms in Fresno, California, had set up a training program in computer skills for high school dropouts and other unemployed workers. Large local firms, including GE, BMW, and Michelin, had worked with the local public school system in Greenville, South Carolina, to establish and staff an Elementary School of Engineering in a poor neighborhood of the city.[57]

James Fallows had spent four years in East and Southeast Asia as a journalist, and he was reminded of industrial policy he had observed there by the similarities with the successful models. "Had a politician labeled [this strategy] 'picking winners' or 'industrial policy,' it would have been stillborn," remarks James Fallows. But "as a series of 'public-private partnerships,' it is a source of civic pride."[58]

As these examples suggest, local programs can succeed when communities engineer partnerships around a shared vision to deliver complementary investments in the workforce, infrastructure, business incentives, and technology. As we saw in the previous chapter in the context of green industrial policies and examine further in chapter 6, this is a common approach underpinning all successful "productivist" policies that target structural changes in the economy. Inspired by this vision, the Biden administration launched several programs directly targeted at good jobs. These programs provided multiyear federal funding to support the development of regional clusters, with a focus on job training, entrepreneurship, and infrastructure. They included the Build Back Better Regional Challenge (BBRC), the Good Jobs Challenge, and the Recompete Program. The programs invited local, cross-sectoral partnerships to submit bids, which were then evaluated according to several criteria, including good jobs creation.[59] The expectation was that the funding would incentivize local initiatives and mobilize coordinating capacity.

To have greater impact, these and other similar programs have to overcome two shortcomings. First, they focus too heavily on manufacturing and energy transition, paying little attention to services, which have the greatest job creation prospects. For example, of the twenty-one projects funded by the BBRC, only a couple revolve around services (health and finance).[60] Second, they lack in ambition and in resources, with budgets in the hundreds of millions rather than billions. This is a footnote compared to the size of the CHIPS and IRA programs, which are in the tens and hundreds of billions of dollars. But they are significant as a proof of concept. They provide a model to emulate and scale up, both in the US and in other advanced economies.[61]

Of all the inputs needed to raise productivity in services, one is of particular significance: technology. While local initiatives and extension services can play an important role in disseminating existing technologies, a good jobs program also requires the development of new technologies. In particular, it needs a dedicated effort at stimulating *labor-friendly* innovations—those that enable workers with a lower education level to perform a greater range of tasks, including those that are typically performed by highly educated professionals.

Promoting labor-friendly technologies

During the early postwar decades, American physicians were increasingly choosing lucrative specialties. The result was a shortage of primary care physicians, leaving many families underserved. Hardest hit were poorer children in rural areas. In response, two physicians at the University of Colorado at Boulder inaugurated a training program for a new medical occupation: the nurse practitioner. Nurse practitioners perform tasks that previously only physicians could do: they order and interpret diagnostic tests and can prescribe treatment. In the words of David Autor, they are elite decision makers.[62] With help from funding from the federal government, nurse practitioner training programs expanded rapidly from the late 1960s on. Today there are 266,000 nurse practitioners in the US, earning a median salary of $126,000. The profession is projected to be among the fastest-growing occupations in the next decade.[63]

A nurse practitioner needs training at the master's level, so the example is not directly relevant to those with less than college degrees for whom good jobs are particularly scarce. But, as Autor notes, it is a useful illustration nonetheless of how it is possible to create job ladders to more remunerative work by enabling workers to perform tasks that were previously beyond reach and that only significantly more trained professionals could perform. The lesson applies to a broad range of services such as care, education, and retail. It represents one of the most important ways in which low-pay, low-status work can be transformed into good jobs.

Autor explains that the transformation in nursing was enabled by both organizational and technological changes. On the organizational front, many obstacles had to be overcome: training, certification, and opposition by physicians who resisted nurse practitioners encroaching on their turf. For example, nurse practitioners obtained the right to be reimbursed directly from the federal government only in 1997, and even then only at 85 percent of a physician's rate.[64] On the technological front, the introduction of new medical technologies, such as diagnostic and testing methods, electronic medical records, and other information and communication technology (ICT) tools, was also critical. These advancements made it possible for nurse practitioners to establish themselves as medical decision makers. Medicine in fact has a long history of new technologies enabling nurses to perform more advanced functions. The stethoscope and sphygmomanometer made taking blood pressure a regular part of a nurse's job. The ophthalmoscope and otoscope similarly moved some health checks from the physician to the nurse. Both transitions were initially resisted but eventually became commonplace.[65]

It is possible to contemplate a similar upgrade for jobs that are typically much less well remunerated and do not require a college education. Consider long-term care.[66] This occupation is set to expand rapidly in future years as the population continues to age and demand for in-home or assisted-living arrangements increases. Despite the high demand for workers in this sector, the quality of the jobs tends to be notoriously poor. Employees are mostly women and disproportionately people of color. Long-term care workers are typically regarded as performing low-skill jobs and are not viewed as "real members of the care team."[67] While regulations that enhance pay and work standards may help improve these jobs, they also risk pricing less experienced care aides out of the market. The surest way to enhance job quality is to raise the productivity of the care workers directly. This would allow care workers to serve their patients better, enhance patients' satisfaction, and reduce the cost of long-term care to make room for better compensation.

Just as with nurse practitioners, this upgrading would require both organizational and technological changes. At present, home care aides are not permitted to undertake simple tasks, such as dressings of bandages or installing nasal or eye drops, which makes it, in the words of Paul Osterman, "difficult to increase the productivity of aides in a way that might underwrite compensation gains."[68] With better training and different work rules, long-term care workers could perform a broader range of tasks. Osterman notes that it might be possible to increase productivity in long-term care through a strategy that mimics Japanese firms' innovations in auto manufacturing. This would require investing in workers' skills, providing workers with greater voice, discretion, and autonomy, and giving them more responsibility for the quality of the service. Care workers that are empowered with greater autonomy and decision making can use their knowledge of residents and patients to customize their services and provide more flexible care (with regard to scheduling, food service, and treatments).[69]

These organizational changes need to be supported by the introduction of new technologies that complement caregivers' skills, such as digital tools that enable caregivers to collect real-time information and respond quickly and efficiently to the needs of individual residents. Many of these tools already exist. They include telemedicine, wearable sensors, and assistive robots. However, few are optimized to enhance caregivers' responsibilities and their relationship with patients. In 2020, Finland introduced a program to integrate new technologies and digital services into home care for older people. The program included technology training for the caregivers and introducing new care work roles.[70] A report on the results notes the following:

> Technology use made professionals' work more versatile . . . and caregivers discovered new ways to be involved in the daily lives of older people. Moreover, professionals considered that technology use aids them in controlling their work, e.g., they were able to direct resources better than before and anticipate contacts. . . . Professionals developed new processes to work, to deal with technology use, and to anticipate and react to the needs of older people. . . . Visits and caring were able to be modified based on needs. Professionals received information easily and they were able to reconsider the urgency of the care they needed.[71]

There could be many productivity benefits from these technologies: lower turnover and burnout on the part of care workers, reduced admissions to more expensive nursing homes, reduced hospitalization rates, better management of chronic conditions, and quicker and smoother transitions out of acute care, in addition to improved customer satisfaction.[72]

Other services can benefit from labor-friendly technologies as well. In retail, managers' excessive confidence in automation, coupled with a lack of trust in their workers, often results in the introduction of technologies that not only bypass workers but also diminish productivity. Zeynep Ton cites examples: employee tracking and monitoring technologies that leave workers dispirited and unmotivated; automated corporate ordering systems that leave stores filled with unsaleable merchandise, such as New York Yankees gear in the Boston area or beach chairs in September; expensive hair care and yoga products in low-income neighborhoods. Each of these mistakes could have been avoided by giving frontline workers greater decision-making powers. By contrast, there are also technologies that empower workers and enable them to be more productive. Ton discusses one retail chain where "an app allowed the store's Tire & Battery Center to find the right tire . . . in under five minutes, whereas it used to take twenty minutes or more. Another app . . . allowed associates to easily access store information, from product prices and locations to who was working what shift that day."[73]

Remote services can also benefit from AI. A study of a Fortune 500 software company by Erik Brynjolfsson, Danielle Li, and Lindsey Raymond found that the introduction of a generative AI tool that provides conversational guidance to customer support agents was particularly helpful to novice and less experienced employees, allowing them to resolve more questions in the same amount of time.[74] The fact that the gains went mostly to less skilled agents is noteworthy. It suggests, as the authors note, that AI enabled novice agents, at least in this instance, to mimic the more productive agents by transmitting the behavioral patterns of the latter to the former. The agents were also treated better by customers, indicating that customer satisfaction increased as well. Generative AI has the potential to improve the productivity of a wide range of occupations beyond medical staff, care workers, and retail workers, including teachers, electricians, and plumbers.[75] Eventually, employers may put less of a premium on college education or professional skills as a result, to the benefit of workers without college degrees.[76]

The right kind of technology can make a big difference. But there is no guarantee that technologies such as AI will in fact help most workers. How technological change affects workers' well-being is complicated; the relationship can go either way. Examples of technological innovation allowing workers to do more skilled work go back to the very early days of the Industrial Revolution. Before the introduction of machines such as the spinning jenny (1764), the water frame (1769), or the spinning mule (1779), cotton textiles were the province of highly skilled craftsmen. Mechanization struck a blow to these craftsmen by permitting ordinary workers, often children, to take their place (though it took a while for the benefits to trickle down to the workers themselves, as we saw). On the other hand, automation and what economists call skill-biased technological change has had the opposite effect in recent decades. Since the early 1980s, the direction of innovation has favored skilled professionals and capitalists. Less educated workers were replaced by machines and better educated professionals, and their wages stagnated. These days digital tools can be used to monitor and track workers or to enhance their agency and decision making, as in the examples above. Innovation is not always the ordinary worker's friend.[77] To reap the full potential of technology, greater focus on and investment in worker-friendly innovation is needed.

The direction of technological change—whom it helps and hurts—depends on many things. One obvious determinant is the relative cost and benefit to businesses of the different types of technologies. When capital is cheap and labor is expensive, we are more likely to see investment in labor-saving and capital-biased technology. During the postwar period, relatively low interest, investment subsidies (i.e., tax credits), and collective bargaining practices raised the return to machinery relative to labor-friendly technologies. Increased import competition from low-wage countries in Asia had the same effect. Venture capital firms that finance a significant part of innovation in the US generally prefer technologies where the rewards to shareholders can be quickly monetized; they naturally undervalue innovations that benefit workers or society at large.

Norms also play a role. Technologists and innovators often view the replacement of labor as inherently desirable and undervalue the contributions of human agency and autonomy. Elon Musk originally built a fully automated plant for Tesla's Model 3 designed to operate without any workers. When the plant failed to reach targeted production levels and brought the company to the edge of bankruptcy, he had to build a conventional assembly line. "Humans are under-rated," he conceded on Twitter.[78] All these biases are magnified when workers have little voice in the workplace and no influence over which technologies are developed and adopted.

These considerations suggest the need for a concerted effort by governments to steer technology more consciously in a labor-friendly direction. I have proposed the launch of a national innovation effort under the US Advanced Research Projects Agency (ARPA) model with a focus specifically on the development of labor-friendly technologies, such as those discussed above.[79] Currently, similar efforts are directed at defense-related technologies (DARPA), advanced energy technologies (ARPA-E), and biomedical and health technologies (ARPA-H). Like its predecessors, this new innovation program—let's call it ARPA-W for ARPA workers—would target the development of new technologies at the frontier of science and technology, where solutions are unclear and many efforts necessarily fail. But it would focus on technologies that are best suited to complement human labor and ingenuity and augment less educated workers' capabilities. It would prioritize technologies that expand the range of tasks these workers can perform and increase their ability to customize services to specific needs and types of customer demand. The overarching objective would be to allow workers to do what they cannot presently do, instead of displacing them by taking over the tasks that they already do.

Discussions of technology are too often shrouded in technological determinism. The direction of technological change is taken to be essentially out of our hands, with the burden of adjustment falling entirely on workers and society at large. To maintain and improve their standards of living, workers are told they have no choice but to acquire the education and skills required by the new technologies. But as we have seen, the direction of technological innovation and its likely impact on future jobs are shaped by the choices we make in institutional arrangements and government policies. By making better choices, we may be able to direct technology to better serve the existing workforce's needs, in addition to preparing the workforce to match the requirements of technology.

Final words

The industrial welfare state was the crowning achievement of the twentieth century. It was underpinned by labor unions and government transfer programs that enabled a combination of productive employment in manufacturing with high levels of job and economic security. In this model, good jobs enabling middle-class living standards were available to most workers. Correspondingly, government policy focused on full-employment macroeconomic policies, on the one hand, and social spending on education, pensions, and social insurance against idiosyncratic risks, such as temporary unemployment, illness, or disability, on the other.

Structural changes have rendered this model inadequate for the twenty-first century. The relative scarcity of good middle-class jobs is driven today by secular trends in technology, deindustrialization, and global competition that are virtually impossible to reverse. These forces have left advanced economies with structural problems that exhibit themselves in the form of bad jobs and depressed local labor markets. These problems now require a strategy that tackles good jobs creation directly, to complement traditional welfare state policies that at best address their symptoms. On top of transfers and social insurance, which redistribute income after the fact, we need a *productivist* approach that reshapes employment, production, and innovation decisions at the source. This approach is necessarily experimental as there are no good models to emulate. But, as we have seen (and examine further in chapter 6), it is not entirely novel; it builds on existing practices in a variety of domains.

5

Fostering Economic Growth to Reduce Poverty

Ethiopia's long-serving prime minister Meles Zenawi was a fan of the East Asian development model. Starting in the late 2000s, he had made a big push for industrialization, courting Chinese and other foreign investors. One of those he succeeded in luring was Zhang Huarong, a Chinese textile tycoon, who in 2011 became the most significant Chinese investor to put up a factory in Ethiopia. Zhang himself came from modest beginnings. He had started with three sewing machines in a small workshop in Jiangxi province. Having lived through China's industrialization miracle, he was alert to Ethiopia's potential. The country seemed to him just like China three decades earlier. In short order, Zhang's company, Huajian, was making shoes in Ethiopia for global brands such as Nine West, Guess, and even Ivanka Trump's fashion line. The company hoped to eventually create as many as 100,000 jobs in Ethiopia.[1]

It was a move that heralded a new dawn for the Ethiopian economy, a beginning that many thought would turn Ethiopia into a manufacturing miracle—a "China in Africa." Foreign investors hoped to capitalize on Ethiopia's advantages. The country had an abundance of cheap labor, in addition to a government intent on attracting foreign investment. Labor costs in China and other Asian countries had begun to rise. The US and Europe maintained especially low import tariffs on manufactured goods made in very poor countries, such as Ethiopia. The country seemed a natural destination for companies looking to outsource their labor-intensive operations. Successive Ethiopian governments' efforts would ultimately yield a total of eighteen industrial parks, populated by investors not only from China but also from India, the US, Turkey, and other countries.

Alas, despite these auspicious beginnings, the Ethiopian manufacturing takeoff never took place. Manufacturing's share in GDP stayed stubbornly low—below 5 percent. The lion's share of manufacturing operations remained tiny enterprises running informally and at very low levels of productivity. The bulk of the increase in manufacturing employment took place in these unproductive firms, leaving little trace in growth statistics. Merchandise exports actually declined relative to GDP. The new industrial parks did create some jobs—a total of 90,000 before military conflict interfered with their operations. However, this number pales in contrast to the two million youth who enter the Ethiopian labor market each year looking for a job.[2]

Ethiopia's industrialization drive failed for many reasons. Foreign companies complained about lousy infrastructure, inadequate skills, burdensome government regulations, high labor turnover, and the absence of local supply chains. Some Chinese managers cited Ethiopians' work ethic as a reason for lagging labor productivity. Ethiopian workers, for their part, found fault with the low wages and poor working conditions. But many if not all of these factors could have been mentioned as obstacles in earlier instances of export-oriented industrialization, whether in South Korea or in China. The more fundamental constraint seems to go deeper, and it is one that all low-income countries are facing today: manufacturing is no longer the growth engine it was three decades ago. Changes in the nature of technology and global competition have made it very difficult today for developing countries to grow on the back of industrialization.

This is a momentous change that demands a fundamental rethink of conventional growth strategy.[3] It is the developing country version of the problem we encountered in the previous chapter, namely, the limited labor absorption capacity of today's manufacturing. Not surprisingly, therefore, it calls for a similar reorientation of policy priorities, from manufacturing to services. This is a huge challenge, since services in developing countries are dominated by highly inefficient micro enterprises and self-owned firms that operate largely informally. In this chapter, I discuss how we can make progress on this challenge, by building on a variety of policy experiments around the world that have shown the way.

I begin by describing how economic growth and poverty reduction happen, so that we can better evaluate the implications of the new context.

How East Asia did it

China is without doubt the most impressive poverty reduction experience in world economic history. In four decades, it managed to cut down the number of people living in extreme poverty by 800 million, a feat that is all the more remarkable given the expansion of its population by 400 million people over the same period. Many other poor nations experienced poverty reduction in the decades prior to the pandemic as well. But China is the main story, accounting on its own for nearly three-quarters of the decline in extreme poverty around the world during those decades.[4] China achieved this transformation first by increasing productivity in agriculture, focusing on the rural areas where most poor people lived, and then by engineering a rapid industrialization that transformed the Chinese economy into the world's manufacturing powerhouse.

Two contradictory narratives exist side by side about what made this miracle possible. On the one side are those who see China as a vindication of neoliberalism.[5] It was China's turn toward markets and its opening to the world economy after Mao's death, these analysts argue, that did the trick. On the other side are those who emphasize the heavy hand of the state. What makes China distinctive for the latter camp is its state-directed and state-dominated economic system.[6]

While each side captures an aspect of China's reality, neither provides the full picture. The neoliberal interpretation distorts China's experience, because it either downplays the contribution of state intervention or views it as a blemish without which the country would have done even better. It also cannot account for the economic failures of so many countries that adhered to the neoliberal playbook much more closely; Mexico provides a particularly striking example, as we saw in chapter 2. The statist interpretation, on the other hand, fails to do justice to the millions of entrepreneurs, such as Zhang Huarong, who were fired up by market incentives and the profit motive. Too many economies in the rest of the world have stagnated under state ownership and regulation for statism to be an adequate explanation. A mash-up of the neoliberal and statist interpretations is more accurate than either one alone.

China was not a typical developing country by any stretch. It is a huge country with a long and proud history of technological innovation, imperial rule, and exam-based, meritocratic bureaucracy. It was governed by a centralized communist regime that had come to power through a peasant revolution. Mao's disastrous experiments with the Great Leap Forward and the Cultural Revolution had left the country ravaged with poverty and famine. Until Deng Xiaoping's reforms started to kick in after 1978, the economy was dominated by collective farms and large state enterprises, both highly inefficient. Private markets in basic commodities, such as food, were illegal, and international trade was highly restricted. China's circumstances are perhaps too peculiar for its specific policies to carry direct relevance for other countries.

China and other East Asian growth miracles stand so tall in the development landscape that we might think development economists focus most of their research on what these nations got right and what that means for other poor economies. But anyone looking for these debates in the leading economics journals would be disappointed. The most prized research in development economics today focuses on narrower impact evaluations of specific interventions in other parts of the world. A typical study might focus on the effects of giving farmers in an Indian district information on the weather, or providing small companies in a sample of Nigerian firms with entrepreneurial training. These are the types of questions that have proved amenable to analysis using modern causal inference methods, such as randomized controlled trials (RCTs). The great advantage of these methods is that results leave little room for debate: the intervention either works or doesn't, and whatever outcome is observed can be attributed directly to the intervention itself. In other words, the results are self-evidently "credible." The disadvantage is that they have kept economists from studying questions of greater significance, such as China's growth strategy, even if the answers are less determinate. Somewhat like the drunkard who searches for his keys under the lamppost because that is where the light shines brightest, economists have focused on issues where there are greater prospects of clear-cut results.

So what broad lessons can we draw from China's experience? The defining feature of China's growth strategy was its pragmatism and gradualism, captured in the Chinese saying, "crossing the river by feeling the stones." It was a strategy that ignored stark boundaries between the state and markets, evading stale ideological debates about the role of the government. In the language of economics, it was gradualist, experimental, and second best. It first targeted poor households in agriculture, then urban areas, and then foreign trade. It road-tested new policies in specific regions—cities or zones—before extending to other parts of the country when successful. Through the 1990s, 40 percent or more of national economic regulations were explicitly labeled as "experimental."[7] (It may not be a coincidence that the share of policies with experimental status declined precipitously after China joined the WTO.) And reforms were carefully designed to avoid second-best complications posed by immovable economic or political constraints.

This often produced heterodox arrangements that left Western economists scratching their heads. For example, economic liberalization took a dual-track form, with market regimes coexisting side by side with heavily regulated segments. Early price reforms in agriculture allowed farmers to sell their grains on free markets, but only once they had delivered their obligatory quota to the government at controlled, below-market prices. This ensured that the government still got access to grains, which it could ration to urban workers at low prices. Similarly, trade reform created special economic zones where foreign investors could import components freely for their export-oriented factories, while the rest of the economy remained heavily protected to safeguard employment in state enterprises. Hybrid institutions, such as the household responsibility system in agriculture and township and village enterprises (TVEs), encouraged private entrepreneurship without undermining communist ideology or placing too many demands on a weak legal system and a poor contract enforcement environment.[8]

China may have raised pragmatism and institutional creativity to an art form, but other East Asian countries benefited from a similar approach as well. The famous gang of four—South Korea, Taiwan, Singapore, and Hong Kong—experienced growth miracles of comparable magnitude to China's, but their policies differed not just with China but among themselves. South Korea, Taiwan, and Singapore, but not Hong Kong, engaged in a heavy dose of industrial policy to upgrade their productive structures. They did so in different ways. South Korea relied on state banks and directed credit, Taiwan on tax incentives, and Singapore on subsidies for foreign investors. South Korea's economy was dominated by large domestic conglomerates, and the government kept foreign investors away early on and delayed opening up to import liberalization. By contrast, Taiwan relied on small firms and Singapore maintained an open economy throughout. Unlike the other three countries, Hong Kong came close to a free market paradise. Milton Friedman, whose *Free to Choose* TV series aimed to spread the gospel on the miracle of the invisible hand, famously opened the series with a segment on Hong Kong. But the state was active even in Hong Kong when it was needed: it invested heavily in construction to meet the housing requirements of one of the most densely populated cities in the world. To this day, nearly half of Hong Kong's residents live in either public or publicly subsidized housing.[9]

Diagnostic versus presumptive strategies

Other countries cannot simply emulate these policies and expect similar miracles, even if there was a single East Asian "model." Their economic and political circumstances differ too much. What they can adopt from East Asia is a certain habit of mind on how to approach economic policy in general. I call this the "diagnostic" approach, to distinguish it from the "presumptive" approach that is common among development practitioners.[10]

The presumptive approach starts with strong priors about what holds economic development back and the appropriate policy remedies. Import-substituting industrialization (ISI) and the Washington Consensus, despite their huge differences, are examples of this frame. For proponents of ISI, the problem was inherent defects in markets—national and international. The answer, then, was to protect the domestic economy from international competition and encourage homegrown industries to replace imported goods. For the Washington Consensus, the problem was too much state intervention. The answer, naturally, was to reduce the role of the state by clamping down on fiscal deficits, liberalizing markets, opening up to trade, and privatizing the economy.

In both cases, the problem and the remedy were universal, paying little attention to country contexts. The requisite policies could be codified in the form of a comprehensive list of reforms (the proverbial laundry list) and "best practices" from supposedly successful countries. When reforms disappointed, as they typically did, proponents responded not by questioning the agenda but by adding more items to the list. Moreover, these policies were complementary, meaning that they could not be implemented selectively. Success required doing them all at once. The Washington Consensus, for example, stressed that trade liberalization needed to be pursued alongside tax reform, product market deregulation, and labor market flexibility. Otherwise, it would not be effective or might even fail. Opening up to capital flows required appropriate fiscal restraint and prudential financial regulation. Otherwise, it might lead to financial crises instead of an investment boost. The ambitiousness of the resulting program gave proponents cover when things went sour: there was always some respect in which governments fell short, to which the failure could be attributed.

The diagnostic mindset, by contrast, starts with relative agnosticism on what works and what doesn't. It tends to be limited in its ambitions at any point, focusing on identifying and removing the most severe constraints or bottlenecks that hold investment and productivity back. It looks for selective, relatively narrowly targeted reforms that can produce large effects. The underlying theory is that there exists lots of slack in poor economies, so simple changes can make a big difference. Instead of best practices and universal remedies, it emphasizes policy experimentation and innovation that provide shortcuts around local second-best or political complications.

There is a litmus test to separate adherents of these two policy frames. Ask the question, Is there an unconditional and unambiguous mapping from specific policies to economic outcomes? Those in the presumptive camp will not hesitate to answer yes for at least a half dozen policies. Those who are in the diagnostic or experimental camp will either say no outright or hedge their bets by naming reforms that are so broad that they have little operational content.[11]

The diagnostic approach is well aligned with the micro-RCT focus that remains fashionable in development economics. The initial promise of RCTs and the so-called credibility revolution was that knowledge would accumulate and practitioners would learn over time which kinds of policies are effective and which are not. This hope was dimmed by the realization that consequences of interventions are context specific: what works in one place does not work in another. A fascinating metastudy by Eva Vivalt analyzed the results from 635 research papers covering twenty types of interventions, such as microfinance or conditional cash transfer programs, from different parts of the world. The results for purportedly similar interventions varied greatly. Individual studies provided poor guidance on not just the magnitude but even the sign of the effect in other settings. They yielded the correct sign (success vs. failure) only 61 percent of the time—little better than a coin toss.[12] In the end, the impact evaluation literature generally reinforced skepticism on universal remedies for economic development.

Hence the significance of learning by experimentation. The experiments might be formal randomized trials, when they are feasible. Or they may take the form of trying something new in one part of the country first and watching informally what unfolds, as in the case of China. The second type of experiment does not always yield clear-cut answers as there could be too many confounding factors. Perhaps the initial site of the experiment was distinctive in some way that influenced the result, or there were other concurrent developments that shaped the outcome. Nevertheless, even though China's policy experiments may not have satisfied the referees of an academic journal, they were still an important source of learning. The predisposition to find out what works through policy innovation and experimentation was at the core of the Chinese approach. It played a big part in producing the most significant poverty reduction experience in history. It remains the most important lesson China has to offer to other developing nations.

The magic of industrialization

Rapid industrialization was a common feature across all East Asian growth miracles. It was also critical in other cases of postwar economic catch-up, in southern Europe (Spain, Portugal), Latin America (Mexico, Brazil), or the Middle East (Turkey). Understanding how industrialization contributed to economic growth and poverty reduction in the past, as well as how it was fostered, can help us sketch the alternative growth strategy required for a postindustrial world.

Poverty reduction and economic growth ultimately both require the same thing: increasing the productivity of labor.[13] There are two broad vehicles through which this end is achieved. The first of these is the accumulation of human and physical capital and the improvement of institutions: increased education; investments in plant, equipment, new technologies, and infrastructure; and better governance. Let's call this the "fundamentals" channel, as this is the bread and butter of standard growth theory and of conventional development advice. As a country's fundamentals improve, workers and the businesses where they are employed become more productive and can make better use of technologies that are already available in the more advanced economies. The second vehicle is the reallocation of resources—workers especially—from less productive to more productive activities. Poor economies are characterized by economic dualism: some modern industries coexist with a large mass of informal, inefficient entities. Fostering new industries and facilitating their expansion can provide a significant boost to economic growth. Let's call this the "structural change" channel of economic growth.

Improvement in fundamentals and structural change are mutually supportive, and they typically operate together in successful countries. The creation of new industries incentivizes investment in human and physical capital and the acquisition of new technologies. Better education and governance facilitate the establishment of new industries. However, as a matter of growth strategy, there are distinct differences. Governments that focus on fundamentals would pay little attention to the structure of the economy, expecting that the requisite structural transformations would happen automatically as fundamentals improved. A government focused on structural change, on the other hand, would directly support the creation and growth of new industries, engaging in the kind of productive development policies (or industrial policies) we have encountered before.

The argument for explicitly targeting structural change is that there are multiple market failures that prevent its unfolding at an adequate rate. Learning externalities, scale economies, and coordination failures all stifle the development of new industries, especially in poor economies. Overcoming these obstacles requires specific government interventions as a remedy. There may be many government failures that act as barriers as well, such as high taxes, corruption, or inadequate infrastructure. As a practical matter, it is typically much easier to alleviate government failures through narrower initiatives that are similarly targeted on new industries, instead of waiting for economy-wide reforms to yield their fruit. For example, specific vocational training courses or regulatory changes aimed at export industries (such as special economic zones) may be more effective than the expansion of the educational system as a whole or broad governance reforms. In other words, a structural change focus serves not only to alleviate market failures but to economize on administrative resources and ease the challenges of economy-wide reform.

Economic development is impossible in the long run without the fundamentals. The accumulation of fundamentals, however, is necessarily a slow process and yields at best medium rates of economic growth.[14] When structural change policies are effective, on the other hand, they yield an immediate growth response and much more rapid economic expansion than with the accumulation of fundamentals alone. High growth in turn facilitates the acquisition of human and physical capital and other fundamentals by relaxing budget constraints. This is indeed the kind of dynamic that East Asian countries perfected. While they improved their fundamentals over time, they owe their exceptional performance to their ability to promote rapid structural transformation—industrialization in particular—through creative and proactive policies of the type I discussed above.

To understand why industrialization is such a powerful force and the role it played in these growth miracles, think of manufacturing as an escalator. There are three features of this escalator that make it very effective. First, it is steep and climbs up very rapidly. The productivity of factory workers tends to rise fast, thanks to learning on the job and the ability to assimilate technology and organizational practices from more advanced economies. In fact, factory work displays a remarkable empirical regularity, which economists call *unconditional convergence*. This means that lagging countries tend to converge to the productivity frontier in manufacturing, even if they face otherwise disadvantageous circumstances, such as poor institutions and low levels of human capital. Not only that, the further they are from the frontier, the more rapid is the growth of their labor productivity. Among all sectors of the economy, only formal large-scale manufacturing exhibits this surprising feature consistently and strongly.[15]

Second, the escalator can keep going virtually without limit. It is as if it operates in an exceedingly tall building where the ceiling reaches high into the skies. This is because manufactured goods are tradable products that can be sold on world markets. Normally, with a good or service that is marketed at home, the size of the market is limited by domestic demand. Try to sell ever greater amounts of cement or taxi rides and you reach the limits of the market; the only way you can increase sales is by cutting prices, which eats into your profits. But a developing nation can expand production of shoes, TVs, or auto parts without regard for the limits of the home market. Consumers abroad are more numerous and much richer. Ultimately, of course, the world market too will be saturated, but that happens late in the game, once the country has become considerably richer and is a significant part of the world economy. Manufacturing enables a country to specialize and grow, far more rapidly and for a much longer period, on the back of a narrow range of exportable products. It makes economic growth a lot easier than developing productive capabilities across the entire range of the economy all at once.

To describe the third feature of this escalator, we have to use the past tense. The escalator was traditionally very wide and could accommodate a huge number of passengers. The passengers in question were the poor farmers who flooded into the cities for factory work. Basic manufacturing operations, such as assembly, could be performed by workers with few skills or educational credentials. This was a great boon for poor nations trying to catch up, since the one resource they had plenty of was workers with little education or professional skills. Outsourcing these operations from the advanced economies to developing nations made a lot of economic sense. Poor nations got to put their people on an escalator out of poverty, while rich nations got cheap consumer products.

The fading of manufacturing

As we have already seen, the escalator has been disrupted by technological developments that render manufacturing much more skill- and capital-intensive. As manufacturing firms in advanced economies came under intense competitive pressure from low-cost exporters during the 1970s and later, they invested heavily in labor-saving machinery.[16] Robots became cheaper and more adept over time: their prices have fallen by more than half since 1990, and even more drastically against labor cost, turning "lights-out" manufacturing into a realistic possibility.[17] Additive manufacturing (or 3D printing) is allowing firms in advanced economies to produce shoes, furniture, auto parts, and many other products customized to consumers' specifications. China's manufacturing has undergone a similar shift toward labor-saving technologies. Consider NIO, the EV firm we encountered in chapter 3. At the end of 2023, the company had a total of around 33,000 employees, of which only 2,231 were actually engaged in manufacturing. Nio's main business is to make cars, yet fewer than 7 percent of its workforce does factory work. The rest are in research, marketing, and administration.[18]

These new technologies in turn set quality and reliability standards that producers in poor countries needed to match in order to succeed within global supply chains.[19] They required skills and capital, which developing nations were short of—precisely the constraints that labor-intensive manufacturing had enabled them to evade.

Return to Ethiopia, the disappointment I highlighted at the beginning of the chapter. If you visit a garment or shoe factory in one of its industrial parks, you will see plenty of workers, typically young women. There are no robots, and the only machines workers operate are ordinary sewing machines. But don't let this fool you into thinking there have not been important changes in the nature of the workforce during the evolution of these industries. I remember listening to the Chinese manager of one of those factories in Ethiopia. She recalled that when they started producing in China some decades earlier, the only qualification they looked for in their employees was basic hand-eye coordination. New hires were asked to hold their two hands out, one with the palm up and the other with the palm down. Then they had to flip them up and down in synchronized fashion, maintaining the opposite orientation of each hand. It was a test that most young Chinese women from the countryside could pass.

Today her firm and other foreign employees in Ethiopia typically require at least a tenth-grade education. Even in the most labor-intensive assembly operations, a good share of the workforce in the industrial parks has education beyond that level (typically vocational training). This may not seem like a lot of education, but it is quite a bit higher than the average level of schooling in the country.[20] This means that the typical young Ethiopian worker has virtually no access to employment in the modern manufacturing sector. It is no surprise that the expansion of manufacturing employment in Ethiopia has remained limited to the inefficient, informal segment without a productivity ladder.[21] Few workers can get on the manu-facturing escalator.

The craze for automation can go too far, and companies some-times rush into technologies that are not ready for prime time. I gave the example of Tesla's "excessive automation" in the previous chapter. Here is another one. Adidas, the athletic footwear company, invested heavily in what it called a Speedfactory. The technology combined 3D printing, robotic arms, and computerized knitting with a small workforce to manufacture running shoes that were cus-tomized to individual preferences and were infinitely malleable in shape. One Speedfactory was set up in Germany in 2015, followed by a second one in the US in 2017. The company thought proxim-ity to final consumers and the ability to respond quickly to their needs would give the technology an edge over mass-produced shoes in China and Vietnam. However, Speedfactories never lived up to the hype. The robots could not handle the large number of steps required to put a shoe together. Adidas eventually closed both of its Speedfactories and went back to sourcing from Asia.[22]

But such cautionary tales have to be viewed as bumps in the road rather than a reversal in the general trend toward ever greater automation. Look at South Korea, which presents a particularly compressed version of the transformation. The country started its industrialization drive during the early 1960s, filling garment fac-tories with hundreds of thousands of former peasants from rural areas and migrants from North Korea. Through the next couple of decades, its economy epitomized labor-intensive production. Today its manufacturing industry is the most automated in the world, with one robot for every ten workers—significantly more than any other country.[23] Meanwhile, manufacturing output and exports have steadily climbed over the years (both in absolute terms and as a share of GDP), while the sector's employment has shrunk by ten percentage points (relative to the total workforce) since the late 1980s.

Countries that have not kept pace with new technologies have fallen behind. Bangladesh, a country that might have replicated the East Asian experience, displays the alternative path. The country was an accidental beneficiary of South Korea's export miracle in garments. As the US and Europe began to protect their home markets against the surge in garment exports from East Asia in the mid-1970s, Korean producers started looking for new production destinations that did not face trade barriers. Bangladesh and other low-income countries were exempt from the import restrictions in Western markets. The Korean firm Daewoo trained Bangladeshi workers and set up the first modern export-oriented garment operation in Bangladesh in 1980. This initial investment was very profitable and spawned an entire ready-made garment (RMG) industry. Most of the 100-plus Bangladeshi workers trained by Daewoo would eventually start their own firms. Thus was born the Bangladesh success story. The number of workers, mostly women, employed in the RMG industry would climb to more than four million, and the country became the second largest exporter of RMGs behind China.

But Bangladesh never became another South Korea or China. Its industry did not diversify beyond RMGs. This produced a stunted productive structure, overspecialized in a very narrow segment of manufacturing with limited backward linkages. One reason is that Bangladeshi industrial policies were not nearly as effective in stimulating new industries. Another is that changes in the technological scene began to impose additional burdens once RMGs had reached some maturity. The path forward and upward was blocked by the need to apply technologies that were expensive and incompatible with Bangladesh's comparative advantage in labor-intensive production. A recurrent theme in industry reports for Bangladesh is the need for greater investment in digital and automation technologies to move up the value chain. While the RMG industry remains labor intensive compared to other manufacturing activities, the use of machines has increased, and less educated workers have run into hard times. The country has experienced a rapid rise in the "skill premium," the wage differential in favor of college-educated workers, indicating a surge in demand for a skilled workforce. Absence of superior technology and lack of skilled workers are regularly cited as the most important constraints that Bangladeshi manufacturing faces.[24]

It stands to reason that Bangladesh—and other countries like it—need to invest in skills, education, and new technologies. Those are all part of the fundamentals of economic development. But remember that industrialization became a growth escalator precisely because it allowed countries an end run around these constraints; it enabled high growth even with slow progress on fundamentals. Rapid economic convergence was achieved by relying not on a country's scarce factors and capabilities but on its abundant ones. The apparent reality that skill and technological upgrading have now become the binding constraints on fostering and deepening industrialization reflects industrialization's diminished role as a vehicle for rapid growth.

Historically, rapidly growing countries could move a third or more of their labor force from farming into manufacturing, reaping the benefits of significant economy-wide productivity gains. Since 1990, practically no country outside of East and Southeast Asia has managed to reach or sustain employment levels in manufacturing exceeding 20 percent of the labor force, with the vast majority of developing nations falling far short of this threshold.[25] Premature deindustrialization seems to have taken over the developing world. Middle-income countries are experiencing declines in manufacturing employment shares at much lower levels of industrialization and of per capita GDP, while low-income countries are finding it virtually impossible to replicate the experience of previous generations of manufacturing success stories.[26] In the few low-income countries where industrialization seems not to have run out of steam, its quality is very poor. Employment growth in these relatively successful instances seems limited to unregistered/informal parts of manufacturing, as in Ethiopia, with formal manufacturing still remaining in the grasp of premature deindustrialization.[27]

It doesn't help that the growth of world trade, including trade in manufactured goods, has slowed down after the global financial crisis of 2008. For the first time in decades, growth of trade in goods is lagging behind growth of global output. Geopolitical tensions, rising trade barriers, and a secular demand shift from goods to services are all playing a role.

The pessimism that such findings foster is sometimes countered by pointing to the prospect of a potentially large relocation of manufacturing away from China. China has more than 100 million workers in manufacturing. Even if a fraction goes to lower-income countries, the argument goes, there could be tremendous scope for industrialization elsewhere. But the reality is considerably more discouraging. Manufacturing employment has already come down significantly in China, with little effect on factory jobs elsewhere. Between 2011 and 2020, China lost thirty-one million jobs in manufacturing—more than the total number of manufacturing workers in the US and Germany combined.[28] One would hardly know this from the country's output and export statistics, which have continued to rise unabated. In view of the increase in labor productivity, this decline in employment evidently has not left much room for others to fill in. Countries like India that expect a large windfall for themselves from the redeployment of jobs from China are likely to be disappointed.[29]

None of this implies that developing countries should write off manufacturing completely. Middle-income countries can still benefit from taking up niche opportunities within global value chains. Low-income countries in Africa are severely underindustrialized and still have some room for developing basic manufacturing sectors. And the green transition, as we have seen, creates new investment possibilities in green industries. A small number of countries may even overcome the headwinds and avoid premature deindustrialization. The most likely to do so at present is Vietnam. This country has experienced a particularly sharp rise in manufacturing employment since the mid-2010s. Its geographic proximity to China and other East Asian exporters has made it the leading beneficiary of, first, rising wage costs in China, then the Trump tariffs on China, and eventually the US emphasis on "friend-shoring." Predictably, in Vietnam as well, "skill shortages" are among the most important constraints export-oriented foreign investors face.[30]

It bears repeating why productive job creation for ordinary workers—whether in manufacturing or, as it now seems necessary, in other parts of the economy—is critical for economic development and poverty reduction. If productive sectors are those that do not absorb labor, we exacerbate the problem of economic dualism in developing countries: a small, modern segment existing within a sea of inefficient, traditional activities. Think of economies that are rich in natural resources, such as oil or diamonds. They can generate some wealth for a few investors or the government, but the rest of the economy is stagnant and good jobs remain scarce. They are, in the language of development economics, *enclave economies*. Overcoming dualism requires creating economic opportunities beyond a narrow slice of the workforce.

The services imperative

Mohamed Bouazizi was one of the many street vendors in Sidi Bouzid, a small town in Tunisia. His father had died when Bouazizi was young, and he now had to take care of his mother and six siblings. He led a difficult life. Each day he would take his cart at midnight to the wholesale market to fill it up with fruits and vegetables. From the early hours of the morning till the evening, he would roam the streets to sell his produce. He would then return home to sleep for a few short hours in the early hours of the evening before starting the cycle over again. He was tired, stressed out, and preoccupied with making a living for his family and paying off his debts.[31] An encounter with the local police on the morning of December 17, 2010, finally set his fuse off. The police harassed him and confiscated his scales, saying he lacked a permit to work as a street vendor. Humiliated and exasperated, Bouazizi went to complain to the provincial governor, who refused to see him. Bouazizi left and returned to the governor's office in short order with a can of gasoline. "How do you expect me to make a living?" he cried out before setting himself on fire.

This was the spark that ignited the Tunisian revolution. Within hours of his self-immolation, Mohamed Bouazizi turned into the symbol of ordinary Tunisians desperate to rid themselves of a political regime that was authoritarian, corrupt, and indifferent to the needs of powerless people like him. The ensuing protests engulfed the country and forced the country's autocratic president, Zine El Abidine Ben Ali, to flee to Saudi Arabia in January 2011.

Mohamed Bouazizi epitomizes the plight of workers engaged in low-pay, precarious, informal work in cities all around the developing world. In fact, he is representative of the typical developing-country worker. A couple of decades ago, we might have thought of the average person in poor countries as a farmer growing food crops on a small plot. But today most residents of poor nations live in urban areas. Vast numbers among them scratch a living doing work similar to Bouazizi's, selling various items on the streets, doing odd jobs, performing repairs, assembling simple goods in a workshop, running a road stand, or managing a tiny shop if a bit luckier. In sub-Saharan Africa and South Asia, 80 percent or more of workers outside of agriculture do informal jobs, meaning they (or their employers) do not pay taxes, are not registered, and do not enjoy the protections of labor laws and other regulations. In the middle-income countries of Latin America, the informal job sector ranges from 40 to 60 percent.

There is a two-way relationship between informality and economic development. As countries get richer, the informal sector tends to decline. But reducing informality is also one way in which overall productivity in the economy can be enhanced. Informal firms are typically very small in scale and inefficient compared to formal enterprises. In a typical African country, more than 80 percent of establishments have fewer than five employees (compared to about half of businesses in the US). Between 30 and 40 percent of the employment is in firms with less than five employees; the corresponding share in the US is around 7 percent.[32] The preponderance of tiny firms and self-proprietorships matters because there is a strong correlation between firm size and productivity: larger firms tend to be more productive. Remember the paradoxical case of Mexico from chapter 2? The country did most everything right by the neoliberal playbook but still stagnated in overall productivity. The proximate cause of this debacle is that almost all the expansion in employment took place in small, informal, inefficient enterprises.[33] Large firms in the northern part of the country that were plugged into North American value chains became more productive, but they did not hire many workers.

The challenge is particularly daunting in lower-income countries where the labor force is still growing very rapidly. In sub-Saharan Africa, the working-age population is expected to expand by twenty million people each year over the next two decades.[34] This means creating 1.67 million new jobs every month! And if widespread poverty and social upheaval are to be avoided, the masses of young people flocking to urban labor markets will have to be provided not just with jobs but with *better* jobs than those that are available at present. Better jobs invariably require higher productivity.

As we have seen, manufacturing is not the answer. Agriculture cannot fill the gap either; while it remains a large employer, it will continue to release workers to the rest of the economy as economic development advances. Future jobs will be overwhelmingly in services, even in the poorest countries. The question is whether we can increase the productivity of these jobs. The good news is that labor productivity in services as a whole (measured as value added divided by number of workers) has performed surprisingly well in the developing world since the early 1990s. While the level of labor productivity in services remains below manufacturing on average, its rate of growth has been faster than in industry (manufacturing plus construction, mining, and utilities) outside East Asia and the advanced economies.[35] This is the opposite of the historical pattern exhibited in the latter group of countries, where services productivity typically lags industrial productivity. This suggests that the traditional worry about stagnant productivity in services may be of lesser concern in today's low-income countries.

Indeed, the rapid growth of developing countries in the two decades before the pandemic was primarily due to the strong performance of their service sector. This was very different from the traditional industrialization-driven growth model. Services contributed to growth both by experiencing rapid productivity growth and by drawing labor from the countryside (where labor productivity was lower). India has been the paradigmatic case of a services-driven economy. But a similar pattern was also found in countries such as Ethiopia (where, as we have seen, industrialization efforts faltered), Ghana, Nigeria, Rwanda, and Zambia, among others.[36] What we can't be sure of is whether this was an exceptional, one-off experience or it heralds a new era, where services can fully substitute for the dynamic role that manufacturing has historically played. A deeper dive into services suggests caution on this front.

It helps to distinguish among different types of services. A World Bank report usefully categorizes services into four broad groups.[37] First, there are global innovator services, such as finance and insurance, IT, and technical and professional services. These are activities that require high levels of education and skill. While India in particular has been successful in competing globally in IT and related services, they cannot be relied on to generate jobs for the bulk of the workforce. A development strategy that focused on such services would inevitably produce stunted, enclave-type economies, in which the vast majority of workers have to rely on trickle-down opportunities to reap the benefits.

Second, we have skill-intensive public services, such as education and health. The opportunities here are limited as well, though some health services (such as home care and community health services) can be provided by less educated workers. Third, we have mostly tradable low-skill services, such as tourism, food, accommodation, and transport. Finally, we have nontradable low-skill domestic services, such as retail and a wide variety of social, community, and personal services. The third category may expand in the future through digital commerce and remote work. But the fourth bucket will remain the largest source of employment in poor economies.

It is the last two categories that present the greatest developmental challenge. Those are the services that will continue to absorb labor in developing countries. They are also the parts of the economy where productivity growth has been very slow and the productivity gaps with the advanced economies are largest. Informality will remain the dominant form of employment in low-income countries in Africa and elsewhere for decades, even under the most optimistic growth scenarios.[38] Increasing productivity in these labor-absorbing services is the key that will unlock poverty reduction and inclusive economic growth.

Productivity policies for labor-absorbing services

Street sellers in developing countries spend a lot of time obtaining their supplies. Fruit-and-vegetable vendors, like Mohamed Bouazizi, have to go to a wholesale market in the middle of the night to replenish their wares for sale during the daytime. The market may be outside the city, many miles away. Reliable and cheap transport, especially when carrying large bags of produce, is typically difficult to find. The round-trip journey can take hours each day. Contrast this with the efficiency of modern multinational retail stores, with their finely optimized supply chains and large-scale orders that keep costs low. Is it a wonder Bouazizi barely made a living for his family or led a stressful life, even leaving aside his troubles with the municipal police? Yet that is the daily reality of as many as a billion street vendors in the developing world.[39]

The founders of a social enterprise in Colombia, known as Agruppa, had an idea. They thought they could use a combination of new technologies and organizational innovations to help street-corner fruit-and-vegetable sellers in Bogotá obtain their supplies more efficiently. They would collect and aggregate orders from individual vendors, source the produce directly from farmers on the outskirts of the city bypassing intermediaries, and deliver it directly to the vendors early in the morning. Agruppa started with a list of five common products (potatoes, plantains, tomatoes, onions, and spring onions), which eventually expanded to twenty-eight items.

Nearly 600 vendors expressed interest and joined the program in its initial run in early 2016. Agruppa's funding came from the World Bank and a group of social investors.[40]

The World Bank matched program participants with a group of nonparticipant vendors, so that researchers could observe the difference the initiative made. They found that Agruppa's services lowered travel time and purchase costs, reduced work stress, and increased the time participant workers spent with family. The effects could have been stronger, were it not for the fact that the vendors still needed to travel to the wholesale market to buy produce not included in the Agruppa service. But because they reduced their total trips to the wholesale market, their sales of non-Agruppa produce fell, cutting into their overall earnings. In any case, the program wound down within two years because Agruppa could not scale up its offerings and coverage sufficiently to sustain itself financially before its funding ran out.

Could such a program have been more effective had it been launched by the government with stronger financial backing? Would it have scaled up successfully and reached more street vendors and small shops? Would the vendors' incomes have risen significantly? Would the government resources spent on it be repaid in the program's social benefits and tax revenues? And had such a program been in existence in Tunisia, would Mohamed Bouazizi have avoided his unfortunate end?

We do not have the answers to these questions. What we do know is that it is only through policy experiments of this kind that we have any hope of raising incomes in labor-absorbing service activities. These policy experiments will look a lot like the industrial policies we have already seen in green industries and manufacturing. They will take the form of governments—and sometimes social enterprises, as in the previous example—collaborating with small and large firms to supply them with the incentives and inputs (including technology) the firms need to become more efficient. They will be targeted, however, at labor-absorbing, low-skill services.

Here is an example of quite a different kind. In July 2018, the government of the state of Haryana, India, launched a collaboration with two large cab aggregators, Uber and Ola, with the goal of expanding the employment of young drivers by the platforms. Saksham Saarthi, as the program was called, was premised on the possibility of mutual benefit. The state government wanted to create jobs for young people who were unemployed or engaged in highly unproductive activities. The companies wanted to expand their activities but faced informational and regulatory hurdles that the government was in a position to address. Ola and Uber each committed to monthly hiring targets and to the expansion of new services, such as bike taxis. The government, in turn, shared with them targeted databases of unemployed youth, organized exclusive job fairs, and popularized the program through media campaigns. It also made some regulatory changes to facilitate the firms' operation. For example, one district had a regulation that prevented drivers from outside the district from obtaining a commercial license; this restriction was removed. Rules and procedures for registering the riding services were simplified across the state. Within a year, 24,000 youth from across the state had been onboarded through the program.

Several things stand out with this program. First, the government did not resort to subsidies or financial incentives. Its assistance to firms took a different form, focused on administrative procedures. In this respect, the program is similar to the local economic development programs we looked at in the previous chapter, where the focus is not on tax incentives or subsidies but on providing critical public inputs to facilitate more productive operation. Second, even though the firms did commit to hiring more drivers, their targets were voluntary. There was no financial penalty if the targets were not met. The conditionality was soft rather than hard: it relied on goodwill and good-faith efforts on the part of the firms rather than explicit, contractual commitments. Third, and relatedly, the government and the firms were engaged in an ongoing and iterative relationship. Frequent meetings ensured the monitoring of outcomes, flexibility, and revisions, when needed, to respond to changing circumstances. These interactions and the mutual understanding they fostered helped build trust between the parties.[41]

A portfolio of programs

The service sector is exceptionally diverse, encompassing informal and formal firms, and enterprises that range from owner-operated units to large platforms. Their needs vary greatly, and so does what the government needs to do to help them become more efficient. The owner of a single-person operation may require supplies and market information, while a medium-sized firm may need access to cheaper credit than is available from commercial banks.[42] Government programs that are not customized or well positioned to offer a variety of services to different kinds of firms are unlikely to be effective. A productivity program targeting labor-absorbing services must necessarily encompass a wide range of initiatives. I sketch four different types of programs here.[43]

The first type works with established firms to incentivize them to expand their employment, either directly or through their local supply chains. These established firms are likely to be large and already productive. They could be global retailers, platforms, mining firms, or manufacturing exporters (with potential to generate upstream linkages with service providers). We have already seen an example of this in the case of Haryana's partnership with two ride-sharing platforms. There may be opportunities of this type especially with global brands that operate locally and either export to foreign markets or serve the home market. The objective is to increase linkages with local providers, upgrading their productive capabilities in the process. Chile's World Class Supplier Program is a private sector initiative that pairs large firms with suppliers to promote innovation and organizational improvements. China's AliExpress is a global retailing platform that assists local small- and medium-sized firms by providing them with market access and information.[44] Many of these arrangements have arisen without government support. Their impact could be much greater if governments were to facilitate their operation and disseminate the model to other parts of the economy.

The second type of program in the portfolio focuses on micro enterprises or smaller firms and aims to enhance their productive capabilities through the provision of specific public inputs. These inputs could be management training, loans or grants, customized worker skills, specific infrastructure, marketing/sourcing, or technology assistance, depending on specific needs. The Agruppa case is an example.

An important consideration here is that the mass of tiny and mostly informal firms that populate low-skill services cannot all be upgraded. Many, if not most, of these firms are condemned to remain inefficient. The heterogeneity in this group also means, however, that some informal firms do overlap with formal firms in their productive capabilities. Some micro or small enterprises that are dynamic can prosper if provided with the requisite support.[45] A significant increase in access to credit, for example, may help a small group of top performers, while having little effect on the performance of the rest.[46] An optimal policy would spend little resources on those with few prospects, facilitating their employees' and owners' transition to more productive, dynamic, and expanding firms. Hence programs targeting small firms necessarily have to be selective, distinguishing entrepreneurs and firms that are dynamic and likely to grow from those that aren't. Separation can be achieved through psychometric evaluations, business plan competitions, or other forms of evaluation of applicants to government programs.

One prominent example is Nigeria's YouWiN! (youth enterprise with innovation in Nigeria) program. This was a business plan competition for young entrepreneurs, launched in 2011, with the aim of encouraging innovation and job creation through the start-up of new businesses and the expansion of existing businesses.[47] The competition comprised an initial application, a four-day training session, submission of detailed business plans, evaluation and selection, and disbursement of grants. The program was publicized through, among others, a high-profile launch by Nigeria's president. The business plans of the finalists were scored on the quality and viability of their business ideas and the number of jobs created. Winners were awarded up to 10 million naira ($64,000 at the then exchange rate) in grants, received further mentorship, and were linked to banks in their regions. An evaluation of the program shows that it had positive impact on the rate of business start-up, employment, profits, and survival of existing firms. These encouraging results have prompted other countries to mount similar initiatives.

The third type of program entails the provision of digital tools or other forms of new technologies, either to workers directly or to firms, that allow workers with little education to perform additional and more complex tasks. The objective here is to enable low-skill workers to do (some of) the jobs traditionally reserved for more skilled professionals. This is the kind of program that we saw in the previous chapter in relation to nursing and home care. But of course it needs to be adapted to the setting of poor countries.

An example is provided by an experiment in Uttar Pradesh, India. In 2012, the Manthan Project provided community health workers (popularly known as ASHA workers) in two districts with a mobile-phone-based multimedia app called mSakhi.[48] ASHA workers traditionally were hampered by inadequate knowledge, lack of supervisory support, onerous reporting requirements, and lack of coordination with auxiliary nurses, who provided additional medical support. The objective of the program was to enhance the capabilities of the workers and thereby improve maternal and newborn health outcomes. The mSakhi app combined self-learning, client management, and reporting in an easy-to-use format. It generated a home visit schedule for each beneficiary and provided video-guided instructions. Upon the completion of a successful pilot run, the technology was extended to five districts in 2015; eventually, its functionality was broadened to other purposes, such as screening for diseases like diabetes and hypertension. Evaluations of the pilot program found that ASHA workers became more productive and adept at using the technology over time. They became more knowledgeable about critical reproductive, maternal, and child topics and more proficient in counseling the beneficiaries and identifying sick newborns who needed immediate medical care.

The fourth program in this portfolio focuses directly on training. It combines vocational training with "wraparound" services—a range of additional assistance programs for job seekers to enhance their employability, job retention, and eventual promotion. Modeled after Project Quest and other similar sectoral workforce development schemes that we saw in the previous chapter, these training programs typically work closely with employers, both to understand their needs and to reshape their human resource practices to maximize employment potential.

Vocational training programs have been of uncertain quality in developing countries, partly due to the difficulties of implementing and scaling up programs with comprehensive wraparound services. One of the encouraging examples is Harambee in South Africa, a social enterprise founded in 2011.[49] Harambee partners with the national and subnational government as well as more than a thousand employers. It has served nearly four million unemployed youth. It recruits unemployed youth, assesses and develops their skills and competencies, works with employers on job matching and creation, and assists youth in the job search process through skills certifications and reference letters. Harambee conducts standardized skills assessments of job seekers and analyzes psychometric and other data to better match them with jobs, as well as providing job-specific training to prepare them for success and retention on their jobs. South Africa has the world's highest unemployment rate for youth, at above 60 percent. Harambee has been a rare bright spot in an otherwise depressing landscape.

None of the specific programs I have discussed here—nor even all of them collectively, as currently configured—will be enough to move the needle significantly on economic growth and poverty reduction in the years ahead. They are merely proof of concept on the potential and feasibility of a different approach. We will need significant amounts of experimentation with these and other similar kinds of initiatives. Governments at all levels, social enterprises, multilateral lenders, and philanthropies will all have to play their part. Local and municipal governments, in particular, will have to step up to the task, since they are often in a better position to address the heterogeneity and diversity of productive structures in services. They will have to exhibit determination and ambition. FDR's call for bold experimentation is perhaps more relevant to developing countries today than at any time: "It is common sense to take a method and try it: If it fails, admit it frankly and try another. But above all try something."[50]

The development-climate connection

Services will have to serve as the main axis of economic development in the future. But the climate transition also opens up opportunities in green industrialization for developing nations, especially for those with key inputs.

Consider Indonesia. In 2014, Indonesia banned exports of nickel ore, hoping to develop a domestic refining industry that would add value to its mineral production and create more jobs. Export bans to encourage downstream processing normally do not work. But this case proved different. It attracted billions of dollars of foreign direct investment from Chinese firms keen to supply their rapidly growing EV and battery industry. Along with the investment came new Chinese technology, which enabled the conversion of low-grade Indonesian ore to battery-grade nickel, slashing costs and driving many of Indonesia's competitors out of the market. Following on the Chinese example, European and South Korean companies lined up to invest in battery plants. Within a decade, Indonesia had catapulted into the world's leading producer of refined nickel. And while mining and smelting are both capital-intensive activities with limited labor absorption potential, as many as 200,000 jobs may have been created in these and related activities.

Success was not without its downside. The nickel smelters required the construction of coal-fired power plants, also financed by Chinese loans, and were a setback to Indonesian plans to phase out coal. Cheap, plentiful, battery-grade nickel will surely benefit the climate, but meanwhile Indonesia's coal consumption and carbon emissions have risen rapidly. High levels of metal from the mines and refineries have seeped into local water sources, creating significant health hazards for the local population.[51]

The Indonesian story illustrates the two sides of the climate transition for developing countries. Climate change imposes significant costs, but it could also be an opportunity. It is a cost because mitigation and adaptation will require significant resources, much of which will have to come from richer nations. I discussed the possibilities and prospects for this in chapter 3. It is an opportunity because it provides an investment strategy—a direction for productivity-enhancing structural change. This strategy could therefore complement the services-oriented approach described above. On its own it would not generate a huge number of new jobs, the Indonesian example notwithstanding. Labor-absorbing low-skill services will remain the major job engine. But it would provide a valuable second axis for productive transformation.

It is one of the counterintuitive implications of the theory of second best that something that would normally be a bad thing in a first-best context could be a good thing in a more realistic second-best situation. This point has been made by Nick Stern and Joe Stiglitz against those who argue that fighting climate change would necessarily undermine the growth prospects of developing countries.[52] Their counterclaim is based on the view that developing countries are starting from a position where they already face rampant market failures and policy inadequacies. Beyond the climate externality, which is global, they suffer from underinvestment in knowledge as a public good; imperfect and asymmetric information, which deters investment; coordination failures throughout the economy, reflected in the underprovision of public goods and networks; widespread externalities in agriculture and health; and pervasive capital market failures that undermine financial intermediation. If governments seriously engage in a climate transition strategy that coincidentally tackles some of these problems, the outcome not only could be superior relative to the business-as-usual scenario but may be even better relative to the counterfactual without a climate change threat.

Nick Stern and his collaborators cite many such opportunities. Investment in R&D and the deployment of renewable energy can lead to broader productivity improvements across wide swaths of the economy. Environmentally friendly urban architecture and improvements in public transport can cut pollution, congestion, and transport costs and render cities both more livable and more efficient. Investments in agricultural biodiversity and natural capital can help both with climate change and with poverty reduction.[53] New seed varieties that are more resilient to extreme weather shocks have been shown to increase farmers' productivity and consumption levels.[54] Africa is especially well positioned in renewables since it has vast potential in solar and wind—39 percent of global renewables potential according to one study—while it holds less than 5 percent of global fossil fuel reserves.[55]

There may even be some job benefits. One study finds that each $1 million shifted from brown to green energy creates a net increase of five jobs.[56] Note, moreover, that the services-based development strategy discussed in this chapter is inherently friendlier to the climate than the traditional manufacturing path with its smokestack industries. "The fastest and most inclusive growth for Africa," declare the authors of a recent study, "is aligned with that of a great green transformation."[57]

Many developing countries are rising to the challenge. Governments ranging from Vietnam to Namibia have pushed to quickly deploy renewables at scale. There is widespread experimentation with green industrial policies to promote domestic production of EVs and batteries and other products, as we have seen in chapter 3 and in the Indonesian example above. It is worth stressing again, however, that the extent and success of the green investment drive in the developing world will depend on the readiness of other nations—the advanced economies and China—to provide access to their financial resources and proprietary technologies.

Final words

Let me be clear: a services-based model of economic development will not deliver the kind of growth rates experienced in East Asia, even in the best-case scenario. Remember the features that made industrialization a powerful growth escalator? One of those is that manufacturing firms can sell their products on world markets and are not constrained by the small size of the home market. This enables a sequential strategy whereby countries initially concentrate on a few manufactured goods where they can be competitive and then diversify into other sectors of increasing sophistication over time. Most of the labor-absorbing services in developing countries are nontradable. Ongoing expansion of one requires the simultaneous expansion of all the others. The growth of retail, say, cannot significantly out-pace the growth of personal services, hospitality, and other domestic services. Services-based development is difficult both because of the challenges of increasing productivity and because of the need for a balanced growth model.

But there is also an upside to this, especially from the standpoint of poverty. The export-oriented industrialization model typically increases inequality early on, as it is the large manufacturing firms and their comparably small number of employees that reap the initial gains. The rest have to wait for their turn to step on the escalator or for the income gains to trickle down. A strategy based on labor-absorbing services, by contrast, attacks poverty directly as it targets the people in urban areas with the lowest incomes. The services model may not deliver very fast growth, but the growth it generates is more inclusive and equitable. It is the most direct route to building a large middle class in the developing world as well.

6

A Productivist Paradigm

There is a common theme running through chapters 3, 4, and 5. Whether it is fostering the green transition, rebuilding the middle class through good jobs, or reducing poverty in the developing world, engineering structural change is key. Meeting each of these objectives requires moving the economy's resources—innovation, organizational capacity, entrepreneurship, capital, and workers—to activities that are more productive and achieve social, environmental, and developmental goals in the process. The strategy that connects all three domains is *productivism*, a paradigm that I describe in greater detail in this chapter.

Market fundamentalists would say structural transformation is a task better left to the operation of markets. Of course, they would readily acknowledge that some tweaking of market forces may be required. We need carbon pricing to ensure private producers, investors, and innovators face the right market incentives. We need public safety nets to ensure that those losing their jobs or unable to work have the financial support they need. But the task of government policy, in their view, should be limited primarily to letting the markets do their job of allocating resources to their best—meaning most profitable—uses.

We have seen time and again that success requires something different: more government intervention than what market fundamentalists would want, but also better government intervention. The task of this chapter is to make the case for governments' role in structural change. It is also to distill what we learn from experience about how governments can be more effective in this role. We need to apply these lessons to all the challenges we discussed in the preceding three chapters. Don't let the label *productivism* turn you off; labels ultimately matter a lot less than what we do.[1] Call it sensible, pragmatic policy making and you'll have it exactly right.

The visible hand

In his aforementioned 1980 TV series *Free to Choose*, Milton Friedman held up a pencil in front of the camera to illustrate the power of markets. It took thousands of people all over the world to make this pencil, Friedman said—to mine the graphite, cut the wood, assemble the components, and distribute the final product all around the globe. No single central authority coordinated their actions; that feat was accomplished by the magic of free markets and the price system. It was Adam Smith's famous invisible hand at work.[2]

Forty-five years later, the pencil story serves a very different narrative—one that gives government policy a much more prominent role. Today China is the world's leading producer of pencils. Yet China was hardly a natural destination for the industry. There are better sources of graphite in Mexico and South Korea. Forest reserves are more plentiful in Indonesia and Brazil. Germany and the United States had better technology when China's industry got off the ground. China had lots of low-cost labor, but so did Bangladesh, Ethiopia, and many other poor countries. Much of the credit belongs to the initiative and hard work of Chinese entrepreneurs and workers. But leaving out the Chinese government's contribution would be like staging *Hamlet* without the prince of Denmark.

The initial investments in technology and labor training were made by China's state-owned firms. The government then stimulated the industry by keeping wood artificially cheap, providing generous export subsidies, and intervening in currency markets to enhance Chinese producers' competitiveness on world markets. As in so many other branches of manufacturing, China's government subsidized, protected, and goaded its firms to ensure rapid industrialization. Friedman himself would have disdained these policies. Yet the tens of thousands of workers that pencil factories in China employ would most likely have remained poor farmers if the government had not given market forces a strong nudge to get the industry off the ground.

Or consider orchids in Taiwan. The industry took off on the island four decades ago thanks to concerted efforts by the Taiwanese government to diversify away from sugar. Sugar had traditionally held an important position in Taiwan's countryside, both as an export commodity and as an employer for a large number of farmers. But it had fallen on hard times due to falling prices on world markets. In many countries, the outcome might have been declining incomes and rising indebtedness for farmers and a depressed rural sector. The Taiwanese government chose instead to mount a comprehensive investment drive to develop a world-class orchid industry. It paid for a genetics laboratory, quarantine site, shipping and packing areas, new roads, water and electrical hookups for privately owned greenhouses, and an exposition hall. It provided low-interest loans to farmers to help them build the greenhouses. Supported by government extension services, a large number of orchid growers, from micro enterprises to medium-sized ones, became part of the orchid cluster and supply chain. Over time, they introduced innovations that allowed, for example, the preservation of seedlings for export to distant destinations, such as the US. Today Taiwan is the world's third biggest exporter of orchids, behind the Netherlands and Thailand.[3]

Maybe it is just East Asian nations that are able to pull these feats off? Consider a case from Latin America. Fundación Chile is a non-profit that acts as a public venture capital fund. It was set up in 1975 with an independent endowment as part of IT&T's compensation agreement with the Chilean government for the telephone company's nationalization under the preceding Allende government. It served as an incubator for new technologies, adapting them to the Chilean context and then selling off the successful ones to the private sector. In 1981, Fundación Chile acquired a small, local aquaculture company. Using Norwegian and Japanese salmon farming technology and through a process of learning by doing, it developed an entire supply chain, from specialized feed to export logistics. The knowledge it acquired was disseminated freely to private firms, producing an explosion of salmon farming. Exports went from 300 tons to 24,000 tons per year by the 1990s, making Chile the second largest exporter of salmon after Norway. In 1988, Fundación Chile's operation was sold to a Japanese company at a competitive auction.[4]

The examples go on. The reality is that virtually all instances of productive transformation since the Industrial Revolution have been the result of combined public-private initiatives. This is as true for countries that are normally associated with free market ideology as for others. Chile has long been lauded as one of Latin America's most successful economies, and as one of its most market oriented. But the state has played a role in all its major exports.[5] The country's largest copper company is state owned, and we have just encountered the salmon story. The forestry sector benefited from generous subsidies, including under the free market radical president Pinochet. The commercialization of fruit has its origins in public R&D and training programs. The wine industry was promoted through supplier development and export credit programs funded by government agencies. Scratch any modern export success story, and more likely than not, you will find the hand of the government hiding beneath.

The US government has always played a significant role in R&D. During the second half of the nineteenth century, land grant colleges and agricultural extension services disseminated know-how and helped create the most productive agriculture in the world. US manufacturing grew, caught up, and eventually surpassed Britain behind high tariff walls. In the postwar period, government funding by the Small Business Investment Company (SBIC) program played a significant role in launching Silicon Valley and laid the groundwork for the subsequent development of the private venture capital industry.[6] The US Department of Defense, through its procurement and R&D programs, enabled all the critical innovations that would eventually constitute the digital revolution. Its Defense Advanced Research Projects Agency (DARPA) is responsible for the internet, GPS, flat-panel displays, and the computer mouse, among other innovations.[7]

"Stop," I hear you say. "We get the message. Government intervention works!" If that's what you are thinking, we are halfway, but only halfway there. The point I want to make is more nuanced. Government policy does work, but not always. It sometimes fails massively. And if we want to apply similar policies to the new domains of services and green industries, we'd better go beyond knee-jerk support for productive transformation policies, think hard about both the successes and failures, and learn how to improve their practice.[8]

What Solyndra teaches us

Here is a cautionary tale. Solyndra was a solar cell company founded in 2005 and one of the first to get funding under an expanded government loan-guarantee program. Then president Obama was keen to develop green technologies. The government provided Solyndra with $535 million in loan guarantees, to supplement $450 million raised from private investors. For Obama, Solyndra was much more than a start-up experimenting with a new technology. It was a company that exemplified the economic transformation he wanted to achieve. The provisional loan commitment to Solyndra in March 2009 was marked by joint appearances by energy secretary Steven Chu and vice president Joseph Biden. Obama personally extolled the company at a visit to its facility in Fremont, California, in May 2010. "Companies like Solyndra are leading the way toward a brighter and more prosperous future," he declared. "The true engine of economic growth will always be companies like Solyndra." But government also had a big role to play. It had to "create the conditions in which students can gain an education so they can work at Solyndra, and entrepreneurs can get financing so they can start a company, and new industries can take hold."[9]

Not unlike the Chinese government (as we saw in chapter 3), the Obama administration hoped to simultaneously accomplish multiple goals with the program. Stimulating demand and employment, spearheading new technologies, competing with China, and environmental benefits were all cited in selling the program to congressional interests and the broader public. The White House talked about positioning "the United States as a global leader in developing and manufacturing cutting-edge clean energy technologies," "continued growth in the renewable energy sector," spurring "innovation and investment in our nation's energy infrastructure," and creating "American jobs."[10] "[If] we want to compete with China, which is pouring hundreds of billions of dollars into this space," said President Obama, "if we want to compete with other countries that are heavily subsidizing the industries of the future, we've got to make sure that our guys here in the United States of America at least have a shot."[11]

By August 2011, a little over a year after President Obama's visit, Solyndra had gone bankrupt. The company had made a gamble that did not pay off: the viability of its business plan depended on silicon prices remaining high. Its technology for producing photovoltaic cells relied on CIGS (copper indium gallium selenide) as the semiconducting material, instead of silicon, which was vastly more common in the industry. CIGS was cheaper than silicon but less efficient at converting solar energy. At the time this seemed a reasonable gamble, as silicon prices had been rising. However, after 2008, silicon prices tumbled precipitously, thanks to new capacity coming online in China. At the new level of prices, Solyndra's technology had no chance to compete with conventional silicon-based photovoltaic cells. The company failed even though it had met its own technological and cost reduction goals. Its bankruptcy became a major source of embarrassment for the Obama administration. Solyndra's offices were searched by FBI agents, and the company's top executives were hauled before Congress (where they invoked the Fifth Amendment). This is what you get when you pick winners, critics scolded. The most damaging consequence may have been that it made it virtually impossible for the US to expand the initiative and truly match China's ambition in renewables—at least until the IRA more than a decade later.

The simplistic version of what went wrong in this case is that the government backed the wrong company (and the wrong technology). But this is the wrong lesson. It is the very nature of innovation that R&D and market outcomes are inherently uncertain. When venture capitalists invest in a variety of firms and technologies, they do not expect that all their investments will succeed. All they hope is that enough of them succeed to pay for the ones that fail. In fact, the calculus of profits under uncertainty ensures that, under an optimal investment strategy, some of the projects will necessarily be failures. If it were otherwise, it would be proof that venture capitalists were too timid and too few projects were financed.[12] As Thomas Watson, the founder of IBM, is said to have advised his managers, "If you want to succeed, raise your error rate." It is no different when new technologies are supported by the government. The failure rate at DARPA, probably the world's most successful innovation agency, is as high as 85–90 percent.[13] At Fundación Chile, the public-private agency that launched salmon exports in Chile, the four most successful investments have more than paid for all the flops.[14]

Similarly, the Department of Energy (DOE), which issued Solyndra's loan guarantee, had backed a variety of green technology projects. We have to consider these projects as a whole, as a portfolio. The true test of the government's success is whether the social return to the overall portfolio is high enough—higher than the government's cost of borrowing. I am not sure whether the DOE ever undertook such a calculation, but we do know that some of the private investments it backed were very successful. In fact, around the same time that Solyndra received its loan guarantee, the DOE also issued a $465 million loan to Tesla to build an all-electric plug-in vehicle, also in Fremont, California. The financial crisis of 2008–2009 had left Tesla in dire financial straits, and the loan was critical to the company's survival. It certainly was a risky investment. But the rest is history, as they say. Tesla would have another brush with bankruptcy in later years, but the company grew to be not only the world's premier EV manufacturer but also its most valuable auto company. We can thank the same government agency that financed Solyndra for enabling this outcome.

If there are lessons from Solyndra, they are about government failures of a different kind. First and foremost, the government was never up front about the experimental and risky nature of the technologies it supported. There was no public messaging about the need to prepare for disappointments or to evaluate the outcomes as a portfolio rather than individually. Worse, the Obama administration publicly showcased and invested political capital in a single firm, Solyndra, before success was assured—and in fact when the downturn in silicon prices had already thrown its future in doubt. As we saw, the firm was showered with special attention from President Obama and his cabinet members. Rather than positioning itself to take credit for successes such as Tesla, the government set itself up for failure. Just imagine if the DOE had insisted on an equity stake in return for its financial support!

The government cannot consistently pick winners, but it can stop backing losers. The worst aspects of the Solyndra debacle could have been avoided if there had been closer scrutiny of the company's progress, or lack thereof. One of the hallmarks of successful innovation programs is that the relevant government agency sets intermediate targets and clear milestones to determine whether projects should continue to receive support or be written off. At ARPA-E (modeled after DARPA, but for advanced energy technologies), award recipients are required to participate in periodic review meetings to enable program directors to assess the work performed and determine whether technical milestones are being achieved. ARPA-E staff members rate progress reports using a traffic light system: red for projects that miss a critical milestone and are at risk of failing; yellow for projects that miss a milestone but are expected to recover; and green for projects that are on track. Red ratings lead to intensified oversight and possible termination.[15] The DOE loan guarantee to Solyndra was not structured in a manner that would have provided similar monitoring. Its application was pushed through the approval process in record time. The drop in silicon prices, which should have raised some red flags, was overlooked.[16] And as Solyndra's financial difficulties mounted, it seems that DOE officials justified the losses by arguing that this was common in all start-ups. The DOE never responded to repeated requests from the Office of Management and Budget to specific questions relating to Solyndra's finances.[17] Senior economists in the administration were concerned about the need for "clear policy principles—and associated metrics for evaluation," but did not ring the alarm bell about possible failures, such as Solyndra.[18]

The final mistake the administration made was to let itself be wooed politically. Solyndra was politically quite active, spending nearly $2 million on lobbying from 2008 to its bankruptcy in 2011.[19] The principal private investor in the firm was a fund-raiser for Obama with access to the White House. He had at least one discussion on Solyndra with White House staff in then vice president Biden's office.[20] Regardless of whether political connections played a role in the quick approval of the loan and its aftermath, this was a bad look.

Solyndra holds important lessons on how to conduct industrial policy, especially in a democracy. First, an ability to pick winners is neither a prerequisite nor even a determinant of the success of productive transformation programs. The failure of an individual investment is not on its own a black mark against such programs. Governments have to acknowledge explicitly and publicly that some projects will fail. The appropriate metric is the performance of the entire portfolio of projects. Second, it is important to change course and cut losses as needed when individual initiatives appear not to be working. This in turn requires two things: clear and measurable yardsticks for progress and continuous monitoring of developments. Having multiple goals—innovation, employment, national security—may make it politically easier to sell industrial policy, but it also makes it more difficult to discern whether the program is on track or not. Finally, the practice of industrial policy must be insulated from political lobbying and rent seeking. Politics does have a role: it is inevitable, and necessary, that the overarching goals of productivist policies will be shaped by politics. But the process by which projects are selected and supported should not be subverted by politically connected firms pulling strings.

Getting productive transformation policies right

In short, some of the critics' concerns about government involve-ment in structural change—though not all—carry weight. Even when they are well intentioned, governments are not omniscient, and they make mistakes. Sometimes short-term political calculations override concerns over the public interest. As we have seen, these considerations do not undermine the case for productivist policies, but they do highlight the need to be careful when designing and implementing them. The real question is not *whether* these policies should be carried out but *how*. Basic economics and the broad expe-rience around the world together provide some helpful answers.

Let's begin with the economics. Markets are generally very effective at directing resources to areas where their contribution to economic well-being is high. When consumers value certain things highly, their willingness to pay is reflected in markets in the form of high prices and prospective profits. This incentivizes entrepre-neurs to supply the goods and services in high demand. When goods and services are no longer in high demand, their prices fall, telling investors and producers to look elsewhere for profit opportunities. This beautiful system can work to maximize a society's productive potential as if there were an invisible hand guiding the allocation of their labor, capital, natural resources, and ingenuity. Economists affectionately call this result the "invisible hand theorem."

One important criticism of markets is that they do not ensure dis-tributional equity, even when they work well and allocate resources efficiently (i.e., to their most productive uses). For one thing, wealth-ier consumers get a disproportionate say in how resources are allo-cated because their preferences shape market demand. One dollar, one vote! More importantly, those who have more to contribute to the economy, whether through hard work or sheer luck, skill, or inheritance, get the far bigger paychecks. These distributional outcomes may violate our sense of social justice.

Market enthusiasts generally do not quarrel that free markets can produce too much inequality. They would argue, however, that intervening in markets for goods, services, labor, or capital is never the best response. If inequality has to be tackled—a big if for libertarians—it would be better to do so by redistributing a limited amount of purchasing power so those who start with limited resources get a leg up. This can take the form of vouchers for education, for example, or a universal basic income (UBI). The welfare state paradigm, while less enamored of markets, essentially takes this idea one big step further. It prescribes broad access to education, health care, and social insurance, either through public provisioning or through an extensive system of social transfers.

What concerns us here is a more fundamental shortcoming of markets: the failure to allocate resources efficiently. When markets fail in this fashion, the structure of economic activity is distorted and does not maximize overall productive potential. This problem goes to the heart of a market system because it calls the invisible hand theorem into question. These are the kinds of problems where productivist policies come into their own. The immediate objective of productive transformation policies is to target and correct such inefficiencies in the allocation of the economy's resources. Typically, they will also serve broader goals, such as the climate, the middle class, and poverty reduction, as we have seen throughout. But they do so by fixing markets directly rather than redistributing resources or ensuring broad access to public services.

There are three circumstances in which markets fail to do their primary job of allocating resources well. First, many economic activities produce externalities—positive or negative—that markets do not price in the decisions of firms or consumers. Environmental externalities, whether local or global (as in the case of climate change), are the best-known instances of negative externalities. On the other hand, technological innovations typically produce positive externalities. When firms learn how to produce solar cells more efficiently, for example, other firms can also reduce their costs by copying the new techniques or poaching the workers and managers who are adept at using them. A third type of externality, which is less well recognized but is central to this book, are good job externalities.[21] When a large employer in a small town shuts down, the economic and social costs can go significantly beyond the wage losses incurred by the workers. Similarly, creating middle-class jobs where good jobs have become scarce creates benefits that extend beyond newly hired workers, if it helps revitalize the community. In the absence of government intervention, economic activities that generate negative externalities are overproduced, and those that generate positive externalities are underproduced.

Coordination failures are the second category of market malfunction. These typically occur in the presence of significant scale economies, when getting a new economic activity or technology off the ground requires complementary investments side by side and along the supply chain. Each of these investments may be unprofitable on their own. For example, there may not be high enough demand for EVs in the absence of a network of fast charging stations. And producing EVs may be too costly if cheap electric batteries, a key input, are not available. At the same time, it makes little sense to invest in fast charging stations or batteries if there isn't a large enough fleet of EVs already being produced.[22] Creating training facilities for specialized technical skills will not be profitable unless there are firms that will employ the graduates. Those firms in turn will not exist unless they already have access to trained personnel in the first place. In such circumstances, profitable clusters of new activities may never exist in the absence of some visible hand coordinating the activities of diverse actors. It is often the government that supplies that visible hand.

Third, as we have already seen, many industrial and service activities require particular types of public inputs—specialized to the needs of certain sectors but not so distinct that it would make sense for each firm to procure them on their own. Workforce development, infrastructure, technical knowledge, regulations, and standards that are specific to a sector are examples. Government has a role in providing these kinds of inputs as well.[23]

One benefit of articulating these rationales explicitly is that they clarify the type of government policy that is called for. In the case of externalities, taxes or subsidies that are directly targeted at the source of the externality are generally the best response. For technological or good job externalities, this means subsidizing the types of investments that produce those externalities. Subsidies for R&D, for solar cell or advanced semiconductor facilities, and for investments by firms that will create jobs that would otherwise be unavailable are some examples. Subsidies may take different forms, such as grants, tax incentives, and cheap loans or loan guarantees.

The other two circumstances require different kinds of government policy. Coordination failures can be addressed at little fiscal cost, in principle, by bringing upstream and downstream investors, potential cluster members, or the different stakeholders together around a table. What is required for success is joint action, not financial incentives. Government guarantees that do not entail budgetary outlays can serve a similar function in certain settings. For example, until the Asian financial crisis, South Korean governments provided informal bailout guarantees to their conglomerates if they invested in priority areas. Since those investments generally proved successful, the guarantees were not called and the government did not incur any fiscal cost. The risk with such guarantees is that they create moral hazard. They may spur investments that are too risky along with those that are jointly profitable.

Customized public inputs typically do require government resources, but these must entail the provision of specific public services rather than financial incentives for firms. If a firm is deterred from investing in a community or a developing nation because of a lack of specialized skills in the workforce or poor transport, providing those inputs is the best way to overcome the obstacle. Subsidies could serve as an inducement as well, but they may not be as effective and may miss the mark entirely. In the worst possible case, firms might end up taking the subsidy but not respond with the sought-after investment.

These considerations are important because economists and policy practitioners both tend to put excessive weight on subsidies when they consider productivist policies. The goals they pursue are often better served with other kinds of remedies. This point has been made forcefully by Tim Bartik, an economist with the W. E. Upjohn Institute for Employment Research and a close observer of local economic development policies in the US. Bartik has found that business services generally are much more effective than subsidies at creating jobs in distressed communities. These services include customized training, technology assistance, entrepreneurship courses, small business development centers, business incubators, and infrastructure. We have seen the role they can play in chapter 4. Yet the resources devoted to these programs are tiny, around $3 billion a year. By contrast, even before the industrial policy programs of the Biden administration, state and local governments spent around $50 billion annually on various kinds of cash incentives and tax breaks for businesses.[24] The magnitude of these subsidies has grown tremendously with the CHIPS and IRA programs. It is a reasonable bet that a reallocation of resources from subsidies to customized public inputs would enhance prospects for local job creation.

The point is of relevance to developing countries as well. Their governments often complain that they do not have the fiscal resources to compete with China or advanced economies when it comes to wooing companies with subsidies. But often what's required may be something different—better coordination of government services, say, or specific regulatory changes. A useful illustration comes from Peru. Piero Ghezzi, the country's minister of production during 2014–2016, decided that he would run industrial policy differently. He set up a series of discussions (*mesas ejecutivas*) with different groups of producers, with the objective of developing a common understanding on the most important bottlenecks that prevented productivity gains and the best way to remove them. When businesspeople sit together with government ministers, the conversation typically focuses on generic complaints about high taxes, bureaucratic red tape, and lack of competitiveness. Ghezzi wanted to have a different conversation, focused on problems specific to each sector. He warned his counterparts from the outset that subsidies or financial incentives were off the table. Don't tell me you want government money, he said; tell me what you or I can do to increase your productivity. The remedies discussed were divided into "your problems" and "my problems"—things that the firms could do on their own and things that the government should help them do better. Out of these conversations came a series of policy initiatives targeted at constraints that had been identified in the process. In forestry, for example, the government adjusted its legislation to facilitate the marketing of timber, simplified procedures for land concessions, established a new technology center to transfer innovations to SMEs, and facilitated the provision of long-term loans from the national development bank.[25]

Overcoming informational limitations

Piero Ghezzi recognized from the outset that he was nowhere near the omniscient policy maker conventional accounts of industrial policy posit. He knew there were problems that prevented productive upgrading in the industries he dealt with. But he didn't know exactly what those problems were. He couldn't simply design an industrial policy scheme and implement it. He needed to engage the firms in dialogue and problem discovery. He recognized also that not all remedies would work as intended. He had to keep the conversation going, monitor outcomes, and change course as required. The *mesas ejecutivas* were a way of institutionalizing this process. Productive transformation policies that work best are those that build in this feature of information revelation and iterative problem solving.

This might sound obvious, but in fact it is not what most analysts think of when they discuss successful industrial policies. Ask an economist or a technocrat what kind of policy setup maximizes efficacy, and you are likely to hear about the need to commit to a fixed set (or schedule) of policies, keep the private sector at arm's length, and apply strict penalties when firms fail to deliver on their promises. Ask them why East Asia's industrial policies appear to have worked better than those elsewhere, and they will explain that governments there followed these strictures. They might add that East Asia is special in that the region has "hard states," meaning that government bureaucrats have considerable autonomy from business and can implement their policies in top-down fashion without interference from private sector actors.

This vision of industrial policy runs into trouble when there is rampant uncertainty about the nature of the underlying problem and the efficacy of alternative remedies. It is perhaps not surprising that it does not correspond well with actual East Asian practice either, conventional wisdom notwithstanding. In a study of Brazil, India, and South Korea, the sociologist Peter Evans found that the distinguishing feature of South Korean industrial policy was what Evans called "embedded autonomy." Yes, South Korean government bureaucrats enjoyed relative autonomy from the private sector in that they could formulate broad policy objectives that they thought were in the national interest and follow through with implementation unimpeded by rent seeking from businesses. But they also exhibited embeddedness, meaning they were engaged in ongoing communication and collaboration with the private sector. Embeddedness provided "institutionalized channels for the continual negotiation and re-negotiation of goals and policies." "A state that was only autonomous," Evans wrote, "would lack both sources of intelligence and the ability to rely on decentralized private implementation."[26] We might worry that close relationships with private firms could render the government prone to capture. (I tell my students to make sure they do not confuse "embedded in" with "in bed with"!) But Evans argued that these links were essential to ensure that governments could get access to the information needed to design workable policies, adjust to changing circumstances, and prod firms along new technological trajectories in the most effective ways possible. The difference with India and Brazil, Evans explained, was less the actual policies employed and more the manner in which the relationship with the private sector was managed.

Chinese industrial policy exhibits many of these elements of embeddedness. The architects of Chinese green industrial policies, write Elizabeth Thurbon and her coauthors, "behaved less like 'top-down commanders' (as authoritarian environmentalism would have it) and more like the collaborative 'catalysts' characteristic of traditional developmental states."[27] They argue this mode of government-business collaboration was critical to the success of their policies. Given the size of the Chinese economy, national policy makers invest significant effort to coordinate with local governments, to combine national resources with local knowledge. In EVs, for example, the government used a form of experimentalism familiar from its previous policy reforms. The national government selected demonstration cities, which received priority in accessing financial incentives from the central government. In return, demonstration cities were expected to put in place complementary policies and raise their own resources.[28] Cities then engaged in close collaboration with local companies and other stakeholders. Early results would be scrutinized by central government officials and experts, policies would be revised and disseminated accordingly, and the programs would be expanded to other regions.[29] As we saw in chapter 3, municipal governments also often acted as venture capitalists, undertaking comprehensive analyses of market and technological conditions before making investment decisions.

Liuzhou City, which achieved very rapid EV take-up, offers a particularly interesting example. Here the municipal government worked very closely with the local EV manufacturer starting from the development phase. An interesting innovation was that the city government engaged in a ten-month public campaign to familiarize residents with EVs, offering free EV rides as well as soliciting suggestions on how to improve the vehicle. The local firm developed EV models that were specifically designed for the city's transport and parking systems. At the same time, the city government introduced a variety of incentives, such as purchase subsidies, reserved parking, and rapid deployment of charging infrastructure.[30]

At the national level, the central government sought to institutionalize its collaboration with the private sector by establishing China EV100 in 2014. The group's members included domestic and foreign manufacturers all along the supply chain, as well as high-level government officials and academics. The association was used as a forum for setting broad goals for the industry, coordinating the introduction of new technologies, generating ideas about new policies, and obtaining feedback from the private sector. A 2019 report set a timetable for the full electrification of vehicles in China.[31]

There is evidence from the US that subsidy programs that combine quantitative criteria and conditionality with flexibility and collaboration can work quite well. An example is the California

Competes Tax Credit program. Under the program, an initial list of awardees is selected through a strict formula that quantifies projected benefits. Administrators then negotiate with firms to finalize the list of recipients. These discussions produce a schedule of incremental employment, wages, and investment targets, which the government monitors annually. Firms that do not stick to their commitments can risk losing their tax credits. The program does not make explicit allowances for the revision of these targets in case of unexpected developments. But prospective applicants are told that program administrators will do their best to work with them to prevent them falling into breach, presumably so long as the firms are acting in good faith. A careful study has found that the program is effective in generating employment, especially in services.[32]

Experimentalist governance

An economist, the old joke goes, is someone who sees something work in practice and asks whether it can work in theory too. The supreme theorist of the collaborative approach discussed in this chapter is Chuck Sabel, a political scientist and legal scholar at Columbia University. Sabel is not an economist, though he is well versed in economics and often collaborates with economists (including me). He has studied how governments make and implement policy in a wide range of settings where there exists high uncertainty about the effectiveness of policies and future technological trajectories, including public schools, environmental regulation, industrial diversification, and social services. Along with Jonathan Zeitlin and other coauthors, he has distilled the lessons into a model of policy making he calls *experimentalist governance*.[33]

The traditional framework of government intervention that economists work with makes several key assumptions. First, the policy maker has clear, well-defined objectives, such as physical investment or exports in a sector. Second, uncertainty is low dimensional. The government may lack precise information about, say, firms' production costs but is otherwise well informed about the consequences of its actions. Relatedly, the economic and technological environment is stable, meaning it is predictable up to a standard and well-behaved error term. Finally, there is little value in direct communication between private actors and the policy maker. This is because firms have the incentive to be strategic, and the only way in which useful information can be elicited from them is by observing their actions rather than listening to what they say. These assumptions yield the conventional principal-agent model, which has proved useful in generating simple regulatory rules.

Experimentalist governance applies in settings where uncertainty is pervasive and background conditions are inherently unpredictable. In such settings, policies cannot be designed and implemented without interacting with private agents. The problem of strategic behavior by firms is real, but it is only one feature of this public-private interaction. Firms too benefit from close interaction, and they have an incentive to build a reputation in what is an ongoing, iterative relationship with government agencies.[34]

Experimentalist governance has four elements, linked in an "iterative cycle." First, the policy maker and the principal stakeholders in the relevant domain establish broad, provisional goals and determine the metrics (qualitative or quantitative) for gauging progress on those goals. An example in our setting might be increasing the number of good jobs in a region or upgrading the productivity of informal firms in a particular service sector. Second, the executing agents—firms, municipal governments, innovators, civil society groups, public service providers, frontline workers—are given broad discretion along with some financial/institutional support to achieve these goals in the ways they see fit. Third, these agents provide periodic reports on their progress and participate in an informal peer review, where results are compared across different experiments. Where progress is unsatisfactory, either the agents take credibly corrective steps or the experiment is abandoned. The conditionality government imposes on agents is soft rather than hard, in the sense that agents are expected merely to show a good-faith effort to meet their commitments rather than to adhere to strict performance criteria. They do not face explicit financial penalties when they miss targets. Finally, the objectives of the program—the metrics for success—and operational procedures are revised and disseminated to a broader circle of agents. And the cycle repeats.[35]

From the perspective of experimentalist governance, what matters most to the effectiveness of productive development policies is not the policy instruments or sectors selected, but the government's ability to navigate these four steps effectively and iteratively. A government evaluates its policy framework not by asking, Which tax breaks or subsidies are we using? Which sectors have we identified? What is the budget we have allocated for productive upgrading? The more important questions are, Do we have the process in place whereby policy makers engage in an ongoing conversation with the private sector on obstacles and opportunities? Do we have the organizational capacity to monitor progress on the ground and respond to the needs that these conversations are helping identify? Can we coordinate the requisite policies across various institutional silos within the government?[36]

The experimentalist framework brings a fresh perspective on state capacity. A nagging question in all discussions of productive development policies is whether government agencies have the capacity to develop and implement the policies that are required. There is no single definition of state capacity. It may refer to human, administrative, or financial resources, ability to nudge the private sector in the desired direction, or independence from the pull and push of day-to-day politics. The examples I have cited throughout notwithstanding, critics often respond to the kind of recommendations that are developed in this book by saying, "Well, our government could never do this because we lack the state capacity."[37]

Experimentalist governance does not require a great deal of state capacity, at least to begin with. It takes as given that government agencies start with little knowledge. Rather than presuming they can discipline firms through explicit penalties or other forms of hard conditionality, it relies on firms' own self-interest to engage in collective problem solving. Neither does it depend on mutual trust between state and private actors. The assumption is trust, along with general state capacity, will grow in the course of the collaboration. The success of productive development policies depends not on preexisting levels of state capacity but on a willingness to develop the capacity over time. The best way to strengthen a muscle is to put it to use.

The experimentalist governance schema above captures the broad outlines of how DARPA/ARPA innovation programs operate in the US. The similarity with China's EV promotion policies is also obvious. Other real-world examples include water quality regulation in Europe and a variety of public-private collaborations in Latin America (as in the Peruvian *mesas ejecutivas* above).[38]

I provide a final illustration, from Sabel's book with David Victor titled *Fixing the Climate*.[39] This book highlights the potential role of experimentalist governance in fostering the innovations that will be essential if climate change is to be addressed. Sabel and Victor discuss how an earlier environmental challenge, the depletion of the ozone layer, was overcome. The Montreal Protocol, signed in 1987, established separate timetables for developed and developing countries to phase out ozone-depleting substances (ODSs). Sabel and Victor argue that the protocol led to an experimentalist regime that set off a chain of innovations. In this case, it wasn't financial incentives but the prospect of regulation that induced firms to look for ODS substitutes. But agencies like the US Environmental Protection Agency provided cooperation and public inputs.

For example, in the case of industrial solvents, the EPA encouraged the formation of research consortia among leading firms and disseminated new technologies. Meanwhile, it goaded holdouts by using the threat of tightening regulatory controls. As significant users, such as AT&T and Nortel, invested in technologies that relied on ODS substitutes, the ODS producers themselves, such as Imperial Chemical Industries (ICI), had to shift to non-ozone-harming materials. In subsectors where innovation did not progress as fast as hoped, exceptions were occasionally made and schedules were extended. Sabel and Victor emphasize that the process of joint problem solving led to the producers reconsidering their own interests, with the result that firms that initially opposed controls eventually became enthusiastic supporters. This was also true for the leading developing countries, who embraced the pollution control efforts once the new technologies became more widely available.[40]

Final words

Productivism prioritizes both the green transition and the broad dissemination of economic opportunity across the economy. It differs from neoliberalism in giving the government an important role in directing structural change and technological innovation to achieve these goals. It places significantly less faith in the ability of markets and large corporations to serve these objectives on their own. It emphasizes the real economy over finance, production over consumption, and revitalizing local communities over globalization.

Productivism also departs from the Keynesian welfare state. It emphasizes that redistribution, social insurance, and macroeconomic management are not enough. A truly inclusive economy, one that gives people dignity and social recognition as productive members of society, also requires interventions on the supply side of the economy to create good jobs for everyone. And productivism diverges from both its predecessors by favoring collaborative, experimental solutions over technocratic ones.

Productivism tackles inequalities where they are created. It intervenes at the source—in employment, production, and innovation—instead of after the fact through redistribution. The old adage goes, If you want to lift someone from poverty, teach them how to fish instead of giving them a fish. The redistributive approach is akin to handing out the fish, while predistribution policies, such as education, amount to teaching people how to fish. The productivist approach, on the other hand, makes sure there are enough fish in the pond in the first place.

7

Remaking Globalization

The year 2008 was an eventful and turbulent one. A financial crisis originating in US markets for mortgage-backed securities had just engulfed the world economy and would eventually produce the most severe downturn since the Great Depression of the 1930s. That year would also prove to be a turning point for globalization. International trade and financial flows, which for decades had grown more rapidly than output, lost their momentum. In the US, imports of goods and services reached their pinnacle in 2008 at 17.4 percent as a share of GDP and began to decline thereafter. China's exports had peaked two years earlier in 2006 at 36 percent of GDP and declined over the next decade by an astonishing sixteen percentage points to 19.6 percent.[1] Before too long, Donald Trump and the COVID-19 pandemic would leave their own deep imprints on these trends, causing decades of deepening economic integration to stall.

Globalization is far from dead. A full-throated deglobalization or radical decoupling between the West and China seems unlikely. What is clearly dead, however, is the version we have come to know as hyperglobalization. Domestic policy agendas—inclusion, resilience, green transition—are now taking precedence over the pursuit of free trade and capital flows. China's priorities always aligned that way; increasingly, Europe and the US are following suit. For no good reason, President Trump has raised import tariffs to levels that would have been unthinkable a few years ago.

For reasons I discussed in chapter 2, we should not mourn hyper-globalization's passing. It provides us with an opportunity to erect a healthier, more sustainable globalization. If hyperglobalization was not foreordained, as I argued in chapter 2, neither is what comes after it. Senseless protectionism à la Trump, which harms all nations—and most of all the country imposing the trade barriers—is not the only path forward. The choices we make will determine whether we create a better or worse version of globalization.

Any consideration of the prospects for the global economy must necessarily center on the US-China relationship. The US has long been the world's dominant power, accustomed to getting its way. China is a rising power and the principal threat to US hegemony over the global economy. The souring of the relationship between these two countries is rooted in geopolitical and economic competition and reflected in broader attitudinal changes among the public.[2] A sound globalization will require that these two giants learn to live with each other. I make the case in this chapter that such a modus vivendi is possible. A world economic order organized around looser rules for globalization can produce peaceful economic coexistence while allowing nations to reap the benefits of international trade and investment. This chapter provides a framework to get us there.

Before we can lay out the framework, we need to accomplish some groundwork. I begin the chapter by discussing where and how the lines between national prerogatives and global cooperation should be drawn. This analysis suggests that the conventional case for global governance—explicit norms and rules that tell countries what they can and cannot do—is overstated. A critical distinction is between true beggar-thy-neighbor policies and global public goods where global governance can play a constructive role, and other, more common types of cross-border spillovers where it is not needed and is likely to backfire. With this distinction in hand, I show how the conversation between the US and China, as well as among other nations, can be structured in a fruitful manner. I then apply the framework to some of the more contentious issues in the global economy: national security, subsidies, human and labor rights, global finance and debt, and international taxation.

The misleading allure of global governance

In April 2023, President Biden's national security advisor, Jake Sullivan, gave a remarkable speech repudiating hyperglobalization and laying out the contours of America's future foreign economic policy. "Much of the international economic policy of the last few decades," he said, "had relied upon the premise that economic integration would make nations more responsible and open." But it had not turned out that way. China's "nonmarket economy" and its massive subsidies in traditional industrial sectors, like steel, as well as key future industries, such as renewables, digital infrastructure, and advanced biotechnologies, were a big problem. The US had lost competitiveness not only in manufacturing but also in the critical technologies of the future. Furthermore, dependence on potentially hostile powers, such as Russia and China, for energy, medical supplies, medical equipment, and critical minerals had created geopolitical vulnerabilities for the West. What the US needs, Sullivan said, is "a foreign policy for the middle class." The US would henceforth look after its own economic and security needs. It would pursue a modern industrial policy targeting critical industries and technologies, focus on securing supply chains instead of reducing trade barriers, and promote good jobs at home. To make sure next-generation technologies work for American democracy and security, it would, among other measures, restrict the sale of the most advanced semiconductor technologies to China.[3]

The speech reflects a fundamental tension at the heart of every country's relationship with the world economy. We want other countries to refrain from doing things that we think harm us, while we want to be free to pursue our own national economic interests as we see fit. For years, China had engaged in policies that protected and promoted its manufacturing, damaging many US industries and communities in the process. The US would now pursue comparable policies to advance its own economic interests—though those interests were now defined differently, to benefit the middle class instead of corporations. Indeed, President Biden's industrial policies under CHIPS and IRA bear more than a passing similarity to China's, as we have seen. Predictably, China blamed the US for attempting to sabotage its economic and technological development, while the EU complained bitterly about American protectionism. The EU was late to the game, but even mainstream policy makers in Europe have become advocates for activist trade and industrial policies.[4]

Where do we draw the line between national prerogatives and global responsibilities? This is the critical question that must be answered in designing a global economic system. How we answer it will determine the future of globalization. At one extreme, we can imagine an extensive set of global rules that nations must either abide by or pay a price for violating. This is the global governance proponents of hyperglobalization hoped to achieve. At the other extreme is a free-for-all, where nations feel entirely unconstrained in pursuing their own perceived economic interests. The anarchic unilateralism of the 1930s is often seen as an example of this.

There is a general presumption that the more global rules we have—the more extensive the global governance—the better. The interwar experience and general reasoning both seem to favor global governance. When what I do affects you, and vice versa, we need rules to regulate our respective behaviors. That is how interdependence is handled within nations, through a constitutional order, laws and decrees, and courts. Does it not stand to reason that the same would be true globally as well? Does interdependence among nations not require a similar set of rules at the global level?

The answers might seem obvious. But I'd like us to consider a different possibility: that the benefits of global governance are oversold, while the costs of free-for-all are exaggerated. Fewer, less constraining global rules may be better than more numerous, more restrictive rules. To get there, we first need to understand how global governance really works in a world where politics is organized nationally and countries have different needs and preferences when it comes to economic regulation. In this real world, attempts at global governance do not produce the desirable effects its well-meaning advocates desire. Second, we might want to reconsider what a free-for-all world would look like. A global system where it is understood (and expected) that nations will exercise autonomy in how they manage their economies may not be as bad as the critics of unilateralism fear. Let me take up each argument in turn.

Let's start with why the domestic analogy does not work. Domestic economic orders are the product of, and are disciplined by, politics. Politics, especially of the democratic kind, is how societies navigate the trade-offs among contending values, rights, and responsibilities. Political institutions ensure representation, checks and balances, accountability, and enforcement. Global economic governance would require an analogous global polity, which simply does not exist. The world does not have a global constitution, global elections, global judiciary, global executive, or global police force. What we have, at best, is a system where national polities appoint delegates to a patchwork of international organizations with minimal enforcement powers, to represent their national interests. This is an unavoidable reality of our world as long as nation-states remain the main locus of politics—in other words, for the foreseeable future.

In the absence of a global polity, more global governance is not necessarily a better thing. (Here is another instance of the second-best theorem!) We need to worry about two kinds of failures in particular.

First, global rules are likely to predominantly reflect the interests of the most powerful nations, and of the most powerful interests within them. Without the kind of institutions of restraint that exist within nation-states, international politics is pure power politics. This is an obvious point, but it is often overlooked—especially by Western policy makers, who tend to perceive themselves as benign actors on the international stage. It is an easy mistake to make since they are themselves the authors of the international rules and norms they expect everyone else to abide by. The "rules-based liberal international order" that the US government likes to bandy about has always been an extension of US national interests. When other nations, and particularly developing nations, look at the international system, they see the US and its allies throwing their weight around rather than a system designed to benefit all.[5] Now that China is a rising major power, it is not surprising that it too wants a much larger say in the rules. "The People's Republic of China harbors the intention and, increasingly, the capacity to reshape the international order in favor of one that tilts the global playing field to its benefit," complained the 2022 US National Security Strategy document.[6] When might makes right, global governance serves to legitimize and enforce powerful states' imposition of their preferences on other nations.

This is not to deny that global rules can still be beneficial, within limits. The postwar Bretton Woods regime was mostly benign. Even though it was designed by the US and (to some extent) Britain, it served as a hospitable environment for most countries to prosper. But it did little to constrain governments' actions, as we have seen. Under hyperglobalization, rules got stricter. The US was occasionally compelled to alter its economic policies in response to WTO rulings, indicating that the constraints, unexpectedly, were sometimes also binding on the regime's chief architect. But when the WTO proved too intrusive, the US had the power to pull the plug and make it impossible for the institution to function.[7]

The second consideration relates to an inherent trade-off between global rules and national differences. Varying historical trajectories, stages of development, and national preferences produce differences across countries in taxation, financial regulation, industrial policies, macroeconomic strategies, health and safety standards, labor market institutions, and state ownership. There is no single economic model that fits all countries. There are stark contrasts between what the US and China consider as appropriate economic management. The US and Europe differ on rules for the internet, consumer health, and the environment, among others. Even within the European Union, national differences in taxation and labor market institutions have been a matter of contention. And future attempts to regulate digital technologies and AI are likely to vary as well. A common set of rules would allow us to reap greater benefits from deep economic integration. But it would come at the expense of reducing some of those differences, which may not be desirable.[8] Uniform global rules prioritizing economic integration are likely to conflict with the diversity of institutional arrangements that countries with varying circumstances require.

These two considerations suggest that we might easily end up with global rules that are of the wrong kind or overly constraining. Instead, we may want to focus our efforts at global governance on domains where there is a particularly strong case for it. I discuss those circumstances in the next section. First, let's turn to the free-for-all regime and consider why it may not lead to undesirable outcomes.

Imagine a world in which all nations, large or small, pursue their own economic interests, with total disregard for the consequences to other nations. This is the anarchic world that proponents of global governance (or its US version, the rules-based liberal international order) want to avoid. The remarkable thing, though, is that this would be for the most part a beneficial anarchy. After all, governments that look out for their economies would never want to cut themselves off from trade; they would seek foreign investment; and they would pursue prudential and macroeconomic policies that ensure financial stability and full employment. All of this would be good for the rest of the world. The Ricardian theory of comparative advantage compels nations to pursue free trade for their own benefit, not for the sake of other nations.

Of course, there are exceptions to the theory. In the presence of market imperfections and in line with the Hamilton-List tradition in economics, governments may want to engage in trade and industrial policies to foster structural change in a particular direction. However, as long as these policies target genuine market failures and do so effectively, they do no harm to other nations. Quite to the contrary. They produce a growing economy and a larger market for other nations' exporters and investors. (There are some exceptions to this, but they are few; I discuss them in the next section.) The same goes for policies that depart from free trade for distributional and social reasons. When governments successfully address problems of equity and fairness at home, their electorates are less likely to support extremists and xenophobes. Ultimately, the best gift a nation can give to the world is to have a healthy economy and cohesive society. The fear that countries looking out for their own interest would undermine the global economy is largely baseless.

All of this presumes that governments pursue policies that genuinely advance national economic (and societal) interests. As the case of President Trump amply demonstrates, this is obviously not the case some of the time, or even perhaps most of the time. Short-sighted political reasons, incompetence, or mistaken economic beliefs can generate policies that harm the domestic economy and the rest of the world. Governments may put up tariff barriers to benefit a tiny rich minority, subsidize industries for no real economic or social reason, or pursue irresponsible policies that produce financial crises. When these outcomes do happen, however, they are rooted in failures of *domestic* governance, not in failures of global governance.

Many economists and technocrats believe that there is nonetheless a role for global governance in such instances. Global rules can tie the hands of the government and prevent it from harming the economy. An international prohibition on subsidies, for example, allows the government to say to its lobbies, "Sorry, as much as I would like to help you, international rules do not allow me to give you the subsidy you are requesting." The downside is that this rule would also prevent the government from acting in cases where there is a genuine economic need for the subsidy, such as in the presence of learning spillovers. To make a case for global governance, we would have to presume global rules can be designed with sufficient detail and flexibility to discriminate between these two cases: prohibit subsidies in the first case but allow them in the second. This seems a tough case to make, especially in view of the power-based features of global governance I have just discussed.

The bottom line is that global governance is not as desirable as it is conventionally presumed, while a free-for-all is not as harmful as commonly thought. Global governance codifies the preferences of hegemonic powers and enforces rules that may be unsuited to lesser nations. A free-for-all does not result in isolationism and autarky. While we cannot rely on governments not to make mistakes or pursue misguided policies, this is a problem that cannot be solved through global governance.

There are two exceptions to the general rule that countries can pursue their own economic advantage without harming the world as a whole or benefiting it. These are global public goods and beggar-thy-neighbor actions. When we look at them closely, we find that their scope is narrower than conventional treatments allow. Nevertheless, a minimal global economic order would need to have provisions for addressing them.

Global public goods

Global public goods refer to national policies whose costs are borne at home but whose benefits are primarily global rather than national. The archetypal example is climate mitigation policies. Climate change is driven by the global stock of greenhouse gases (GHGs) in the atmosphere. It does not matter where the GHGs are emitted or which country invests in mitigation policies. A country that is small enough in the world economy has, on its own, an imperceptible effect on the global stock of GHGs so has little incentive to bear the costs of mitigation. Even larger countries, whose emissions would make a difference, would prefer to free ride on other countries' mitigation efforts.

This is the problem that has long stymied global efforts to fight climate change. It remains the one area where global governance, in the form of a global carbon pricing or cap-and-trade program, for example, would make the greatest contribution. We saw in chapter 3 that progress on climate has come from a different direction. A mix of foreign policy, commercial, and technological motives has pushed China, the US, and the EU, unilaterally and each in their own way, toward more aggressive climate policies than most analysts thought would be feasible in the absence of global cooperation. In other words, leading nations have found ways to "privatize" the benefits of mitigation, keeping some of the benefits for themselves and reducing free-riding incentives along the way. The climate-related global public good that remains the most severely underprovided at present is that of financial and technological transfers needed to bring developed countries along. As discussed in chapter 3, this is a responsibility that falls largely on advanced economies and China.

Other than climate change, it is difficult to identify policy domains that are strictly global public goods. When commentators use the term in relation to the global economy, they typically have in mind policies that have broadly positive effects on other countries, particularly in large economies. Maintaining open trade, financial stability, and macroeconomic balance are some examples. As we have discussed, these are things that benefit the home economy first and foremost. Technological knowledge and R&D also produce positive externalities for other nations to the extent that they spill over across national borders. But the nations that invest in R&D typically reap the greatest benefits, so they have plenty of incentive to do it alone, even though those incentives may fall short of what would be adequate from a global standpoint. Investments in early warning and other public health systems to prepare for and address pandemics are similar. Finally, global poverty reduction is sometimes considered a global public good. But that interpretation depends on considerations of global fairness and justice, which raises different types of questions.

Beggar-thy-neighbor policies

Beggar-thy-neighbor (BTN) policies are the second category that requires global cooperation. The term is often used broadly to denote policies that harm other nations. But I prefer a narrower definition, which gives us greater analytical purchase on the question of global governance. We need a tighter definition of BTN policies; otherwise, the list of policies that would need to be brought under global governance would not make much sense.

Consider some examples. Increased public spending on tertiary education in a country with a comparative disadvantage in skill-intensive goods will reduce the country's disadvantage, improve its external terms of trade, and harm the countries it trades with. Investment in R&D has the same effect for a country with a comparative disadvantage in high-tech products. Policies that incentivize saving will widen a country's trade surplus, potentially reducing employment in other nations. Judicial reforms that enhance the efficiency of contract enforcement will make a country more attractive for foreign investors, drawing multinational companies away from other locations. In a world of economic interdependence, the list of policies with cross-border spillovers is virtually endless. It would be not just impossible but also senseless to try to bring them all under a global discipline.

Some readers might object that all these policies are prima facie desirable policies, regardless of the impacts on other nations. What global rules should constrain, they might argue, are policies that are not so desirable. But this takes us down another rabbit hole. Who is to judge whether a particular policy is desirable or not? And if a country's government argues a contested policy—say, a particular industrial policy—is actually beneficial and serves an important economic function, is there any reason to believe that an international body would reliably know better?

So here is the narrow definition of BTN policies that I think does a better job of drawing the relevant distinction. A policy is BTN when the benefit provided to the domestic economy is *made possible* by the harm that it generates to other nations. In other words, the negative cross-border spillover must be a necessary condition for the policy to benefit the home economy. No harm done to other nations, no gain at home. Under this definition, none of the illustrations above is an example of a BTN policy. In each case, the home government would presumably want to pursue those policies—to enhance education, R&D, saving, the judiciary—even if no other countries were harmed, and indeed, even if there were no other countries in the world.

Genuine BTN policies exist, but they are a small subset of policies with negative cross-border spillovers. The term itself was first used in an economics context by Joan Robinson, a Cambridge colleague of Keynes, to describe the detrimental consequences of some of the policies governments resorted to during the Great Depression of the 1930s. In a situation of generalized unemployment, noted

Robinson, a country could boost employment at home through policies targeting a trade surplus. Examples of such policies were competitive currency devaluations or export subsidies. As she noted, what made this possible was the switch in aggregate demand from foreign to home goods.[9] The increase in employment was enabled by a corresponding decrease in employment in the rest of the world. This feature makes these policies a classic instance of BTN. Note that the argument requires Keynesian unemployment. Otherwise, the same policies may simply produce inflation (which undoes the gain in competitiveness of home goods and has little effect on other nations); or even if they have an impact on the trade balance, they may not alter employment levels.

Another example is provided by what economists call *optimum tariffs*. These are tariffs that enable a country to exploit its monopoly power on world markets. They produce gains for the home economy by improving its terms of trade (and correspondingly deteriorating other countries' terms of trade). The gain at home is the direct result of the loss imposed on the rest of the world. Export taxes that restrict sales on world markets when the home country has market power work similarly.

Trade policy to extract monopoly profits from foreign nations is different from trade policy to protect an infant industry or employment in a particular industry at home. The former is a clear instance of BTN, while the latter is not.[10] Of course, protective tariffs may also cause terms of trade losses for other countries, when the applying country is a large economy with market power. But abuse of market power is not the government's objective, and the monopoly rents are an incidental by-product. Indeed, in this case the government applying protection would be willing to give up the monopoly rents. That is exactly what happened when the advanced economies wanted to protect their garment, auto, steel, and other sectors against the rapid increase in exports from newly industrializing countries and Japan during the 1970s and 1980s. They agreed to have the trade restrictions applied by exporting nations, so that the rents were captured by the exporters instead of the importing countries. Exporters got the monopoly profits while the importers got the protection. Prominent examples were the Multifiber Arrangement (1974–1994) and the voluntary export restraints (VERs) of the 1980s. These arrangements were banned when the WTO went into effect in 1995.

Whether they generate monopoly profits or not, trade or financial restrictions that have the objective of undermining another country's economy are also patently BTN policies. This is an area of considerable controversy in light of US export controls on China in advanced semiconductors. The US government has defended these controls on national security grounds, while the Chinese government is convinced the objective is to sabotage China's technological development. I return to this issue later in the chapter.

A final example is tax haven policies. Countries can maintain low taxes on corporations for a variety of reasons. Typically, the purpose is to offer an attractive environment for investors—domestic and foreign alike—thereby promoting capital accumulation and economic growth. Such policies cannot be considered BTNs, even if they result in international corporations moving their investments from high- to low-tax economies. Countries may evaluate the trade-offs among the pros and cons of corporate taxation differently: Who is to judge what the correct tax rate is? In some cases, though, governments set low tax rates not to attract physical investment but to generate tax revenues by inducing corporations to shift paper profits from higher-tax jurisdictions. These are pure tax havens. They produce anomalies such as companies booking tens of billions of dollars in profits in countries where they employ only a handful of people and have no physical investment.[11] Since these policies are beneficial only to the extent that they shift profits from elsewhere, they are a clear instance of BTN.

A general feature of BTN policies is that they are negative sum for the world as a whole. Each of the policies described previously generates global inefficiencies, even as they benefit the home country. An implication is that, if other nations retaliate by imposing similar policies, *all* countries are left worse off.[12] Therefore, countries that take the likelihood of retaliation into account may be less prone to engage in them—and more willing to condone prohibitions as a rule, as I argue in the next section.

In short, while many policies generate cross-border spillovers, it is BTN policies that are the more clearly objectionable. I don't claim to have provided an exhaustive list of BTN policies here. But the list is surely not as long as that for cross-border spillovers. This is useful because it lowers the demand on global governance and reduces the burden it must bear.

New rules of the road

One reason hyperglobalization floundered and cannot be revived is that it was premised on a convergence in policies on trade, finance, industry, regulation, and taxation across the world. Countries were expected to embrace a similar model of a market economy, providing maximum freedom for international corporations and financial institutions to roam the world. Trade and financial arrangements sought a common set of rules for governments. Using a traffic analogy, this was like telling drivers the speed at which they should travel on the highway, regardless of whether they are on bicycles or in racing cars. I take a different approach here. I accept as desirable, or at least inevitable, that countries will want to maintain different policies. Instead of harmonizing them away, my approach focuses on managing the frictions produced by the resulting spillovers to make it possible for different policy regimes to live side by side. Returning to the traffic example, the goal is to allow individual vehicles to drive at different speeds. However, this more permissive set of rules still requires guidelines on what they must do when they come to an intersection where they encounter other vehicles.

To see how such a global order might work, let's focus on the most difficult relationship that it would have to manage: the US-China conflict. I assume that both countries are interested in building an economic order that maximizes the benefits to themselves and minimizes the harms, but that their approach to the global economy is not zero sum. The latter qualification is important. It would be violated if one or both countries were to view economic relations from a purely geopolitical lens, whereby one country's gains is another's loss. That would likely be the case if the US were to seek permanent global primacy over China, or if China were to upset the prevailing status quo in Taiwan or the South China Sea unilaterally through military force. It is difficult to see how under those circumstances economic relations would not become part of an entirely different kind of game, where economic interdependence is weaponized by both parties for geopolitical and military ends.[13]

Leaving that possibility aside, let's imagine the two countries tell each other the following: We are two nations with very different economic systems that will not converge anytime soon, if ever. Given our divergent economic models and interests, it is very unlikely we could agree on a common set of rules to apply in different domains of the global economy, such as trade, financial regulation, intellectual property, digital economy, subsidies, and so on. Instead of substantive rules, let's instead negotiate procedural rules on how we sort out our differences. Here is a simple idea that neither one of us should have any difficulty with. Let's agree that there are four distinct buckets in which our policies can be placed. Each bucket calls for a different approach. These buckets are described below, but what's important is that we don't have to agree from the beginning which bucket any specific policy belongs in.[14]

The first bucket is for *prohibited policies*. Any policy that both nations agree should be banned would go here. Despite their differences, the two nations should be able to agree that some kinds of practices are illegitimate and unacceptable. For example, the inviolability of national borders is a principle to which both nations subscribe. Invading another country other than for reasons of self-defense is something that ought not be done. Of course, countries occasionally do violate these principles, as when the US invaded Iraq in 2003 and Russia invaded Ukraine in 2022. The widespread acceptance of certain actions as prohibited does not necessarily prevent states from engaging in them. But it does mean that states understand where the lines have been drawn in terms of what is acceptable and what is not. Explicit transgressions normally entail reputational costs, such as loss of legitimacy and support in the international arena.

In economics, the idea that nations should not engage in BTN policies, defined narrowly as in the previous section, is the closest we have to a shared norm. We might reasonably expect China and the US to put BTN policies in this bucket, as they are explicitly meant to harm others. The two nations also understand that they would both be worse off if each were to resort to them. Of course, there will necessarily be disagreements about whether specific policies constitute BTN or not. These disagreements will be part of future discussions and negotiations. As with other global norms, the goal is to draw clear borders around the types of actions that are illegitimate and wrong.

For other types of policies, countries retain full "property rights"; that is, governments are regarded as entitled to act in any way they see fit. The second bucket is for policies that nevertheless may be amenable to *mutual negotiations and adjustments*. As previously discussed, many policies create spillovers abroad. As long as those are not of the BTN kind, they would not be regarded as prohibited (and included in the first bucket). But there is the possibility that the two countries could work out a mutual bargain of the sort where "you refrain from that policy, and I will do something else for you in return." The traditional GATT model of tariff negotiations was based on this approach. Large economies would agree to reduce tariffs vis-à-vis each other. The bilateral tariff reductions would then be extended to other nations through the most-favored-nation rule. There are a large number of areas where the US and China could engage in negotiations of this kind, to their mutual benefit.

Any policy that creates a benefit at home that is of lower value than the cost it imposes on the other country (with benefits and costs valued by the countries where they are incurred) is in principle amenable to being placed in the second bucket. In such instances, the country that is harmed can essentially provide a transfer (or a policy of equivalent benefit) to the harming country for the latter to desist from the policy. Economically inefficient policies are generically of this kind. Therefore, mutual negotiations have the potential to discipline policies that are clearly inefficient and provide a way for countries to gradually move toward globally efficient outcomes. But countries retain the freedom to choose their own policies, unless the other country offers them a bargain that they prefer.

Not all policies will allow such mutual negotiations. The value that a country places on a particular action may be larger than the cost incurred by the other nation. There may be strategic standoffs, with nations misrepresenting their respective costs and benefits. Or there may not be an obvious way in which the other nation can reciprocate. Policies of this kind belong in our third bucket of *autonomous actions*. These are policies where countries are expected to act unilaterally. We expect the majority of policies with actual or potential spillovers to end up in this category.

A minimal requirement when countries go their own way is that countries act in a "well-calibrated" manner. The policies should be justifiable to the other side, in the sense that they must serve broadly legitimate objectives and have a plausible causal link to the intended outcomes. Autonomous actions should not be taken for the purpose of punishing or weakening the other side. When actions are taken in response to the other government's behavior, they should be directly linked to the damage being done by the other side's policies and intended solely to mitigate its negative effects. They should not be undertaken to retaliate or escalate a conflict.

The third bucket allows self-help but not sanctions or punishment. Governments would obviously have considerable leeway in how they interpret these restrictions. But the acting government should be able to provide an account for its action: I am doing this because I want to increase employment, productivity, resilience, etc., and this is how this policy is expected to achieve this outcome. I am doing this because I want to weaken your economy or because I think you should run your economy the way I run mine would not be acceptable explanations on their face value. This gives the home side the chance to explain what it is doing and why, and the other side an opportunity to question the motives for and effectiveness of a policy. It is the difference between a jungle where no one knows the rules and one where the parties commit to certain basic guidelines—though there is still no third party to enforce those guidelines. Ultimately, the threshold for autonomous action is a low one. The requirement that a policy be well calibrated is essentially a vehicle for inducing a conversation between the two sides that might not otherwise take place.

So far we have considered problems that involved just the two parties and could be solved bilaterally. Some problems require joint action by a multitude of governments. Global public goods, discussed earlier, are the premier example of that. Such problems would go in our fourth bucket of *multilateral governance*. This is where we'd expect issues related to climate change, global pandemics, and debt resolution (as we will see later) to end up. The US and China as major powers would have an important leadership role in tabling problems and framing answers. But participation and acceptance from a much broader group of countries would be required for effective solutions.

This road map presumes little agreement or trust on the part of governments. By organizing a discussion about which issues belong in which bucket, it aims to advance each country's understanding of the motives and aspirations of the other. Over time, it might enhance trust and make it easier to address problems that earlier proved tractable. In the rest of the chapter, I discuss how the framework applies to some of the key areas of friction between the US and China, starting with trade and investment restrictions motivated by national security.

Small yard, high fence

In the speech I quoted from earlier in the chapter, Jake Sullivan used a memorable phrase to describe US trade and investment regulations vis-à-vis China in technologies that posed national security concerns. To ensure new technologies advance US security and democracy, rather than undermining them, he said the US would protect critical technologies with "a small yard and high fence."[15] The US would restrict exports of the most advanced semiconductor technologies to China. Incoming and outgoing investment flows would similarly be screened for national security. The US has a long tradition of export controls on high technology, dating from the Cold War with the Soviet Union. As geopolitical competition with China heats up, these restrictions have once again come to the fore. Effectively, the US has decided to apply its version of the Chinese maxim "open the window but place a screen on it" (see chapter 2).

Placing restrictions on trade and investment to protect national security is one of the most natural prerogatives of every nation-state. US policy is distinctive in this regard only insofar as a large share of cutting-edge technologies are developed by US firms, often with funding or other kinds of assistance from the federal government. What stands out in Sullivan's speech is the self-imposed discipline— the commitment that such restrictions would be tough but applied sparingly ("a small yard and high fence"). In particular, the measures would focus "on a narrow slice of technology and a small number of countries." In a speech then treasury secretary Janet Yellen gave shortly before Sullivan, the approach was spelled out further.

> Let me be clear: these national security actions are not designed for us to gain a competitive economic advantage, or stifle China's economic and technological modernization. Even though these policies may have economic impacts, they are driven by straightforward national security considerations. . . . There are key principles that guide our national security actions in the economic sphere. First, these actions will be narrowly scoped and targeted to clear objectives. They will be calibrated to mitigate spillovers into other areas. Second, it is vital that these tools are easily understood and enforceable. And they must be readily adaptable when circumstances change. Third, when possible, we will engage and coordinate with our allies and partners in the design and execution of our policies.[16]

The approach laid out in these statements is closely aligned with the framework of the previous section. Essentially, the US administration was telling China the following: These trade and investment restrictions are not aimed at enhancing our economic competitiveness at China's expense. Neither do they target the weakening of China's economic and technological development. Their sole purpose is to ensure US national security. For these reasons, they cannot be considered BTN policies and do not belong in the first bucket of prohibited actions. Moreover, there is nothing China could offer us that would dissuade us from protecting our security interests (so bucket two does not apply either). We are exercising our prerogative to act unilaterally, which means we are in the third bucket. In accordance with bucket three rules, our actions will be well calibrated. We will apply the measures only in a very small range of technologies where there is a clear national security case. And we will not escalate into other areas unrelated to national security.

Hence the Biden administration appeared to have situated its policies clearly and publicly within the rules of the game I have offered. This is important regardless of whether it fully abided by those rules. Having done so, it provided others, and China in particular, a yardstick against which its actions could be evaluated. It signaled to China the limited aims of the measures, laid out the standards against which they could be judged, and thereby opened the door for a bilateral conversation, where China could articulate its concerns on the same terms as the measures themselves. It was an invitation to be constructive rather than to escalate.

When our rules work, they will direct controversy to questions on whether the principles are being applied properly instead of questions on the principles themselves. This seems to have been the case in this instance. Predictably, China complained about the policies, but the criticism focused on the misuse of export controls rather than the export controls or the national security argument per se. Chinese concerns centered on the scope of the controls, which expanded over time to a wider range of technologies, a larger number of Chinese companies, other countries that are allies of the US, and measures beyond trade and investment regulations.[17]

The Chinese reaction was in fact muted compared to some of the commentary by Western observers. Edward Luce of the *Financial Times* claimed the initial suite of export restrictions amounted to "a full-blown economic war on China." Gregory Allen of the Center for Strategic and International Studies wrote that it constituted "a new US policy of actively strangling large segments of the Chinese technology industry—strangling with an intent to kill."[18] In light of such views, the measured Chinese response was especially encouraging. It was precisely what the framework was designed to encourage.

It is not entirely clear that the US approach under Biden was a fully successful case of autonomous action, one that safeguarded national security while limiting damage to the Chinese economy and to relations with China. There were too many ways the experiment could unravel. There was bound to be considerable overlap between what the US counted as a legitimate response to a national security threat and what China thought was the weaponization of trade and investment. Over time, it seemed that the US government began to take too expansive a view of its national security interests, turning more and more of its economic relations with China into a zero-sum game. It failed to do a convincing job of explaining, both to its domestic audience and to China, the specific security threats caused by technologies that are restricted. There was further loss of trust when the US apparently failed to respond to good-faith efforts by Chinese firms to address stated national security concerns.[19] With Trump coming into office in 2025, whatever remained of the doctrine was jettisoned.

However, it was to the Biden administration's credit that it articulated a standard against which its behavior could be judged. The "small yard, high fence" test was a declaration of self-restraint. Even if did not ensure trade and investment restrictions remained tightly targeted on clear national security objectives, it gave others a way of calling the US out. It was an invitation to China not only for understanding ("we are doing this solely for national security; you would do the same") but also to question US policy when it seemed to violate its own principle.

Subsidy wars

Next to national security, subsidies are the biggest bone of contention in the West's economic relations with China. The US and European nations have long complained that Chinese industrial competitiveness was built on the back of government subsidies. These recriminations have intensified in the context of China's green industrial policies in solar, EVs, and batteries. The liberal use of subsidies in the US IRA and CHIPS programs has also drawn the ire of the European Union and developing nations.

A major innovation under the WTO was a ban on subsidies when they harmed the trade of other nations. The restriction applied, with some narrow exceptions, to all countries except for the poorest. In the language of our framework, subsidies were treated as BTN policies and placed in the first bucket of prohibited actions. However, this was a clear case of overreach. A closer look at what subsidies do would suggest that they belong in the second or third buckets, where countries retain autonomy. Affected countries in turn ought to be free to respond, if they wish, in order to shield their economy, as long as their response is calibrated.

Governments use subsidies for a variety of reasons. Throughout the book, we have seen cases where subsidies promoted learning, innovation, the green transition, or good jobs. But there may be other motives as well. Governments may resort to subsidies to promote exports for their own sake or for purely political reasons to enrich cronies of the ruling group. In some instances, subsidies could be considered BTN, but these are relatively rare. During periods of generalized Keynesian employment, subsidies act like currency devaluations and can similarly export unemployment. Subsidies could be used for predatory purposes, to drive competing firms out and jack up prices later.

The subsidies that typically raise other nations' ire are very different from BTN policies. In fact, they are closer to the opposite: from a purely economic standpoint, they are a gift to a country's trading partners. A government that subsidizes its firms enables those firms to sell on world markets at lower prices. Consumers in the rest of the world enjoy lower prices thanks to the subsidy. If a tax on exports raises prices on world markets, thus beggaring other nations, a subsidy (which is a negative tax) enriches them! It is true, of course, that competing firms in other countries lose competitiveness and market share and may even have to fold. But the same is true whenever a country enhances its comparative advantage in certain products, regardless of whether this happens through cuts in costs, increased productivity, or sundry other reasons. In all those cases, there are gains in aggregate to the rest of the world while certain firms may be harmed. The economic consequences for trade partners are exactly the same. (There may be a legitimate concern about the fairness of subsidized trade, of course. I pick this point up later; for now, allow me to stick to the economic case.)

One feature of BTN policies, as we saw, is that they are efficiency-reducing for the world as a whole. And they leave all nations worse off when they result in retaliation. Neither of these considerations applies as a rule to subsidies. As we have seen, there are many circumstances in which subsidies perform a valuable function—when there are innovation externalities, learning spillovers, and benefits to the local community from good jobs. Even when they are not perfectly suited to the objective and lack effectiveness compared to alternatives, they could be economically useful in a second-best sense. When governments employ subsidies in this fashion, they help markets perform better. They and their trading partners both end up richer.

In fact, the economic benefits they generate for the rest of the world can be even larger. This is because many of the externalities addressed by the subsidies spill over across national boundaries. We have seen how China's green subsidies have helped speed up the green transition in the rest of the world. The innovations in the semiconductor industries of East Asia and elsewhere promoted by government subsidies have produced technological learning in other countries as well.[20] And subsidies that create good jobs and strengthen the middle class help the world economy by fostering cohesive societies that are less likely to turn autarkic and xenophobic.

All of this presumes that governments use subsidies for economic and social purposes that are desirable and legitimate. Obviously, this will often not be the case. Governments can make mistakes or use subsidies for political ends while ruining their economies. It would be desirable to rein in the use of subsidies in such cases. The complication is that it is difficult to distinguish benign subsidies from their malign versions. It is generally sensible to defer to the home government's judgment on this, especially when the costs of inefficient subsidies are borne by the home economy.

Imagine a hypothetical scenario between a subsidizing government and a foreign government that feels it is adversely affected. The aggrieved government says, "You are hurting my industries; you must desist!" The home government responds, "I am fostering innovation and promoting technological development. That will be good for you, too, in the long run, if you can ignore the pain that some of your firms feel in the short run." Aggrieved government: "Only if it were so. You are just helping some of your inefficient firms. You and I will both end up worse off." Home government: "To be perfectly honest, you may be right. I cannot be certain that my policy is good for the economy. What I can say is that if I am wrong, it is primarily my own taxpayers and consumers who will bear the cost. They are the ones who pay the taxes that finance the subsidies. They will be the ones who pay higher prices if the innovation does not materialize. And as the government, I will be the one that will pay the political price of my mistake. Your economy, meanwhile, is benefiting, at the very least, from the lower prices due to my subsidies." Aggrieved government: "OK, I take the point. But it does not quite solve the problem I have with my firms that are losing market share to yours. I reserve the right to respond. This conversation will continue."[21]

But what about subsidy wars? What if all countries start playing by the same rules? Would this not be a race to the bottom? This is a common concern, but it is misplaced. When all countries promote their industries for legitimate goals (learning externalities, say), the collective outcome would be greater prosperity. In fact, in view of the cross-border spillovers from innovation, the more pertinent worry is that there is too little subsidization going on all around, rather than too much! This is certainly the case with green subsidies. As we saw in chapter 3, green industrial policies are an important complement to, and a partial substitute for, carbon pricing. When carbon is not priced at its true social costs, a subsidy war in renewables and green industries is actually a good thing: it is what the doctor ordered in our inevitably second-best world.[22]

So much for the economics of subsidies in the international economy. We cannot discuss subsidies without also raising questions of fairness. There is a difference between becoming more competitive through innovation versus undercutting others through government handouts. We can imagine the aggrieved government in the above hypothetical to argue, "Nothing you say alters the fact that your subsidies have artificially created an unlevel playing field between your firms and mine. What am I supposed to tell those firms when they come to me and complain that they are being forced to compete with firms whose costs are covered by their government?"

The question of fair trade deserves a broader discussion, which I turn to in the next section. With respect to subsidies proper, the home government can be expected to respond in the following manner: "I understand the fairness argument. We can do one of two things. You could offer me a deal that I consider generous enough that entices me to remove my subsidies (bucket 2). Or you could simply go it alone and put up some tariffs to protect your affected firms. But if you go the latter route, I expect you to apply a narrowly targeted remedy—one that provides no more than the needed margin of protection, does not escalate the conflict, or aim to punish me (bucket 3)." Aggrieved government: "Got it. That makes sense."

The US and the EU eventually responded to China's green subsidies with tariffs of their own. Effectively, they chose to act within the third bucket, though it is questionable that their response was fully aligned with our framework. The US claimed the tariffs were "carefully targeted," but the new tariffs were quite high (rising to 100% in the case of EVs). More seriously, the rhetoric around the action demonized China, depicting the country as a norm breaker, engaged in unfair nonmarket practices and flooding global markets.[23] Setting such a tone disregarded what China as the home government might have said in concluding the previous dialogue: "If you put up countervailing tariffs, do not go on a rampage about how China is 'a bad actor' violating the rules-based global economic order. We are both doing what makes sense in a complicated and politically divided world."

Dealing with labor and human rights

The third set of issues I apply the framework to is labor and human rights. While labor and human rights are typically treated differently, they both raise a similar question: How should nations respond— or respond under commonly accepted rules—when they import goods from countries in which there are fundamental violations of rights? From a narrowly economic perspective, it does not matter how comparative advantage is created. Whether it comes about through exploitation of workers or through technological advances, comparative advantage creates economic gains from trade. As we have already seen in the case of subsidies, however, this is an unsatisfactory answer. Ultimately, fairness will intrude in international economic relations.

Two perspectives have prevailed to date. The traditional approach was to keep the two issues as distinct as possible. Outside of some very narrow cases—prison or slave labor perhaps— importing countries could not treat imported goods differently based on the circumstances of their production. A T-shirt was the same for trade policy purposes regardless of whether it was produced by workers with a full set of rights or by children toiling in an unsafe factory. To this day, WTO rules do not allow countries to restrict imports when exporting nations commit flagrant violations of worker rights. The second approach is to introduce explicit labor conditions into trade agreements to ensure minimum standards of labor rights are observed among trade partners. For example, the US-Mexico-Canada free trade agreement (USMCA, the successor to NAFTA) contains a labor chapter with enforceable provisions that require adherence to core labor standards and freedom of collective bargaining.

Developing countries have generally preferred the first approach, as it minimizes the risk of protectionism in advanced economies using worker/human rights as a cover. They have been concerned that labor conditions demanded by rich countries may be unsuited at low levels of development and could undercut their comparative advantage in labor-intensive products. The worry is not entirely misplaced. Along with core labor rights, the USMCA included a specific wage provision aimed at reducing outsourcing to Mexico.[24]

Both of these approaches are variants of global governance, though with very different and contradictory intent. The first prohibits countries from taking labor conditions under consideration, while the second imposes a minimum floor on labor rights as a precondition for free trade. The tension between these two approaches means that global norms on what's permitted and prohibited remain at present a patchwork. In a small number of cases, such as the USMCA, countries have been able to agree on and codify some principles. In other cases, guiding norms are either missing or ineffective because they conflict with basic moral intuitions. The first bucket of our framework is largely empty.

We then need to consider how to handle these issues in the second or third buckets. One possibility is that countries reach mutual bargains, bilaterally or in small groups, that establish some common understanding on rights as part of a trade agreement. The USMCA is one example. Another more ambitious case is the European Union itself, which requires broad protection of humanitarian and democratic rights as a precondition of membership. These are instances of the second bucket at work.

A more common outcome is unilateral action when there are concerns about labor or human rights in exporting nations. The US has periodically and selectively blocked imports in such cases. A 2021 law, for example, resulted in a ban on all goods produced in or originating from the Xinjiang region of China, where the Muslim Uyghur minority is subject to forced labor and other human rights abuses. In 2017, France passed pioneering legislation requiring all large companies based in France (those with more than 5,000 workers) to publish an annual "vigilance" plan. Companies are required to identify and eliminate potential human rights and environmental abuses throughout their global supply chain, including subcontractors as well as subsidiaries. These are well-calibrated and targeted responses in the sense of our third category.

The French law applies only to French companies and does not affect imports from foreign firms with no (or small) presence in

France. A broader type of action within this bucket would be a social safeguard measure analogous to current antidumping and safeguard practices. Existing trade laws, sanctioned by the WTO, permit countries to impose import tariffs when imported goods are sold below cost or, under certain conditions, when they cause "material injury" to a domestic industry. There are no similar laws that protect labor specifically or ensure trade does not violate commonly held moral principles at home.

As in the case of subsidies, one may reasonably object to imports that are produced under exploitative conditions. There could be two distinct grounds for concern. One is that such imports entail unfair competition for domestic labor: putting our workers in direct competition with workers elsewhere whose wages are kept low through oppressive practices. The other is that consuming goods produced under such conditions makes us morally complicit in human rights abuses. The latter objection would apply even in those cases where the goods in question, or close substitutes, are not produced at home and no domestic workers are affected adversely.

One can envisage the extension of prevailing laws to cover such concerns, by enabling countries to impose trade restrictions on partners or specific types of imports where production involves practices that violate broadly held norms at home.[25] To pass the well-calibrated test, the legislation would have to impose a clear, publicly verifiable test on the nature of the violation. It would require demonstration of a systematic abuse of collective bargaining rights, employment of child labor, disregard of basic health and safety requirements, and so on. It would also provide a vehicle for opponents of the restriction, including the exporting country, to express their own perspective on the issue. An important objective in setting up a process of this kind would be to distinguish cases where there are genuine human and labor rights abuses from cases where wages in the exporting countries are depressed due to low labor productivity. The latter case would constitute crass protectionism and may be less justifiable to trade partners in the kind of dialogue envisaged under the third bucket.

Another important distinction is between trade measures that protect a country's own values and those that target the transformation of another country's practices. While our framework is quite permissive on the former, it takes a harder line on the latter. In practice, what makes Western actions on humanitarian or political grounds particularly contentious from the perspective of China or other targeted countries is that they are often presented as punishment for transgressions, and perceived in addition as questioning the legitimacy of the political regime in place. Sanctions of this sort have a long and checkered history. They rarely work, especially when they take aim at fundamental prerogatives of sovereign countries. Using trade remedies to uphold a country's own values and practices rather than to denigrate those of another country is generally more legitimate and workable. The distinction, however, may be difficult to make in practice. One country's protective effort is another's sanction. This makes the language governments use to describe what they are doing and why all the more important.

Global finance and debt crises

In global finance, our principles allow countries considerable room to manage capital flows, including through capital controls on inflows and outflows. This is important because proponents of hyperglobalization have greatly exaggerated the benefits of financial globalization, even more so than for free trade. The free flow of capital around the world was supposed to transfer savings from rich to poor nations, increase investment rates, discipline irresponsible macroeconomic policies, and enable smooth consumption growth paths. To facilitate this agenda, middle-income developing countries were branded as "emerging markets" by multilateral organizations to render them more attractive to international capital markets. "Frontier markets" became the analogous label for poorer developing nations in subsequent decades. Unfortunately, none of the original predictions was borne out, and in many cases, the outcomes were exactly the opposite. Investment and growth rates did not increase, while income distribution deteriorated.[26] Access to foreign finance allowed many governments to engage in more irresponsible fiscal and monetary policies, for far longer, than would have been possible otherwise. Developing countries were buffeted by a series of costly financial crises as a result of sharp reversals in capital flows.

Countries suffering these crises bear the lion's share of the responsibility. Too often they were reckless in throwing themselves open to fickle, short-term capital flows in search of short-term yields. They benefited in the short run as the inflows boosted domestic consumption. But they also became more dependent on financial flows and more fragile. Once the inevitable "sudden stop" occurred, they found themselves in the midst of a long and drawn-out process of debt renegotiation with their creditors. The list of sovereign and banking crises under financial globalization is too long, but it goes from Mexico in 1994 through the East Asian financial crisis that engulfed Thailand, South Korea, and Indonesia in 1997–98 to the most recent cases of debt distress in Sri Lanka, Zambia, Kenya, and Ghana.

Having become a major lender, China enabled greater flows to developing countries in the context of its Belt and Road Initiative. The upside was the construction of some major infrastructure projects. But Chinese finance also exacerbated the inherent instability of financial globalization. It created more debt, often in ways that lacked transparency. And it greatly complicated the process of debt resolution by aggravating the coordination problem among creditors. As I write these lines, Kenya is recovering from deadly riots in its capital Nairobi that were sparked by the extreme fiscal austerity the government felt it had to undertake in order to pay back its Chinese and other creditors.

Nobody forces a country to take on too much debt. Avoiding the buildup of debt is almost entirely the responsibility of individual governments. We are squarely in bucket three in this phase of financial crises. Capital controls were once frowned upon by global financial institutions and discouraged. Luckily, the IMF and other international organizations have gradually moved away from treating free capital flows as a norm that all countries should eventually adhere to. Accordingly, governments in developing countries can feel free to curb surges in capital flows and regulate short-term borrowing to avoid excessive indebtedness. Advanced economies that are home to private lenders might complain. But the complaints would have little legitimacy as long as capital controls are designed to protect domestic economic stability and are not punitive.

But once the crisis strikes, the problem becomes multilateral. It requires achieving a three-way coordination among official lenders, private lenders, and the indebted government. The government may be willing to take the requisite measures but will typically need additional financing to get over tough times. Official lenders may be willing to provide assistance in return for a credible government adjustment program, but in the absence of a separate agreement with private creditors, the bulk of new money would leak out as debt service to private creditors. Individual private creditors, on the other hand, want others to take haircuts while they get paid in full. Each party has an interest in free riding, which delays any debt restructuring and makes reaching agreement very difficult. Given these incentives, establishing a debt resolution framework that could be readily applied in debt crises is a global public good, requiring the tools of bucket four.[27] This point has been generally recognized, and there have been various attempts at developing a global framework. But we are not any closer to effective global governance in this domain today than we were in the 1980s. This makes it imperative for countries to take their own unilateral precautions in order to protect themselves from the downsides of financial globalization.

International taxation

Tax havens are BTN policies, as we have seen. This places them within our first bucket and makes it appropriate to institute global prohibitions against them. At the same time, countries may have legitimate reasons to maintain low tax rates on corporations to attract real investment. A global regime for corporate taxation must therefore also be permissive toward the latter kind of policies.

An important first step was taken when leading nations signed an agreement in October 2021 to set rules on global taxation of corporations. The agreement established a global minimum tax of 15 percent on large corporations (with earnings above €750 million). This is arguably low enough that it still leaves some headspace for countries that want to maintain corporate tax regimes that are attractive to investors. It also required that a portion of the global profits of the world's largest corporations (those with annual global turnover exceeding €20 billion) be returned to countries where they do business, even if their nominal headquarters were located elsewhere. In many ways, this was a landmark agreement. It demonstrated an unprecedented level of global cooperation in an area where many rich countries had long resisted global controls. It became possible only after the US changed its position on global taxation, along with its general souring on hyperglobalization.

Yet the agreement also displays the downsides of global governance when the agenda is captured by powerful players. It is estimated that the bulk of the additional tax revenues generated will accrue to rich nations. Probably more seriously, as part of the agreement, developing countries were required to abstain from imposing digital service taxes and other "unilateral measures" on multinational corporations in the future. In light of the rapidly growing importance of the digital sector, this is a significant constraint on the ability of developing countries to raise revenues. In the words of one critic, developing countries were "asked to take a blind leap of faith by signing a legally binding agreement to give up certain taxing rights in return for a completely uncertain, and potentially harmful, revenue outcome."[28] Yet again, less powerful nations might be better off operating within the second or third buckets than in the first one.

More recently, Gabriel Zucman and his collaborators have floated the idea of a global tax on super-rich individuals. The baseline proposal is an annual tax equivalent to 2 percent of the net worth of those with more than $1 billion in wealth.[29] There are about 3,000 individuals around the world who would have to pay the tax. Zucman estimates that it would raise $200–$250 billion per year, which could go to pay for important global public goods, such as climate finance for developing countries. The idea is supported by Brazil, France, and Spain, but the US is yet to get on board. The logic for such a tax is impeccable. The problem it faces is not just one of global cooperation—why should rich countries tax themselves to pay for poor countries?—but also one of inaction on the part of national governments. Countries such as the US could do a lot more to tax those at the top income levels and increase the progressivity of their tax regime on their own.[30] Their failure is due as much to poor domestic governance as it is to inadequate global governance.

Final words

Ambitious attempts at global governance are best restricted to the relatively few policy domains where BTN policies and global public goods predominate. The spillovers that independent national policies create have to be managed mostly through loose rules of the road. The framework I have developed in this chapter provides a manual for managing the interface among different national policy regimes in the interest of enlarging the space for self-help in the international economic system.

Self-help is a friend of the global economy, not its enemy. China's pragmatic and unorthodox economic policies produced unprecedented economic growth. Western protests about the policies notwithstanding, they produced significant benefits for the rest of the world by creating a vast market for foreign exporters and investors and, more recently, engineering a remarkable reduction in the prices of renewables. Similarly, if American and European unilateralism succeeds in producing more prosperous, cohesive, and secure societies at home, this will be to the world's benefit. Prioritizing domestic economic, social, and environmental goals does not necessitate a deepening US-China conflict or a weaker global economy. Neither does it pose a great obstacle to progress in the developing world. Developing nations that have devised appropriate growth strategies have prospered thanks to their own efforts, despite many global rules rigged against them and the glaring absence of critical global public goods.

The US continues to criticize China for allegedly pursuing mercantilist and protectionist policies and violating the norms of a "liberal" international order. Chinese policy makers accuse the US of turning its back on globalization and waging economic warfare on China. The irony is that the two sides have become more similar in their conduct of economic policies. China placed a screen on its open window; the US put a high fence around a small yard. In an interdependent global economy, it is inevitable that many policies targeting national economic well-being and domestic social and environmental priorities will have some undesirable side effects on others. The US will continue to put its economic, social, environmental, and national security concerns first, and China will not abandon its state-driven economic model. Cooperation will not be the order of the day. But it may become a bit easier if both countries recognize that their policies are neither too different nor necessarily harmful to the other side.

Of course, nothing prevents nations such as the US from pursuing policies that harm their own economies, alongside others'. (The Trump administration provides an unfortunate illustration of this.) Regrettably, there is little that global governance can do in such instances. Global rules cannot enforce good behavior when self-interest itself fails to do so.

8

A New Progressive Agenda

The backlash against neoliberalism and hyperglobalization that swept the world over the last decade was predictable. When markets are placed ahead of social contracts, the result is a deepening of social conflicts and the rise of populist politics. As economies become more integrated with each other, societies and polities disintegrate from within. Economic history and economic theory both provided plenty of hints regarding the unsustainability of the post-1990s arrangements.[1]

It remains to be seen what will come out of the passing of the old order. The reelection of Donald Trump in 2024 after four years of progressive leadership certainly gives cause for some pessimism. Many on the left were understandably shocked and disillusioned by the Democrats' failure at the polls. But there is reason for hope. Neoliberalism and hyperglobalization were shaped over several decades; it will take more than four years for a coherent alternative to emerge and capture the public's imagination. Ideas and practices in today's global economy still remain in flux. A progressive alternative to create inclusive, sustainable economies does exist. This chapter pulls on the threads of the arguments in the preceding chapters to outline such an alternative.

How the left lost its way

Surprisingly, the immediate political beneficiaries of the backlash against neoliberalism and hyperglobalization were populists of the right—those who emphasized national, religious, and cultural identity against the supposed threat posed by foreigners, Muslims, and immigrants. The turning point came in 2016, as Britain voted for withdrawal from the EU and Americans elected Donald Trump as president. Both were landmark events and highlighted the success of the far right in mobilizing a disaffected plurality to their cause. The populist right managed to attract previously unimaginable levels of support in many other nations, including France, Germany, Italy, and the Netherlands.

The left was mostly missing in action early on. This is somewhat of a paradox. One may have expected parties of the left to be in the best position to address the economic grievances unleashed by hyperglobalization. Economic insecurity, disappearing jobs, corporate power—traditionally, these had been the bread-and-butter issues of the left. Until recently, though, the left was unable to mount a significant and popular response against the rise of the right. The only meaningful programmatic innovation came with President Biden's wholesale adoption of industrial policies and rejection of the prevailing centrist policy consensus. But as the 2024 presidential election revealed, Bidenomics did not prove hugely popular despite some clear economic successes. Trump won decisively in 2024, wrote the veteran political consultant James Carville, "by seizing a swath of middle-class and low-income voters focused on the economy. . . . [A] lot of Americans perceive [Democrats] as out to lunch on the economy—not feeling their pain or caring too much about other things instead."[2]

The left was paralyzed by its earlier embrace of the policies that had generated the crisis. The Democrats in the US and Labour in the UK were staunch supporters of hyperglobalization, under Bill Clinton and Tony Blair, respectively. In Germany, Gerhard Schröder's Social Democrats took Clinton's and Blair's "third way" as their inspiration. French Socialists were the architects of the financial integration that moved the EU away from any conceivable social model. As I noted in chapter 2, paradigms get established when their putative opponents turn into proselytizers. In that sense, neoliberalism's true enablers were the center-left politicians who regarded it as not just inevitable but also desirable—as long as it was softened around the edges with social transfers to the poor and some half-hearted attempts at redistribution.

There were many reasons that the left got sidetracked into a narrative that alienated its working-class base. But one that stands out is the role played by the educated elite. As Thomas Piketty has shown, the left relied increasingly on voters with greater levels of education.[3] In effect, educated voters replaced the unionized manufacturing workers leftist parties had traditionally relied on but whose numbers were getting thin. This turned left-of-center parties into representatives of the "Brahmin left," to use Piketty's term, instead of workers. Important to this story is that the educated elite were also undergoing their own transition. They were moving away from a Keynesian, social democratic worldview to a more market-friendly, government-skeptic one. This transition was both led by and reflected in the economics profession's turn to market fundamentalism. Hence leftist parties became the chief torch bearers of a technocratic paradigm in love with markets and disdainful of collective action, mirroring the changes both in their class base and in the views of the educated elite.

The left is changing and in some ways is in a somewhat better position today. The Labour Party in Britain won in a landslide in July 2024, ending fourteen years of Conservative rule. The left-wing Popular Front coalition in France came first in the second round of the parliamentary elections that same week. President Biden took the US into uncharted territory with new industrial and green policies, though the strategy evidently did not deliver a payoff at the polls in November 2024. Clearly, the parties of the left have not yet overcome their identity crisis. And they have yet to discover a reliable route to electoral victory. How should they reposition themselves? Should they double down on redistribution, as the Popular Front in France has done? Should they uphold fiscal responsibility, as with

Britain's Labour Party? Should they embrace industrial policies à la Biden, and to what purpose? How should they handle issues such as immigration, the environment, or transgender rights on which the cultural elite hold very different views from the general public?

The American electorate's turn to the right can be interpreted in one of two ways. One possibility is that culture wars have become the dominant cleavage in US politics, and economic policies are slated to remain a sideshow. On a strict interpretation of this theory, the approach advocated in this book would have little political traction. It may bring economic benefits, but it will not necessarily win votes for its advocates and practitioners.

The other possibility is that the left has done too little so far to win the working class back. Biden-style industrial policies were an important start, but they focused too much on manufacturing and neglected productive upgrading in the service sectors that employ the vast majority of the electorate. We cannot return to a mythical past in which organized labor in manufacturing forms the backbone of the middle class. An effective strategy for rebuilding the middle class requires a more comprehensive and better-targeted approach that recognizes the new technological and competitive realities of the day, along the lines sketched in this book.

This argument does not require that we dismiss the political salience and significance of culture wars. But it cautions us that we should not treat cultural divides as primordial and unchangeable. Economic insecurity contributes to cultural polarization by deepening the division between the winners and losers from economic and social change. As the Yale political philosopher Jason Stanley puts it, "People who feel slighted (materially or socially) come to accept pathologies—racism, homophobia, misogyny, ethnic nationalism, and religious bigotry—which, under conditions of greater equality, they would reject."[4]

Moreover, the left's conventional welfare state remedies are no longer a good sell to voters with middle-class aspirations, especially those who do not come from traditional manufacturing backgrounds. One reason Democrats lost Hispanic voters to Trump in 2024 is that they were viewed as the party that distributes welfare benefits to those who do not work.[5] Many hard-working people, such as recent immigrants who have had to overcome significant obstacles, want the government to reward initiative rather than joblessness. Of course, leftist parties will always support those who are on the losing side of economic change. But they cannot afford to be defined exclusively by an agenda of welfare benefits and redistribution.

An agenda fit for purpose

If the progressive left is to revive, it will have to reconnect with working people and convince them it offers a credible path to middle-class prosperity. It must achieve these goals while providing concrete answers to the climate crisis and without blocking the paths of developing countries to poverty reduction.

Those are the challenges I have covered in these pages. While the book is not meant as a political tract, it does offer the basis for a new progressive economic policy. It calls for a recalibration of the mindset for progressives along several dimensions. In particular, it suggests the left must turn up the dial on good jobs (over redistribution), labor-absorbing services (over manufacturing), and productivity (over job quality mandates). The left must be an advocate for structural transformation, in the service of both good jobs and the green transition. It must not shy away from micro interventions in production, investment, and technology that serve this agenda and extend beyond broad, economy-wide regulations and macro policies. These interventions cannot be top down. They must entail iterative collaboration with firms, innovators, and other stakeholders that necessarily take an experimental form. This type of policy making is not a pipe dream, and I have given examples throughout the book. The ultimate goal of these interventions is to enhance productivity, especially of workers with lower education levels. The left must also reconcile with patriotism, distinguishing it from ethno-nationalism.

Let me take up each of these points briefly by way of recap.

I have said plenty in this book on the importance of good jobs. These are jobs that provide a ladder to the middle class. They are critical both to social cohesion and to democratic resilience. Social transfers and redistribution, even where they are feasible, are not an adequate substitute. People appreciate income, regardless of its source. But what gives meaning to their lives and provides dignity and social recognition is the contribution they make to society, in large part through their work. Transfers make people feel inadequate rather than valued. Nor do they repair the breakdown in social and community life that ensues when factories close or move elsewhere.

The philosopher Michael Sandel makes an important distinction between two conceptions of justice: distributive justice and contributive justice.[6] Distributive justice answers the question, Who should get what? Traditional welfare state arrangements are largely built on this conception. They aim to ensure everyone has adequate levels of income and equitable access to public services, including social insurance. Contributive justice, on the other hand, relates to the opportunities individuals have to contribute to the economic and social life of their communities. The ability to perform work that is respected and rewarded, because it deserves respect and reward, is an essential, if not *the* essential component of this. Contemporary liberals, notes Sandel, "have been offering working-class and middle-class voters a greater measure of distributive justice— fairer, fuller access to the fruits of economic growth. But what these voters want even more is a greater measure of contributive justice— an opportunity to win the social recognition and esteem that go with producing what others need and value."[7] Progressives would do well to update their conception of justice and pay more attention to the requirements of contributive justice.

Creating good jobs requires micro interventions that target structural change directly. Investing in education and health remains as important as ever, but it is not enough when the available technologies and production incentives create a chronic shortage of good-paying jobs for those with less than a university education. Similarly, macroeconomic management can ensure full employment, but it has at best an indirect effect on the composition of jobs that are created. Enhancing incentives for activities and technologies that raise demand for less educated workers is a necessary complement to these conventional strategies. The requisite policies have a flavor of successful industrial policies of the past, but they are specifically for good jobs (and do not focus on manufacturing).

The green transition similarly calls for a structural focus. Progressive economists have long hailed carbon pricing as the most essential tool in the fight against climate change. While the logic of the argument is impeccable, the real world has not proved very amenable. Instead, we have seen how industrial policies encouraging solar, wind, electric vehicles, and batteries have put us on the right track and substituted, in a second-best fashion, for a carbon tax. These green industrial policies are now also facilitating the phasing out of carbon, by broadening the political coalition in favor of the green transition. It is an important economic and political lesson: generating economic opportunities in well-identified sectors works and sells better than economy-wide policies with clear losers and uncertain winners.

Many of the new policies have taken the form of government subsidies. But successful programs of structural change go beyond subsidies and often are better conducted without relying on subsidies. Public-private collaboration, investment coordination, and provision of specific public inputs are often much more effective at achieving structural transformation than cash incentives. Evidence around the world suggests this requires a new type of policy making that is problem driven, experimental, and iterative, rather than top down and technocratic.

Such efforts do not have to start anew. They are not a radical departure from practices that already exist, albeit often under the radar screen and at small scale. In the US, they range from successful local development partnerships to ARPA-style agencies. In China and other successful nations of East Asia, they take the form of "embedded" industrial policies. Similar experiments, such as a public venture fund in Chile, a coordinated supply provision to street vendors in Colombia, and a collaboration with ride-share providers in Haryana state in India, abound in the rest of the world. These and the other examples we have seen in the book constitute proof of concept. The best counterargument to the claim "it cannot be done" is that it is already being done.

Experiments come with mistakes. One of the key challenges the left faces is to extricate industrial policy from the failures that have given it a negative reputation. Many believe that industrial policy can be successful only in authoritarian countries, such as China. We have seen plenty of examples that suggest otherwise. What matters is not individual failures but the results of the program as a whole. Governments cannot pick winners, but they can let losers go. The real risk lies elsewhere—in the possibility that the rediscovery of industrial policies will not be matched by an adequate recognition that the policies have to operate today in a very different economic context.

In particular, the left has yet to fully face up to the reality that manufacturing jobs are not coming back. Services are the main provider of employment, and they will remain so in the future. A good jobs strategy necessarily has to focus on services. None of the talk about reshoring, competitiveness, digitalization, and the green transition sounds realistic when it comes to jobs. Nor does protectionism against China. Approaches that focus on manufacturing will fail to have much political appeal when few workers are in manufacturing and even fewer have a realistic prospect of being employed there. The left can no longer win by targeting an auto or steel worker; its program must appeal to a care or retail worker.

Boosting both wages and jobs in labor-absorbing services requires higher productivity for workers in these sectors. Government or collective-bargaining-mandated improvements in working conditions can be detrimental to job creation in the absence of commensurate increases in labor productivity. We have seen examples in the book of how this trade-off can be avoided through organizational and technological innovations. When appropriately targeted, such innovations enable less educated workers to undertake a wider range of more sophisticated tasks, directly improving their productivity. Automation and other forms of labor-saving innovation are not the only possible model for the future. But the alternative path requires dedicated effort by governments to engage in the innovation process and incentivize labor-friendly technologies.

Since productivity is at the core of this agenda, it is crucial that the left not only makes peace with it but embraces it wholeheartedly.

The concept has been tainted because it is typically hijacked by conservatives and right-wing economists for their cause. It is associated with economic growth that benefits only those at the top and with trickle-down economics. But productivity is the foundation of prosperity, as much for those at the low and middle range of the income distribution as for those at the top. Without productivity gains that accrue directly to workers with less education and to regions that are left behind, it is impossible to achieve an inclusive society.

Developing countries have very different circumstances, but ultimately the strategy they need to follow is not that different. As we have seen, export-oriented industrialization has run out of steam. Poverty reduction and growth strategies based on services have become inevitable. This is a difficult lesson to embrace for progressive forces in the developing world, who remain enamored by manufacturing. But trying to replicate the East Asian growth model will produce disappointment on the economic front and leave most workers in precarious, unproductive, informal jobs. Increasing the productivity of jobs in services is essential for equity, economic growth, and ultimately social and political stability.

We must recognize that East Asian rates of growth will be virtually impossible to attain in the future. Services do not provide as powerful a growth escalator as manufacturing traditionally did. What should make the strategy appealing to progressives, however, is that, unlike the trickle-down approach, it reaches people in the lower-income rungs directly. Economic growth is achieved through the dissemination of productive opportunities throughout society, in advanced and developing economies alike. Indeed, the merging of social and economic agendas is a key advantage of the services imperative.

Another critical feature of the experimental approach I have sketched here is that it rejects ideological distinctions between markets and the state. Its pragmatism grounds it in existing practice, enlarged in scale and extended to other domains. It does not seek wholesale institutional transformation from the outset. It should allay voters' possible concerns about radicalism from the left. But it also opens up a path for possibly more comprehensive institutional reform over time. It allows progressives to maintain far-reaching ambitions of structural transformation even as they start from gradualist beginnings.[8]

Patriotism for progressives

In the introduction, I discussed some trade-offs that might arise as countries pursue their own agendas. When advanced countries try to shore up national security and their middle classes, they might undercut the economies of poor countries. When developing countries attempt to industrialize, they might raise carbon emissions and contribute to global warming. If major powers do not put aside their national interests and cooperate on a large number of fronts, the world economy as a whole might suffer.

But a closer look suggests that many of these trade-offs are less real than they appear. They are the product of outmoded conceptions of what is required to achieve national goals. Rebuilding the middle class in the advanced countries does not have adverse effects on developing countries if it focuses on where the jobs really are. Reducing poverty in poor nations does not have adverse effects on the climate if the most effective growth strategy is pursued. Even in climate, where the global governance argument is strongest, the greatest progress to date has come from localities, nations, and regions following their own parochial interests. The best gift that a nation can give to the rest of the world is to take care of its own economy, society, and environment. And the best kind of global governance is that which empowers individual nations to help themselves, subject to minimal and widely acceptable rules of the road.

That is also the sense in which patriotism is a progressive value. Patriotism does not preclude concern for broader global issues, such as the climate or poverty. Patriotism is to be distinguished from the right-wing conception of nationalism, which is exclusionary. The latter draws boundaries between "us" and "them" on the basis of ethnicity, religion, or national origin. It has a zero-sum understanding of the world: *we* are in a bad state because *they* are taking advantage of us. The ethno-nationalist remedy consists of punishing *them* so *we* can advance. Patriotism, on the other hand, privileges compatriots as cocitizens, without setting up false and misleading dichotomies that attach blame to outsiders. It focuses attention on problems that we can solve—our own.

A crucial difference between the right and the left is that the right thrives on deepening divisions in society, while the left (when successful) overcomes these cleavages through reforms that bridge them. Hence a paradox: Earlier waves of reforms from the left—Keynesianism, social democracy, the welfare state—both saved capitalism from itself and eventually rendered their specific remedies superfluous. We need a similar response today, fit for contemporary realities. Otherwise, the winners will remain the far-right populists who inevitably lead the world to deeper division and greater conflict.

ACKNOWLEDGMENTS

I am lucky to have been on the Harvard Kennedy School's faculty for the bulk of my professional career. HKS is an ideal place for scholarship in the service of the real world. I am deeply indebted to the students, scholars, and practitioners I have gotten to know there, and whose contributions over the years have been central to the development of my own ideas.

As usual, my wife, Pınar Doğan, was the first to read the manuscript. Her comments, encouragement, and support have been indispensable. My three children—Deniz, a budding ethicist and philosopher; Odile, a healer of trauma victims; and Delphine, a seeker of justice for refugees—have contributed through the pride, joy, and fulfillment they add to my life. My mother passed soon after the first draft was completed; she remains an inspiration, as in all my previous books.

Roberto Mangabeira Unger, with whom I have taught a course on the future of political economy for many years, has directly or indirectly inspired many of the ideas in this book. Jeff Frieden, Robert Lawrence, Chuck Sabel, Rob Stavins, Ernie Cortes, and two anonymous reviewers for Princeton University Press provided valuable feedback. Andrew Wylie and Jacki Ko deftly steered my original proposal into the right hands. Jessica De Simone provided expert editorial assistance. I am also grateful to the Hamilton Project at the Brookings Institution for the invitation to write a policy essay on industrial policy.

I am especially grateful to the Hewlett Foundation and its former director, Larry Kramer, who generously funded the Reimagining the Economy Program (RtE) at HKS. The RtE program has been my intellectual home for the last three years. Codirector Gordon Hanson's patient and systematic approach to evidence gathering and empirical analysis is a model of scholarship; he has been an ideal intellectual companion. Research fellow Rohan Sandhu's contributions, both in research and with administration, have been critical to the launch and flourishing of the program. Vidit Doshi and Huw Spencer have helped develop and extend my ideas to the British context. Natasha Khwaja, Samira Mathur, and Peter Reid have provided research assistance through the preparation of mini case studies on labor-absorbing services and green industrial policies. Bringing researchers, practitioners, and students together, the RtE program is deepening our understanding of the public-private initiatives that are discussed in this book and needed all over the world.

NOTES

Introduction: In Search of Democracy, Prosperity, Sustainability

1. Rawls himself did not advocate a global extension of his maximin principle on the grounds that redistributive justice applied only within prevailing political boundaries.

1: Overcoming the Triple Challenge

1. On the need to complement carbon pricing with subsidies for green technologies, see Daron Acemoglu, Philippe Aghion, Leonardo Bursztyn, and David Hemous, "The Environment and Directed Technical Change," *American Economic Review* 102, no. 1 (2012): 131–166.

2. On British Columbia's fuel tax, see Brian C. Murray and Nicholas Rivers, "British Columbia's Revenue-Neutral Carbon Tax: A Review of the Latest 'Grand Experiment' in Environmental Policy," *Energy Policy* 86 (November 2015): 674–683. On California's cap-and-trade program, see Christian Lessmann and Niklas Kramer, "The Effect of Cap-and-Trade on Sectoral Emissions: Evidence from California," *Energy Policy* 188 (2024), and Greenhous Gas Reduction Fund, "Annual Report to the Legislature on California Climate Investments Using Cap-and-Trade Auction Proceeds," April 2023, https://ww2.arb.ca.gov/sites/default/files/auction-proceeds/cci_annual_report_2023.pdf. Lessmann and Kramer estimate California's program has reduced emissions from the power sector by 48 percent but has not had much effect on emissions from the industrial sector.

3. The idea that the middle class is a driving force for democracy goes all the way back to Aristotle, who foresaw that it would be a counterforce against both anarchy and repression. As he wrote, "the middle class is least likely to shrink from rule, or to be over-ambitious for it . . ." (John Zumbrunnen, *ADEF 2017–2018*, p. 19, https://wisc.pb.unizin.org/adef20172018/chapter/2-2-aristotle-politics/.) On the relationship between polarization in incomes and values on the one hand and authoritarianism on the other, see Sharun Mukand and Dani Rodrik, "The Political Economy of Liberal Democracy," *Economic Journal* 130, no. 627 (April 2020). Eli G. Rau and Susan Stokes, "Income Inequality and the Erosion of Democracy in the Twenty-First Century," *Proceedings of the National Academy*

of Sciences 122, no. 1 (2025), https://doi.org/10.1073/pnas.2422543121, provide evidence that income inequality is a robust predictor of democratic erosion. Mordecai Kurz examines the tension between free market capitalism and democracy in *Private Power and Democracy's Decline* (Cambridge, MA: MIT Press, 2025).

4. In general, the higher the income inequality, the larger the gap between average income (or per capita income) and the median level of income (the income level at the fiftieth percentile).

5. Michael J. Sandel, *The Tyranny of Merit: Can We Find the Common Good?* (New York: Picador, 2021); Michele Lamont, *Seeing Others: How Recognition Works—and How It Can Heal a Divided World* (New York: Simon & Schuster, 2023).

6. The empirical literature is summarized and discussed in Dani Rodrik, "Why Does Globalization Fuel Populism? Economics, Culture, and the Rise of Right-Wing Populism," *Annual Review of Economics* 13 (2021): 133–170. The study on the 2016 US presidential election is David Autor, David Dorn, Gordon Hanson, and Kaveh Majlesi, "A Note on the Effect of Rising Trade Exposure on the 2016 Presidential Election," January 6, 2017, https://mpra.ub.uni-muenchen.de/112889/.

7. The productivity figures are calculated from data provided by Groningen Growth and Development Centre. See Klaas de Vries, Gaaitzen de Vries, and Marcel Timmer, "Patterns of Structural Change in Developing Countries," in *Routledge Handbook of Industry and Development,* ed. John Weiss and Michael Tribe (London: Routledge, 2015): 65–83. Employment numbers are from the St. Louis Fed (Federal Reserve Bank of St. Louis, "FRED Economic Data," https://fred .stlouisfed.org/).

8. These figures are from the St. Louis Fed ("FRED Economic Data," https:// fred.stlouisfed.org/).

9. German data are from the St. Louis Fed ("FRED Economic Data," https://fred .stlouisfed.org/). South Korean data are from de Vries et al., "Patterns of Structural Change in Developing Countries." Chinese data are from an unpublished source provided by the Development Research Centre of the State Council of China.

10. My Harvard colleague Robert Z. Lawrence makes this argument forcefully in *Behind the Curve: Can Manufacturing Still Provide Inclusive Growth?* (Washington, DC: Peterson Institute for International Economics, 2024).

11. The World Bank's poverty estimates are available at data.worldbank.org.

12. Halsey Rogers, Shwetlena Sabarwal, Chris McCahan, Jaime Saavedra, and Norbert Schady, "Learning Losses: What to Do about the Heavy Cost of COVID-19 on Children, Youth, and Future Productivity," World Bank, September 20, 2022, https://thedocs.worldbank.org/en/doc/e52f55322528903b27f1b7e61238e416 -0200022022/related/WBG-LearningLosses-flier-10-09-22-e-version.pdf.

13. "For the Poorest Countries, Climate Action Is Development in Action," World Bank, December 2, 2023, https://www.worldbank.org/en/news/feature /2023/12/02/for-the-poorest-countries-climate-action-is-development-in -action.

14. In 1990, 760 million people in China (65 percent of the population) lived in extreme poverty. By December 2020, this number had been brought to zero, according to the Chinese government. See Homi Kharas and Meagan Dooley,

"The Evolution of Global Poverty, 1990–2030," Brookings Global, Working Paper no. 166, February 2022, https://www.brookings.edu/wp-content/uploads/2022/02/Evolution-of-global-poverty.pdf.

15. In economists' jargon, modern, formal manufacturing exhibits unconditional convergence to the productivity frontier, which means that factories in poor countries tend to catch up with labor productivity levels in advanced countries even in the presence of disadvantageous circumstances, such as bad policies or geographical obstacles. See Dani Rodrik, "Unconditional Convergence in Manufacturing," *Quarterly Journal of Economics* 128, no. 1 (February 2013): 165–204.

16. I have presented the evidence on manufacturing's declining role in promoting economic growth in several research papers. See Dani Rodrik, "Premature Deindustrialization," *Journal of Economic Growth* 21, no. 1 (March 2016); Dani Rodrik, "Prospects for Global Economic Convergence under New Technologies," in David Autor et al., *An Inclusive Future? Technology, New Dynamics, and Policy Challenges* (Washington, DC: Brookings Institution, 2022); and Xinshen Diao, Mia Ellis, Margaret McMillan, and Dani Rodrik, "Africa's Manufacturing Puzzle: Evidence from Tanzanian and Ethiopian Firms," *World Bank Economic Review* 0 (2024): 1–33, https://doi.org/10.1093/wber/lhae029.

17. The classic reference, from which an extensive literature has developed, is R. G. Lipsey and Kelvin Lancaster, "The General Theory of Second Best," *Review of Economic Studies* 24, no. 1 (1956–1957): 11–32.

18. Franklin D. Roosevelt, "Franklin D. Roosevelt Speeches: Oglethorpe University Address," May 22, 1932, https://publicpolicy.pepperdine.edu/academics/research/faculty-research/new-deal/roosevelt-speeches/fr052232.htm.

19. John Maynard Keynes, "An Open Letter to President Roosevelt," 1933, https://la.utexas.edu/users/hcleaver/368/368KeynesOpenLetFDRtable.pdf. While Keynes approved of FDR's methods, he also expressed concern in the letter that FDR was not sufficiently prioritizing recovery efforts (to increase aggregate demand and purchasing power) over structural economic and social reforms.

20. Albert O. Hirschman, *The Strategy of Economic Development* (Boulder, CO: Westview Encore, 1988) (new edition with a new postscript by the author); Philipp H. Lepenies, "Possibilism: An Approach to Problem-Solving Derived from the Life and Work of Albert O. Hirschman," *Development and Change* 39 (2008): 437–459, https://doi.org/10.1111/j.1467-7660.2008.00487.x.

21. The "Washington Consensus" was a term coined by the late John Williamson to denote a common set of policies being put in practice by technocratic politicians in Latin America in the aftermath of the debt crisis of the early 1980s. See John Williamson, "What Washington Means by Policy Reform," in *Latin American Readjustment: How Much Has Happened*, ed. John Williamson (Washington, DC: Peterson Institute for International Economics, 1990): 7–40. As described originally by Williamson, this was a rather loose list of policies that was not highly prescriptive and did not go too far. For example, it called for only moderate trade liberalization and did not include capital account liberalization (which Williamson personally did not favor). Over time, to Williamson's dismay, the term became

associated with a much more detailed and ideological set of policy prescriptions promoting economic liberalization and hyperglobalization.

22. See Dani Rodrik and Charles F. Sabel, "Building a Good Jobs Economy," in *A Political Economy of Justice*, ed. Danielle Allen et al. (Chicago: University of Chicago Press, 2022): 61–95; and Charles F. Sabel and Jonathan Zeitlin, "Experimentalist Governance," in *The Oxford Handbook of Governance*, ed. David Levi-Faur (Oxford, UK: Oxford University Press, 2012): 169–183.

23. See the previous note and other writings of Charles Sabel, including Charles Sabel and David Victor, *Fixing the Climate: Strategies for an Uncertain World* (Princeton, NJ: Princeton University Press, 2022). My thinking on policy experimentation has also been greatly influenced by Roberto Mangabeira Unger, with whom I have long taught a course on the future of political economy. See Unger, *Democracy Realized: The Progressive Alternative* (London: Verso Books, 1999).

24. Thomas L. Friedman, "Has Our Luck Run Out?," *New York Times*, April 30, 2019, https://www.nytimes.com/2019/04/30/opinion/trump-climate-change .html; Erna Solberg and Hugh Evans, "Global Cooperation Is Our Only Hope to Recover from the COVID-19 Pandemic," *Time*, August 13, 2021, https://time .com/6090103/global-cooperation-covid-19/. At the time the piece was written, Solberg was the prime minister of Norway and Evans the CEO of Global Citizen.

25. I owe this formulation to Vivien A. Schmidt, who has described the EU as "policy *without* politics" and the national level as "politics *without* policy": Schmidt, *Democracy in Europe: The EU and National Polities* (Oxford, UK: Oxford University Press, 2006).

26. A July 2020 survey found 36 percent of Americans support leaving the WTO, while 28 percent oppose withdrawal. The rest are "indifferent" or "unsure": Anne Kim and Andrea Durkin, "Do Americans Want the US to Leave the WTO?," Hinrich Foundation, July 30, 2020, https://www.hinrichfoundation.com/research /tradevistas/wto/us-attitude-wto/.

27. Dani Rodrik, "What Do Trade Agreements Really Do?," *Journal of Economic Perspectives* 32, no. 2 (Spring 2018): 73–90.

28. Agreements under the WTO were of course shaped largely by rich-country interests. But the WTO's General Council and the dispute settlement process do not privilege them explicitly.

29. Jayati Ghosh, "For Global Tax Reform, the Devil Is in the Details," *Project Syndicate*, March 12, 2024, https://www.project-syndicate.org/commentary/un -subject-to-tax-rule-is-better-than-oecd-version-by-jayati-ghosh-2024-03.

30. For an elaboration on this argument, see Dani Rodrik, "Putting Global Governance in Its Place," *World Bank Research Observer* 35, no. 1 (February 2020): 1–18.

31. The problems with hyperglobalization are discussed in my book *The Globalization Paradox* (New York: W. W. Norton, 2011).

32. White House, "Remarks by National Security Advisor Jake Sullivan on Renewing American Economic Leadership at the Brookings Institution," April 27, 2023, https://www.whitehouse.gov/briefing-room/speeches-remarks/2023/04 /27/remarks-by-national-security-advisor-jake-sullivan-on-renewing-american -economic-leadership-at-the-brookings-institution/.

2: The Failures of Hyperglobalization

1. Tony Blair, "Tony Blair's Conference Speech 2005," *The Guardian*, September 27, 2005, https://www.theguardian.com/uk/2005/sep/27/labourconference.speeches.

2. William J. Clinton, "Remarks at Vietnam National University in Hanoi, Vietnam," November 17, 2000, https://www.presidency.ucsb.edu/documents/remarks-vietnam-national-university-hanoi-vietnam.

3. My translation from the original, quoted in Martin Marcussen, "Globalization: A Third Way Gospel That Travels World Wide," International Studies Association, March 2000, https://ciaotest.cc.columbia.edu/isa/mam01/.

4. Dani Rodrik, *The Globalization Paradox: Democracy and the Future of the World Economy* (New York: W. W. Norton, 2011).

5. Gary Gerstle, *The Rise and Fall of the Neoliberal Order: America and the World in the Free Market Era* (Oxford, UK: Oxford University Press, 2022).

6. There is some uncertainty about what Friedman said or meant by this, but it takes little away from the story. See "We Are All Keynesians Now," Wikipedia, September 6, 2023, https://en.wikipedia.org/wiki/We_are_all_Keynesians_now.

7. Search for "neoliberal" or "neoliberalism" in Google Scholar, and you will not encounter a single entry from a self-avowed neoliberal articulating and defending the concept. Instead, you will find one critical piece after another: "Neoliberalism: A Critical Reader," "The Terror of Neoliberalism," "Elite Transition: From Apartheid to Neoliberalism," "Profit over People: Neoliberalism and the Global Order."

8. Dani Rodrik, "Rescuing Economics from Neoliberalism," *Boston Review*, November 6, 2017, https://www.bostonreview.net/articles/dani-rodrik-rescuing-economics-neoliberalism/.

9. Letter from Keynes to Roy Harrod sent in July 1938; see Oleg Komlik, "What Is Economics? Read Keynes' Definition," Economic Sociology & Political Economy, April 3, 2018, https://economicsociology.org/2018/04/03/what-is-economics-read-keynes-definition/. On economics as a science of models, see Dani Rodrik, *Economics Rules: The Rights and Wrongs of the Dismal Science* (New York: W. W. Norton, 2015).

10. Carlos Diaz-Alejandro, "Trade Policies and Economic Development," in *International Trade and Finance: Frontiers for Research*, ed. P. B. Kenen (Cambridge, UK: Cambridge University Press, 1974): 93–150.

11. Under the Social Democratic Party, the Swedish government's share of ownership in the economy rose from 14 percent in 1950 to 44 percent in 1975. See Matt Bruenig, "The Dramatic Rise of Public Ownership in Midcentury Sweden," People's Policy Project, October 8, 2018, https://www.peoplespolicyproject.org/2018/10/08/the-dramatic-rise-of-public-ownership-in-midcentury-sweden/.

12. Silvia Nenci, "Tariff Liberalization and the Growth of World Trade: A Comparative Historical Analysis of the Multilateral Trading System," *World Economy*, February 2012, https://www.researchgate.net/publication/228122454_Tariff_Liberalization_and_the_Growth_of_World_Trade_A_Comparative_Historical_Analysis_of_the_Multilateral_Trading_System.

13. John G. Ruggie was the clearest exponent of this view. He used the concept of "embedded liberalism" to describe the postwar economic order as one where external liberalization was subject to the constraints of management of the domestic economy. See Ruggie, "International Regimes, Transactions, and Change: Embedded Liberalism in the Postwar Economic Order," *International Organization* 36, no. 2 (Spring 1982): 379–415.

14. Christine Lagarde, "Updating Bretton Woods," International Monetary Fund, *Finance & Development,* June 2019, https://www.imf.org/en/Publications/fandd/issues/2019/06/christine-lagarde-future-of-bretton-woods-straight.

15. International rules that reach behind national borders and have broad effects on domestic policies and institutions have a precedent, of course, in the gold standard. See Jamie Martin, *The Meddlers: Sovereignty, Empire, and the Birth of Global Economic Governance* (Cambridge, MA: Harvard University Press, 2022), on the establishment of arrangements during the interwar period under the economic and financial section of the League of Nations and the Bank for International Settlements that institutionalized those practices to resuscitate the pre–World War I international economic order.

16. A slew of academic papers in the early 1990s produced highly inflated estimates of the positive effects of trade integration on economic growth. For a review and critique of this literature, see Francisco Rodriguez and Dani Rodrik, "Trade Policy and Economic Growth: A Skeptic's Guide to the Cross-National Evidence," in *Macroeconomics Annual 2000*, ed. Ben Bernanke and Kenneth S. Rogoff (Cambridge, MA: MIT Press, 2001): 261–325.

17. In my book *The Globalization Paradox*, these tensions were captured in the form of a trilemma: it is impossible to have hyperglobalization, the nation-state, and mass politics all at once; we can have at most two out of the three. The gold standard regime combined advanced globalization with national sovereignty, but could not be sustained when leading nations became more democratic. The Bretton Woods system combined national sovereignty with democracy, explicitly giving up deep global integration. A third utopian possibility would be to combine hyperglobalization with democracy through some form of global federalism that transcends the nation-state.

18. Michael Clemens, Lant Pritchett, and Claudio E. Montenegro, "The Place Premium: Wage Differences for Identical Workers across the US Border," World Bank Policy Research, Working Paper no. 4671, July 2008, https://papers.ssrn.com/sol3/papers.cfm?abstract_id=1233047.

19. Dani Rodrik, "Feasible Globalizations," in *Globalization: What's New?*, ed. Michael A. Weinstein (New York: Columbia University Press, 2005): 196–213.

20. Rodrik, *Globalization Paradox.*

21. In the terminology of economics, economic development requires structural change, and the process of structural change is rife with market failures, such as coordination failures and learning externalities. See Dani Rodrik, *One Economics, Many Recipes: Globalization, Institutions, and Economic Growth* (Princeton, NJ: Princeton University Press, 2007).

22. On China's economic strategy and how it worked, see Dani Rodrik, "Growth Strategies," in *Handbook of Economic Growth*, ed. Philippe Aghion and Steven N. Durlauf, vol. 1A (Amsterdam: North-Holland, 2005): 967–1014; Yingyi Qian, *How Reform Worked in China: The Transition from Plan to Market* (Cambridge, MA: MIT Press, 2017); Yuen Yuen Ang, *How China Escaped the Poverty Trap* (Ithaca, NY: Cornell University Press, 2016); and Sebastian Heilmann, "Policy Experimentation in China's Economic Rise," *Studies in Comparative International Development* 43 (2008): 1–26.

23. An interesting question on which we can speculate is whether China's economic miracle would have happened if *other* countries were not pursuing hyperglobalist policies. It is true that Chinese exports likely would not have increased as rapidly if the US, Europe, and other major markets were not as open or responded, as during the 1970s and 1980s, with protective barriers to surges of imports. On the other hand, it is also the case that other notable export-oriented growth miracles of the postwar era—Japan, South Korea, Taiwan—all happened under the Bretton Woods regime when barriers to trade were quite a bit higher.

24. Xinshen Diao, Margaret McMillan, and Dani Rodrik, "The Recent Growth Boom in Developing Economies: A Structural-Change Perspective," in *The Palgrave Handbook of Development Economics: Critical Reflections on Globalization and Development*, ed. Machiko Nissanke and José Antonio Ocampo (Cham, Switzerland: Palgrave Macmillan, 2019): 281–334. For a perspective that links developing economies' growth to hyperglobalization, see Dev Patel, Justin Sandefur, and Arvind Subramanian, "A Requiem for Hyperglobalization: Why the World Will Miss History's Greatest Economic Miracle," *Foreign Affairs*, June 12, 2024, https://www.foreignaffairs.com/china/requiem-hyperglobalization.

25. Shannon K. O'Neil, "Lopez Obrador Can Save Mexico by Embracing Globalization," Council on Foreign Relations, May 29, 2020, https://www.cfr.org/blog/lopez-obrador-can-save-mexico-embracing-globalization.

26. Between 1960 and 1980, per capita GDP in Mexico grew at an annual rate of 3.4 percent. Between 1990 and 2010, average growth was less than 1 percent. For a discussion of Mexico's productivity problem, see Santiago Levy Algazi, *Under-Rewarded Efforts: The Elusive Quest for Prosperity in Mexico* (Washington, DC: Inter-American Development Bank, 2018), https://flagships.iadb.org/en/Under-Rewarded-Efforts.

27. Eduardo Bolio, Jaana Remes, Tomás Lajous, James Manyika, Eugenia Ramirez, and Morten Rossé, "A Tale of Two Mexicos: Growth and Prosperity in a Two-Speed Economy," McKinsey Global Institute, March 1, 2014, https://www.mckinsey.com/featured-insights/americas/a-tale-of-two-mexicos.

28. O'Neil, "Lopez Obrador Can Save Mexico."

29. For a summary and discussion of the literature on the distributional consequences of trade, see Dani Rodrik, "A Primer on Trade and Inequality," *Oxford Open Economics*, supplement for *IFS Deaton Review: Inequalities in the Twenty-First Century* (2023), https://drodrik.scholars.harvard.edu/publications/primer-trade-and-inequality.

30. Dani Rodrik, "The Rush to Free Trade in the Developing World: Why So Late? Why Now? Will It Last?," in *Voting for Reform: Democracy, Political Liberalization, and Economic Adjustment*, ed. Stephan Haggard and Steven B. Webb (New York: Oxford University Press, 1994): 61–88.

31. On the costs of redistribution to compensate trade's losers, see Pol Antràs, Alonso de Gortari, and Oleg Itskhoki, "Globalization, Inequality and Welfare," *Journal of International Economics* 108 (2017): 387–412.

32. Mark Muro and Joseph Parilla, "Maladjusted: It's Time to Reimagine Economic 'Adjustment' Programs," Brookings, January 10, 2017, https://www.brookings.edu/articles/maladjusted-its-time-to-reimagine-economic-adjustment-programs/. On the politics of compensation, see Jeffry Frieden, "A Place for Politics," International Monetary Fund, *Finance & Development*, March 2024, https://www.imf.org/en/Publications/fandd/issues/2024/03/A-Place-for-Politics-Jeffry-Frieden.

33. See the studies discussed in David Dorn and Peter Levell, "Trade and Inequality in Europe and the US," *IFS Deaton Review of Inequalities* (2021), https://ifs.org.uk/inequality/wp-content/uploads/2021/11/IFS-Deaton-Review-Trade-and-inequality-in-Europe-and-the-US.pdf. The two studies mentioned in this paragraph are Shushanik Hakobyan and John McLaren, "Looking for Local Labor Market Effects of NAFTA," *Review of Economics and Statistics* 98, no. 4 (2016): 728–741; and David H. Autor, David Dorn, and Gordon H. Hanson, "The China Syndrome: Local Labor Market Effects of Import Competition in the United States," *American Economic Review* 103, no. 6 (2013): 2121–2168.

34. Nicolai Suppa, "Unemployment and Subjective Well-Being," Global Labor Organization (GLO), Discussion Paper no. 760 (January 2021), https://www.econstor.eu/bitstream/10419/228706/1/GLO-DP-0760.pdf.

35. William Julius Wilson, *When Work Disappears: The World of the New Urban Poor* (New York: Alfred A. Knopf, 1996). More recently, the economists Anne Case and Angus Deaton have documented the rise in "deaths of despair" among less educated American men: Case and Deaton, *Deaths of Despair and the Future of Capitalism* (Princeton, NJ: Princeton University Press, 2020).

36. Dani Rodrik, "Why Does Globalization Fuel Populism? Economics, Culture, and the Rise of Right-Wing Populism," *Annual Review of Economics* 13 (2021): 133–170.

37. "The Long Trend of Falling Corporate Taxes Is Being Reversed," *The Economist,* January 10, 2022, https://www.economist.com/special-report/2022/01/10/the-long-trend-of-falling-corporate-taxes-is-being-reversed.

38. Cited in Marcussen, "Globalization: A Third Way Gospel That Travels World Wide."

39. William J. Clinton, "Full Text of Clinton's Speech on China Trade Bill," *New York Times,* March 9, 2000, https://archive.nytimes.com/www.nytimes.com/library/world/asia/030900clinton-china-text.html. Clinton continued: "The more China liberalizes its economy, the more fully it will liberate the potential of its people—their initiative, their imagination, their remarkable spirit of enterprise. And when individuals have the power, not just to dream but to realize their dreams,

they will demand a greater say. . . . When China joins the WTO . . . it will have fewer instruments, therefore, with which to control people's lives. . . . So if you believe in a future of greater openness and freedom for the people of China, you ought to be for this agreement."

40. Henry S. Rowen, "The Short March: China's Road to Democracy," *National Interest*, September 1, 1996, https://nationalinterest.org/article/the-short-march -chinas-road-to-democracy-416.

41. As Aaron L. Friedberg notes, "At the end of the Cold War, the United States and its allies decided to waive what had become, in effect, a requirement for full membership in the Western system in order to incorporate both Russia and China as fully as possible within it, despite the fact that neither had yet made a successful transition to liberal democracy. The assumption was that integration would speed that transition": Friedberg, "China's Understanding of Global Order Shouldn't Be Ours," *Foreign Policy*, January 24, 2018, https://foreignpolicy.com/2018/01/24 /niall-ferguson-isnt-a-contrarian-hes-a-china-apologist/.

42. "Henry Kissinger at 99: How to Avoid Another World War—interview by Niall Ferguson," *Sunday Times Magazine*, February 20, 2023.

43. John J. Mearsheimer, *The Great Delusion: Liberal Dreams and International Realities,* Henry L. Stimson Lecture Series (New Haven, CT: Yale University Press, 2018).

44. The concept of weaponized interdependence is due to Henry Farrell and Abraham L. Newman, "Weaponized Interdependence: How Global Economic Networks Shape State Coercion," *International Security* 44, no. 1 (Summer 2019): 42–79.

3: Making the Green Transition Happen

1. Friederike E. L. Otto et al., "Climate Change Increased Extreme Monsoon Rainfall, Flooding Highly Vulnerable Communities in Pakistan," *Environmental Research: Climate 2*, no. 2 (March 2023), https://doi.org/10.1088/2752-5295 /acbfd5; Max Bearak, Raymond Zhong, and Ihsanullah Tipu Mehsud, "Deadly Floods Devastate an Already Fragile Pakistan," *New York Times*, August 29, 2022, https://www.nytimes.com/2022/08/29/climate/pakistan-floods-monsoon.html.

2. See "Mapped: How Climate Change Affects Extreme Weather around the World," Carbon Brief, August 4, 2022, https://www.carbonbrief.org/mapped-how -climate-change-affects-extreme-weather-around-the-world/.

3. "Ethiopia Drought, 2015—a Livelihood Crisis," World Weather Attribution, July 24, 2015, https://www.worldweatherattribution.org/ethiopia-drought-2015/.

4. Linnia R. Hawkins, John T. Abatzoglou, Sihan Li, and David E. Rupp, "Anthropogenic Influence on Recent Severe Autumn Fire Weather in the West Coast of the United States," *Geophysical Research Letters* 49, no. 4 (February 2022), https://doi.org/10.1029/2021GL095496.

5. Sihan Li, Friederike E. L. Otto, "The Role of Human-Induced Climate Change in Heavy Rainfall Events Such as the One Associated with Typhoon Hagibis," *Climatic Change* 172, no. 7 (2022), https://doi.org/10.1007/s10584-022-03344-9.

6. "Extreme Sahel Heatwave That Hit Highly Vulnerable Population at the End of Ramadan Would Not Have Occurred without Climate Change," World Weather Attribution, April 18, 2024, https://www.worldweatherattribution.org/extreme -sahel-heatwave-that-hit-highly-vulnerable-population-at-the-end-of-ramadan -would-not-have-occurred-without-climate-change/.

7. "Summary for Policymakers," in *Climate Change 2023 Synthesis Report: The Sixth Assessment Report of the Intergovernmental Panel on Climate Change*, ed. IPCC Core Writing Team, Hoesung Lee, and Jose Romero (Geneva, Switzerland: IPCC, 2023): 1–34, https://doi.org/10.59327/IPCC/AR6-9789291691647.001.

8. D. Tirpak and P. Vellinga, "Emissions Scenarios," in *Climate Change: The IPCC Response Strategies* (Washington, DC: Island Press, 1990): 9–42, https://www .ipcc.ch/site/assets/uploads/2018/03/ipcc_far_wg_III_chapter_02.pdf. Also see IPCC Working Group I, "Policymakers Summary," in *Climate Change: The IPCC 1990 and 1992 Assessments* (Geneva, Switzerland: IPCC, 1999): 63–85, https:// www.ipcc.ch/site/assets/uploads/2018/03/ipcc_far_wg_I_spm.pdf.

9. Kingsmill Bond et al., "X-Change: Electricity—on Track for Net Zero," Bezos Earth Fund, July 2023, https://rmi.org/wp-content/uploads/dlm_uploads/2023 /07/rmi_x_change_electricity_2023.pdf.

10. Alison F. Takemura, "Chart: Renewables Are on Track to Keep Getting Cheaper and Cheaper," Canary Media, September 1, 2023, https://www .canarymedia.com/articles/clean-energy/charts-renewables-are-on-track-to -keep-getting-cheaper-and-cheaper; International Energy Agency, *World Economic Outlook 2023*, October 2023, https://www.iea.org/reports/world-energy -outlook-2023.

11. Ivy Tyn, "Infographic: China's Solar Capacity Growth in 2023 Sets New Record," S&P Global, February 8, 2024, https://www.spglobal.com /commodityinsights/en/market-insights/latest-news/energy-transition/020824 -infographic-china-solar-capacity-coal-electricity-renewable-energy-hydro-wind.

12. Asker Voldsgaard and Mogens Rüdiger, "Innovative Enterprise, Industrial Ecosystems, and Sustainable Transition: The Case of Transforming DONG Energy to Ørsted," in *Handbook of Climate Change Mitigation and Adaptation* (Cham, Switzerland: Springer, 2022): 3633–3684, https://doi.org/10.1007/978-3-030-72579 -2_160; "Ørsted's Renewable-Energy Transformation," McKinsey Sustainability, July 10, 2020, https://www.mckinsey.com/capabilities/sustainability/our-insights /orsteds-renewable-energy-transformation. On government subsidies, see "Feed-In Premium Tariffs for Renewable Power (Promotion of Renewable Energy Act)," IEA 50, September 9, 2013, https://www.iea.org/policies/4888-feed-in-premium -tariffs-for-renewable-power-promotion-of-renewable-energy-act.

13. "CAT Net Zero Target Evaluations," Climate Action Tracker, December 14, 2023, https://climateactiontracker.org/global/cat-net-zero-target-evaluations/.

14. Arik Levinson, Karl Dunkle Werner, Matthew Ashenfarb, and Annelise Britten, "The Inflation Reduction Act's Benefits and Costs," US Department of the Treasury, March 1, 2024, https://home.treasury.gov/news/featured-stories /the-inflation-reduction-acts-benefits-and-costs; John Bistline, Neil Mehrotra, and Catherine Wolfram, "Economic Implications of the Climate Provisions of

the Inflation Reduction Act," Brookings Institution, March 30–31, 2023. Bistline et al. estimate that the tax credit provisions of the IRA pass a social cost-benefit test handily, based on a carbon price of around $200.

15. Elizabeth Thurbon, Sung-Young Kim, Hao Tan, and John A. Mathews, *Developmental Environmentalism: State Ambition and Creative Destruction in East Asia's Green Energy Transition* (Oxford, UK: Oxford University Press, 2023): 106.

16. Thurbon et al., *Developmental Environmentalism*, 106–134; Keith Bradsher and Joy Dong, "What China's E.V. City Says about the State of the Economy," *New York Times*, January 29, 2024, https://www.nytimes.com/2024/01/27/business /china-hefei-ev-city-economy.html. On the explosion of public venture capital in China in general, see Jinlin Li, "Government as an Equity Investor: Evidence from Chinese Government Venture Capital through Cycles," March 2022, http://dx.doi .org/10.2139/ssrn.4221937. Li shows that public VC is countercyclical, as in the case of Nio-Hefei, with governments playing a more active role during market downturns.

17. This vignette brings to mind Tesla's experience with the US federal government. The company collapsed during the Great Recession of 2008–2009 and was revived only through a $465 million loan from the Department of Energy: "TESLA," US Department of Energy, Loan Programs Office, https://www.energy .gov/lpo/tesla. The US government would have been well advised to take an ownership share at the time!

18. Paolo Gerbaudo, "The Electric Vehicle Developmental State: BYD Exemplifies Transformations in Chinese Industrial Policy," *Phenomenal World*, April 11, 2024, https://www.phenomenalworld.org/analysis/byd/.

19. Thurbon et al., *Developmental Environmentalism*.

20. According to one study, industrial subsidies in China amount to 1.73 percent of GDP, three to four times the level in the US or leading European nations. Direct subsidies to BYD amounted to more than 3 percent of the company's revenues: Frank Bickenbach, Dirk Dohse, Rolf J. Langhammer, and Wan-Hsin Liu, "Foul Play? On the Scale and Scope of Industrial Subsidies in China," Kiel Policy Brief 173, April 2024, https://www.ifw-kiel.de/publications/foul-play-on-the-scale-and -scope-of-industrial-subsidies-in-china-32738/.

21. For example, under the Golden Sun program initiated in 2009, solar installations were reimbursed for 50–70 percent of their investment costs. When this scheme produced delays and cost overruns, the government shifted to a generation-based subsidy: Xue Gao and Jiaha Yuan, "Policymaking Challenges in Complex Systems: The Political and Socio-Technical Dynamics of Solar Photovoltaic Technology Development in China," *Energy Research & Social Science* 64 (June 2020), https://www.sciencedirect.com/science/article/pii/S2214629620300037.

22. Ignacio Mauleón, "Photovoltaic Learning Rate Estimation: Issues and Implications," *Renewable and Sustainable Energy Reviews* 65 (2016): 507–524, https://doi.org/10.1016/j.rser.2016.06.070. For a detailed empirical analysis of municipal subsidies for solar in China and their effects on capacity and productivity, see Ignacio Banares-Sanchez et al., "Chinese Innovation, Green Industrial Policy and the Rise of Solar Energy," March 18, 2024, https://economics

.unibocconi.eu/sites/default/files/files/media/attachments/ray_of_hope__
_paper%288%2920240412112838.pdf.

23. Gao and Yuan, "Policymaking Challenges in Complex Systems."

24. Thurbon et al., *Developmental Environmentalism*, 133.

25. Hongyang Cui and Hui He, "Liuzhou: A New Model for the Transition to Electric Vehicles?," International Council on Clean Transportation, December 18, 2019, https://theicct.org/liuzhou-a-new-model-for-the-transition-to-electric-vehicles/. Cited in Thurbon et al., *Developmental Environmentalism*, 198.

26. For a comparative analysis of successes and failures in shipbuilding, semiconductors, and EVs, see Lee Branstetter and Guangwei Li, "The Challenges of Chinese Industrial Policy," *Entrepreneurship and Innovation Policy and the Economy* 3, no. 1 (2024): 77–113, https://www.journals.uchicago.edu/doi/10.1086/727768.

27. Li, "Government as an Equity Investor."

28. Joseph Webster, "China's Wind Industrial Policy 'Succeeded'—but at What Cost?," Atlantic Council, EnergySource, May 1, 2023, https://www.atlanticcouncil.org/blogs/energysource/chinas-wind-industrial-policy-succeeded-but-at-what-cost/.

29. "US Won't Allow Chinese Imports to Kill New Industries: Yellen," *Asia Financial*, April 8, 2024, https://www.asiafinancial.com/us-wont-allow-chinese-imports-to-kill-new-industries-yellen.

30. The Biden administration began with a social cost of carbon estimate of $51 per ton, but the Environmental Protection Agency proposed in 2022 to raise it to $190: EPA, "EPA External Review Draft of Report on the Social Cost of Greenhouse Gases: Estimates Incorporating Recent Scientific Advances," US Environmental Protection Agency, 2022.

31. The two policies are identical when there is no uncertainty. When there exists uncertainty about demand or supply elasticities, the cap-and-trade system might be preferable to the carbon tax when the cost of missing emission targets is weighted more heavily than the unanticipated costs imposed on producers and consumers. The classic paper on this is Martin L. Weitzman, "Prices vs. Quantities," *Review of Economic Studies* 41, no. 4 (October 1974): 477–491. For a broad comparison of the theoretical and practical differences of the two approaches, see Robert N. Stavins, "The Relative Merits of Carbon Pricing Instruments: Taxes versus Trading," *Review of Environmental Economics and Policy* 16, no. 1 (2022): 62–82, https://doi.org/10.1086/717773.

32. On the need to complement carbon pricing with innovation subsidies, see Daron Acemoglu et al., "The Environment and Directed Technical Change," *American Economic Review* 102, no. 1 (February 2012): 131–166. On spillovers in solar panels, see Todd D. Gerarden, "Demanding Innovation: The Impact of Consumer Subsidies on Solar Panel Production Costs," *Management Science* 69, no. 12 (2023): 7799–7820, https://doi.org/10.1287/mnsc.2022.4662.

33. Pierre Friedlingstein et al., "Global Carbon Budget 2023," *Earth System Science Data* 15, no. 12 (2023): 5301–5369, https://doi.org/10.5194/essd-15-5301-2023.

34. Esther Duflo has argued that the North owes poor nations a "moral debt" of $500 billion a year, due to the increase in mortality that Northern emissions

generate: Simon Mundy, "Esther Duflo: Rich World Owes $500bn in 'Moral Debt' to Poor Countries," *Financial Times,* April 22, 2024, https://www.ft.com/content /2fa5787c-7139-405d-aecc-b07a493cb304. This figure does not take into account, however, historical emissions, where the North played an even bigger role.

35. Vera Songwe, Nicholas Stern, and Amar Bhattacharya, "Finance for Climate Action: Scaling Up Investment for Climate and Development," November 2022, https://www.lse.ac.uk/granthaminstitute/wp-content/uploads/2022/11/IHLEG -Finance-for-Climate-Action-1.pdf.

36. World Bank, "State and Trends of Carbon Pricing 2023," World Bank, https://openknowledge.worldbank.org/handle/10986/39796. The European Union's emissions trading system (ETS) stands out as the most significant, where carbon prices have fluctuated between $60 and $100 per ton in recent years. Prices in China, New Zealand, California, and Quebec ETS regimes are much lower.

37. The World Bank uses as the requisite carbon price $61 per ton or higher. Recall that the EPA's recommendation is a carbon price of $190.

38. "CAT Net Zero Target Evaluations," Climate Action Tracker, December 14, 2023, https://climateactiontracker.org/global/cat-net-zero-target-evaluations/.

39. Alexander F. Gazmararian and Dustin Tingley, *Uncertain Futures: The Politics of Climate Change* (Cambridge, UK: Cambridge University Press, 2023): 1; Dionne Searcey, "Wyoming Coal Country Pivots, Reluctantly, to Wind Farms," *New York Times*, March 3, 2021, https://www.nytimes.com/2021/03/03/climate /wyoming-coal-country-wind-farm.html; Jason Plautz, "How Wyoming's Carbon County Came to Embrace Renewable Energy," *Energy Wire*, July 19, 2023, https:// www.eenews.net/articles/how-wyomings-carbon-county-came-to-embrace -renewable-energy/.

40. Gazmararian and Tingley, *Uncertain Futures.* The authors find that nearly 70 percent of local officials in fossil fuel communities in the US believe a government commitment to invest in their communities is unreliable.

41. Chris Martinez et al., "These Fossil Fuel Industry Tactics Are Fueling Democratic Backsliding," Center for American Progress, December 5, 2023, https:// www.americanprogress.org/article/these-fossil-fuel-industry-tactics-are-fueling -democratic-backsliding/.

42. Victoria Bassetti and Kelsey Landau, "Seizing Opportunities for Fuel Subsidy Reform," Brookings, February 25, 2021, https://www.brookings.edu/articles /seizing-opportunities-for-fuel-subsidy-reform/.

43. "Tracking the Impact of Fossil-Fuel Subsidies," International Energy Agency, https://www.iea.org/topics/energy-subsidies.

44. Gazmararian and Tingley, *Uncertain Futures*, 4; Jonas Meckling, "Making Industrial Policy Work for Decarbonization," *Global Environmental Politics* 21, no. 4 (2021): 134–147; Réka Juhász and Nathan J. Lane, "The Political Economy of Industrial Policy," NBER, Working Paper no. 32507, May 2024.

45. Walter Frick, "Biden's Second-Best Economic Agenda," *ProMarket*, March 28, 2023, https://www.promarket.org/2023/03/28/bidens-second-best -economic-agenda/.

46. Gazmararian and Tingley, *Uncertain Futures.*

47. Robinson Meyer, "Biden's Long Game on Climate," HeatMap, May 24, 2024, https://heatmap.news/politics/biden-climate-policy#.

48. "Industry Profile: Oil & Gas," OpenSecrets, https://www.opensecrets.org/federal-lobbying/industries/summary?id=e01&cycle=2022; "Industry Profile: Renewable Energy," OpenSecrets, https://www.opensecrets.org/federal-lobbying/industries/summary?id=E12.

49. John Burn-Murdoch, "How Red Texas Became a Model for Green Energy," *Financial Times*, May 24, 2024, https://www.ft.com/content/ef2f6f8e-60df-4ccd-8c4f-ef5cd0eb3176.

50. "Red States Are Big Winners of Biden's Landmark Laws," CNN, February 14, 2024, https://www.cnn.com/2024/02/14/business/manufacturing-jobs-biden/index.html.

51. Dan Lashof, Lori Bird, and Jennifer Rennicks, "4 Things to Know about US EPA's New Power Plant Rules," World Resources Institute, May 3, 2024, https://www.wri.org/insights/epa-power-plant-rules-explained; Lisa Friedman and Coral Davenport, "E.P.A. Severely Limits Pollution from Coal-Burning Power Plants," *New York Times*, April 25, 2024, https://www.nytimes.com/2024/04/25/climate/biden-power-plants-pollution.html.

52. Thurbon et al., *Developmental Environmentalism*, 48.

53. "China National ETS," International Carbon Action Partnership, 2022, https://icapcarbonaction.com/system/files/ets_pdfs/icap-etsmap-factsheet-55.pdf.

54. Centre for Research on Energy and Clean Air [@CREAClean Air], tweet on July 18, 2024.

55. Tom Delreux and Frauke Ohler, "Climate Policy in European Union Politics," *Oxford Research Encyclopedia of Politics*, March 26, 2019, http://dx.doi.org/10.1093/acrefore/9780190228637.013.1097.

56. In 1993, 73 percent of Germans surveyed thought global warming was a "very serious" problem, versus 47 percent of Americans: Steven R. Brechin, "Comparative Public Opinion and Knowledge on Global Climatic Change and the Kyoto Protocol: The US versus the World?," *International Journal of Sociology and Social Policy* 23, no. 10 (2003): 106–134.

57. European Commission, "Citizen Support for Climate Action," 2023, https://climate.ec.europa.eu/citizens/citizen-support-climate-action_en.

58. Jon Birger Skjærseth and Jørgen Wettestad, "Making the EU Emissions Trading System: The European Commission as an Entrepreneurial Epistemic Leader," *Global Environmental Change* 20, no. 2 (2010): 314–321, https://www.fni.no/getfile.php/131538-1467555911/Filer/Publikasjoner/JBS-JW-GEC-2010-2.pdf.

59. Skjærseth and Wettestad, "Making the EU Emissions Trading System."

60. Skjærseth and Wettestad.

61. None of this is to suggest that climate denialism has been overcome. But the recent political backlash against proclimate policies is at least partly a response to their increased adoption: Edoardo Campanella and Robert Z. Lawrence, "The Populist Revolt against Climate Policy," *Foreign Affairs,* July 25, 2024, https://www.foreignaffairs.com/united-states/populist-revolt-against-climate-policy.

62. Joseph E. Aldy, "How Big Is the 'Biggest Climate Spending Bill Ever'? Key Factors Influencing the Inflation Reduction Act's Clean Energy Impacts," Harvard Kennedy School, Faculty Working Paper no. RWP24-007, November 2024.

63. Joseph R. Biden Jr., "Remarks by President Biden on the Anniversary of the Inflation Reduction Act," White House, August 16, 2023, https://www.whitehouse.gov/briefing-room/speeches-remarks/2023/08/16/remarks-by-president-biden-on-the-anniversary-of-the-inflation-reduction-act/.

64. Jonathan Packroff, "Battery Production: Germany First EU Country to Match US Subsidies," *Euractiv*, January 8, 2024, https://www.euractiv.com/section/economy-jobs/news/battery-production-germany-first-eu-country-to-match-us-subsidies/.

65. It is worth adding that in response to CBAM several non-EU countries with significant exports to the EU are developing their own carbon pricing schemes to escape the tariffs.

66. Songwe et al., "Finance for Climate Action."

67. Benjamin H. Bradlow and Alexandros Kentikelenis, "Globalizing Green Industrial Policy through Technology Transfers," *Nature Sustainability* 7 (April 2024): 685–687, https://doi.org/10.1038/s41893-024-01336-4.

68. Annika Seiler, Hannah Brown, and Samuel Matthews, "Just Energy Transition Partnerships: Early Successes and Challenges in Indonesia and South Africa," Center for Global Development, July 25, 2023, https://www.cgdev.org/publication/just-energy-transition-partnerships-early-successes-and-challenges-indonesia-and-south.

69. Sean Sweeney, "The Fad Is Dead: Why 'Just Energy Transition Partnerships' Are Failing," *New Labor Forum* 33, no. 2 (Spring 2024), https://newlaborforum.cuny.edu/2024/04/16/the-fad-is-dead-why-just-energy-transition-partnerships-are-failing/.

70. Reza Baqr, Ishac Diwan, and Dani Rodrik, "A Framework to Evaluate Economic Adjustment-cum-Debt Restructuring Packages," Harvard Kennedy School, January 2023, https://drodrik.scholars.harvard.edu/publications/framework-evaluate-economic-adjustment-cum-debt-restructuring-packages.

71. Lili Bermel et al., "U.S. Leadership in Scaling Capital for Multilateral Clean Energy Finance," Research Commentary Series, CEEPR, MIT, June 2024, https://ceepr.mit.edu/wp-content/uploads/2024/06/MIT-CEEPR-RC-2024-04.pdf.

72. Larry Elliott, "IMF Should Give Poor Countries $300bn a Year to Fight Climate Crisis, Says Joseph Stiglitz," *The Guardian,* October 13, 2023, https://www.theguardian.com/environment/2023/oct/13/poorest-countries-should-get-300bn-a-year-to-fight-climate-crisis-says-joseph-stiglitz; Task Force on Climate, Development and the IMF, "Re-channeling Special Drawing Rights for a Climate Resilient and Just Transition: Prospects for a Resilience and Sustainability Trust," October 2021, https://www.bu.edu/gdp/files/2021/10/TF_Policy-Brief_FIN.pdf.

73. Maurice Obstfeld and Edwin M. Truman, "The IMF's Special Drawing Rights Alone Are No Silver Bullet for Needed Climate Finance," Peterson Institute for International Economics, November 20, 2023, https://www.piie.com/blogs

/realtime-economics/imfs-special-drawing-rights-alone-are-no-silver-bullet-needed-climate.

74. Joe Lo, "Global Billionaires Tax to Fight Climate Change, Hunger Rises Up Political Agenda," *Climate Home News*, April 19, 2024, https://www.climatechangenews.com/2024/04/19/global-billionaires-tax-to-fight-climate-change-and-hunger-rises-up-political-agenda/; Emmanuel Saez and Gabriel Zucman, "A Wealth Tax on Corporations' Stock," *Economic Policy* (April 2022): 213–228, https://gabriel-zucman.eu/files/SaezZucman2022EP.pdf.

75. Bradlow and Kentikelenis, "Globalizing Green Industrial Policy."

76. Martin Guzman and Joseph E. Stiglitz, "Post-Neoliberal Globalization: International Trade Rules for Global Prosperity," *Oxford Review of Economic Policy* 40, no. 2 (Summer 2024): 282–306, https://doi.org/10.1093/oxrep/grae022.

77. Guzman and Stiglitz, "Post-Neoliberal Globalization."

78. Amar Bhattacharya, Homi Kharas, and John W. McArthur, "Developing Countries Are Key to Climate Action," Brookings, March 3, 2023, https://www.brookings.edu/articles/developing-countries-are-key-to-climate-action/; Hannah Ritchie, "Global Inequalities in CO_2 Emissions," Our World in Data, August 31, 2023, https://ourworldindata.org/inequality-co2.

79. Bradlow and Kentikelenis, "Globalizing Green Industrial Policy."

80. See, for example, Hannah Ritchie, *Not the End of the World: How We Can Be the First Generation to Build a Sustainable Planet* (London: Chatto and Windus, 2024), https://www.nottheendoftheworld.co.uk/.

4: Building a Good Jobs Economy

1. The first of these interviews is taken from Don Gonyea, "Stuck between Clinton and Trump: Rust Belt Union Voters Face a Tough Choice," National Public Radio, June 2, 2016, https://www.npr.org/2016/06/09/481351312/union-voters-in-ohio-not-satisfied-with-the-choice-of-clinton-or-trump. The second and third are from Elizabeth Dias, Haley Sweetland Edwards, and Karl Vick, "Voices from Democratic Counties Where Trump Won Big," *Time*, no date given, https://time.com/voices-from-democratic-counties-where-trump-won-big/.

2. For a discussion of this research, see Dani Rodrik, "Why Does Globalization Fuel Populism? Economics, Culture, and the Rise of Right-Wing Populism," *Annual Review of Economics* 13 (2021): 133–170.

3. The researcher is Lainey Newman. See Newman and Theda Skocpol, *Rust Belt Union Blues: Why Working-Class Voters Are Turning Away from the Democratic Party* (New York: Columbia University Press, 2023), 19.

4. Ana Faguy, "Six Trump Voters on Why He Won Their Support in 2024," BBC News, November 6, 2024, https://www.bbc.com/news/articles/cwyg5jdgzylo.

5. Steven Levitsky and Daniel Ziblatt, *How Democracies Die* (New York: Viking, 2018).

6. Aristotle, *Politics*, in *Aristotle in 23 Volumes*, vol. 21, translated by H. Rackham (Cambridge, MA: Harvard University Press, 1944): 4.1295b.

7. For a theoretical exploration of the relationship between income and identity cleavages on the one hand and liberal democracy on the other, see Dani Rodrik and Sharun Mukand, "The Political Economy of Liberal Democracy," *Economic Journal* 130, no. 627 (April 2020): 765–792.

8. William Easterly, "The Middle Class Consensus and Economic Development," *Journal of Economic Growth* 6 (2001): 317–335. For other studies in the same vein, see Charles Kurzman and Erin Leahey, "Intellectuals and Democratization, 1905–1912 and 1989–1996," *American Journal of Sociology* 109, no. 4 (January 2004): 937–986, https://www.jstor.org/stable/10.1086/378929; and Chunlong Lu, "Middle Class and Democracy: Structural Linkage," *International Review of Modern Sociology* 31, no. 2 (Autumn 2005): 157–178, https://www.jstor .org/stable/41421642.

9. Eli G. Rau and Susan Stokes, "Income Inequality and the Erosion of Democracy in the Twenty-First Century," *Proceedings of the National Academy of Sciences* 122, no. 1 (2025), https://doi.org/10.1073/pnas.2422543121.

10. Kamala Harris, "Remarks by Vice President Harris at a Campaign Event in Raleigh, NC," August 16, 2024, https://www.whitehouse.gov/briefing-room /speeches-remarks/2024/08/16/remarks-by-vice-president-harris-at-a-campaign -event-in-raleigh-nc/.

11. Marco Rubio, "Rubio Argues for American Industrial Policy in Legislative Efforts to Combat China," May 18, 2021, https://www.rubio.senate.gov/rubio -argues-for-american-industrial-policy-in-legislative-efforts-to-combat-china/.

12. "Job Quality," Organisation for Economic Co-operation and Development, no date given, https://www.oecd.org/statistics/job-quality.htm.

13. Jonathan Rothwell and Steve Crabtree, "Not Just a Job: New Evidence on the Quality of Work in the United States," Gallup, 2019, https://omidyar.com/wp -content/uploads/2020/09/GreatJobsReport2019_rprt_102219_es.pdf.

14. Laura Silver, Patrick van Kessel, Christine Huang, Laura Clancy, and Sneha Gubbala, "What Makes Life Meaningful? Views from 17 Advanced Economies," Pew Research Center, November 2021, https://www.pewresearch.org/global/wp -content/uploads/sites/2/2021/11/PG_11.18.21_meaning-in-life_fullreport.pdf.

15. See Michael J. Sandel, *The Tyranny of Merit: Can We Find the Common Good?* (New York: Picador, 2021); and Michele Lamont, *Seeing Others: How Recognition Works—and How It Can Heal a Divided World* (New York: Simon & Schuster, 2023).

16. Morgan Kelly, Joel Mokyr, and Cormac Ó Gráda, "The Mechanics of the Industrial Revolution," *Journal of Political Economy* 131, no. 1 (2023): 59–94.

17. From John Forster, *The Life of Charles Dickens* (1872), quoted in Liam O'Farrell, "Warren's Blacking Factory, the First Workplace of Charles Dickens," no date given, https://www.liamofarrell.com/2020/12/warrens-blacking-factory/.

18. Thierry Pech, "Two Hundred Years of the Middle Class in France (1789– 2010)," *L'Économie politique* 49, no. 1 (2011): 69–97, https://www.cairn-int.info /article-E_LECO_049_0069-two-hundred-years-of-the-middle-class.htm.

19. Frank Levy and Peter Temin, "Inequality and Institutions in 20th Century America," National Bureau of Economic Research, Working Paper no. 13106,

May 2007, https://www.nber.org/system/files/working_papers/w13106/w13106
.pdf.

20. Newman and Skocpol, *Rust Belt Union Blues*, 49–59.

21. Dani Rodrik, "An Industrial Policy for Good Jobs," policy proposal for the Hamilton Project, September 2022. On changes in manufacturing technology and their impact on labor demand, see Daron Acemoglu and Pascual Restrepo, "Automation and New Tasks: How Technology Displaces and Reinstates Labor," *Journal of Economic Perspectives* 33, no. 2 (2019): 3–30. On the factors driving employment deindustrialization more broadly, see Robert Z. Lawrence, *Behind the Curve: Can Manufacturing Still Provide Inclusive Growth?* (Washington, DC: Peterson Institute for International Economics, 2024).

22. David H. Autor and David Dorn, "The Growth of Low-Skill Service Jobs and the Polarization of the US Labor Market," *American Economic Review* 103, no. 5 (2013): 1553–1597; David Autor, David Mindell, and Elisabeth Reynolds, *The Work of the Future: Building Better Jobs in an Age of Intelligent Machines* (Cambridge, MA: MIT Press, 2020); Eurofound, *Income Inequalities and Employment Patterns in Europe before and after the Great Recession* (Luxembourg, Belgium: Publications Office of the European Union, 2017); Organisation for Economic Co-operation and Development, *The Future of Work: OECD Employment Outlook 2019* (Paris: OECD Publishing, 2019).

23. Rakesh Kochhar and Stella Sechopoulos, "How the American Middle Class Has Changed in the Past Five Decades," Pew Research Center, April 20, 2022, https://www.pewresearch.org/short-reads/2022/04/20/how-the-american
-middle-class-has-changed-in-the-past-five-decades/. See also Janet Gornick, "The U.S. Middle Class Isn't Shrinking, but It Is Getting Squeezed as Inequality Rises," Stone Center on Socio-Economic Inequality, June 4, 2020, https://
stonecenter.gc.cuny.edu/the-u-s-middle-class-isnt-shrinking-but-it-is-getting
-squeezed-as-inequality-rises/.

24. Kochhar and Sechopoulos, "How the American Middle Class Has Changed."

25. Donald Trump, "Remarks by President Trump at Whirlpool Corporation Manufacturing Plant," White House, August 6, 2020, https://trumpwhitehouse
.archives.gov/briefings-statements/remarks-president-trump-whirlpool
-corporation-manufacturing-plant/.

26. Zolan Kanno-Youngs, Madeleine Ngo, and Don Clark, "Intel Receives $8.5 Billion in Grants to Build Chip Plants," *New York Times*, March 20, 2024, https://www.nytimes.com/2024/03/20/us/politics/chips-act-grant-intel.html. The sentiment is paralleled in Europe. An EU report produced by Enrico Letta, a former prime minister of Italy, writes: "At the turn of the century and for much of the subsequent decade, the shift [toward deindustrialization] was widely regarded as a feasible and even beneficial option. However, it is now evident that this is no longer the case": Letta, *Much More Than a Market—Speed, Security, Solidarity: Empowering the Single Market to Deliver a Sustainable Future and Prosperity for All EU Citizens*, April 2024, 10, https://www.consilium.europa.eu/media/ny3j24sm
/much-more-than-a-market-report-by-enrico-letta.pdf.

27. Taiwan Semiconductor Manufacturing Company Limited, "TSMC Arizona," https://www.tsmc.com/static/abouttsmcaz/index.htm.

28. The Biden administration expects "25,000 direct construction and manufacturing jobs, along with thousands of indirect jobs": Joseph R. Biden Jr., "Statement from President Joe Biden on CHIPS and Science Act Preliminary Agreement with TSMC," White House, April 8, 2024, https://www.whitehouse.gov/briefing-room/statements-releases/2024/04/08/statement-from-president-joe-biden-on-chips-and-science-act-preliminary-agreement-with-tsmc/.

29. Rodrik, "An Industrial Policy for Good Jobs," figure 5.

30. Heidi Garrett-Peltier, "Green versus Brown: Comparing the Employment Impacts of Energy Efficiency, Renewable Energy, and Fossil Fuels Using an Input-Output Model," *Economic Modelling* 61 (February 2017): 439–447, https://www.sciencedirect.com/science/article/abs/pii/S026499931630709X. See also Guillermo Montt, Kirsten S. Wiebe, Marek Harsdorff, Moana Simas, Antoine Bonnet, and Richard Wood, "Does Climate Action Destroy Jobs? An Assessment of the Employment Implications of the 2-Degree Goal," *International Labour Review* 157, no. 4 (December 2018): 519–556.

31. Katharina Bergant, Rui C. Mano, and Ippei Shibata, "How the Green Transition Will Impact U.S. Jobs," International Monetary Fund, December 13, 2022, https://www.imf.org/en/News/Articles/2022/12/12/cf-how-the-green-transition-will-impact-us-jobs.

32. Giovanni Marin and Francesco Vona, "Climate Policies and Skill-Biased Employment Dynamics: Evidence from EU Countries," *Journal of Environmental Economics and Management* 98 (November 2019), https://doi.org/10.1016/j.jeem.2019.102253.

33. US Bureau of Labor Statistics, "Employment Projections: Occupational Projections Data," https://data.bls.gov/projections/occupationProj.

34. Waldman, Adelle, *Help Wanted: A Novel* (New York: W. W. Norton, 2024), 110.

35. Waldman, *Help Wanted*, 116.

36. Richard Freeman and James Medoff, *What Do Unions Do?* (New York: Basic Books, 1984).

37. Heidi Shierholz, Celine McNicholas, Margaret Poydock, and Jennifer Sherer, "Workers Want Unions, but the Latest Data Point to Obstacles in Their Path," Economic Policy Institute, January 23, 2024, https://www.epi.org/publication/union-membership-data/.

38. European Trade Union Institute, "Trade Unions," worker-participation.eu, https://www.worker-participation.eu/National-Industrial-Relations/Across-Europe/Trade-Unions2.

39. Arindrajit Dube, "Using Wage Boards to Raise Pay," Economics for Inclusive Prosperity, February 2019, https://econfip.org/policy-briefs/using-wage-boards-to-raise-pay/.

40. Zeynep Ton, *The Case for Good Jobs: How Great Companies Bring Dignity, Pay, and Meaning to Everyone's Work* (Cambridge, MA: Harvard Business Review Press, 2023).

41. Waldman, *Help Wanted*, 131–138.

42. Acemoglu and Restrepo, "Automation and New Tasks," talk about so-so technologies, which reduce labor's share of value added while increasing productivity only slightly.

43. This accounts for why services have become more expensive over time, relative to goods, and why they are cheaper in developing countries. It is also the source of the Baumol cost-disease argument, whereby increasing services costs crowd out other activities in the economy. See William J. Baumol and William G. Bowen, *Performing Arts: The Economic Dilemma. A Study of Problems Common to Theater, Opera, Music and Dance* (New York: Twentieth Century Fund, 1966).

44. Gordon H. Hanson, Dani Rodrik, and Rohan Sandhu, "The U.S. Place-Based Policy Supply Chain," NBER, Working Paper no. 33511, February 2025.

45. Good Jobs First maintains a useful database of these subsidies at "Subsidy Tracker: Discover Where Corporations Are Getting Taxpayer Assistance across the United States," https://subsidytracker.goodjobsfirst.org/.

46. "Update on Virginia's Prime Deal with Amazon," Virginia Justice Democrats, June 7, 2023, https://vajusticedemocrats.com/2023/06/07/update-on-virginia8217s-prime-deal-with-amazon/.

47. On Amazon, see "Amazon Tracker: Discover How Much the Public Is Subsidizing One of the Largest Retailers," Good Jobs First, https://goodjobsfirst.org/amazon-tracker/; and Ike Brannon, "Amazon Tax Subsidies Are Inefficient Job Creators," *Forbes*, April 28, 2023, https://www.forbes.com/sites/ikebrannon/2023/04/28/amazon-tax-subsidies-are-inefficient-job-creators/?sh=e7859e759d02. On the high fiscal cost of subsidies in relation to the number of jobs created, see Timothy J. Bartik, "Bringing Jobs to People: Improving Local Economic Development Policies," Aspen Institute, August 2020.

48. The California Competes tax credit program is an example. See Matthew Freedman, David Neumark, and Shantanu Khanna, "Combining Rules and Discretion in Economic Development Policy: Evidence on the Impacts of the California Competes Tax Credit," *Journal of Public Economics* 217 (January 2023), https://doi.org/10.1016/j.jpubeco.2022.104777. Interestingly, the study finds larger impacts on employment in services rather than manufacturing, contrary to policy makers' expectations.

49. Chiara Criscuolo, Ralf Martin, Henry G. Overman, and John Van Reenen, "Some Causal Effects of an Industrial Policy," *American Economic Review* 109, no. 1 (2019): 48–85.

50. James J. Heckman, Robert J. Lalonde, and Jefferey A. Smith, "The Economics and Econometrics of Active Labor Market Programs," in *Handbook of Labor Economics*, ed. Orley C. Ashenfelter and David Card, vol. 3A (New York: Elsevier, 1999): 1865–2097; Jochen Kluve and Christoph M. Schmidt, "Can Training and Employment Subsidies Combat European Unemployment?," *Economic Policy* 17, no. 35 (October 2002): 409–448; Jochen Kluve, "The Effectiveness of European Active Labor Market Programs," *Labour Economics* 17, no. 6 (December 2010): 904–918; David Card, Jochen Kluve, and Andrea Weber, "Active Labour Market Policy Evaluations: A Meta-analysis," *Economic Journal* 120, no. 548 (Novem-

ber 2010): F452–F477; Marco Caliendo and Ricarda Schmidl, "Youth Unemployment and Active Labor Market Policies in Europe," Institute of Labor Economics (IZA), Discussion Paper no. 9488, November 2015.

51. On sectoral training programs, see Lawrence F. Katz, Jonathan Roth, Richard Hendra, and Kelsey Schaberg, "Why Do Sectoral Employment Programs Work? Lessons from WorkAdvance," *Journal of Labor Economics* 40, no. S1 (2022): S249–S291; Sheila Maguire et al., "Tuning In to Local Labor Markets: Findings from the Sectoral Employment Impact Study," Public/Private Ventures, 2010, https://ppv.issuelab.org/resources/5101/5101.pdf; Anne Roder and Mark Elliott, "Nine Year Gains: Project QUEST's Continuing Impact," Economic Mobility Corporation, April 2019, https://economicmobilitycorp.org/wp-content/uploads/2019/04/NineYearGains_web.pdf; Kelsey Schaberg, "Can Sector Strategies Promote Longer-Term Effects? Three-Year Impacts from the WorkAdvance Demonstration," September 2017, https://www.mdrc.org/sites/default/files/WorkAdvance_3-Year_Brief.pdf; and Richard Hendra et al., "Encouraging Evidence on a Sector-Focused Advancement Strategy: Two-Year Impacts from the WorkAdvance Demonstration," Manpower Demonstration Research Corporation, August 2016, https://www.mdrc.org/sites/default/files/2016_Workadvance_Final_Web.pdf.

52. See Dani Rodrik and Stefanie Stantcheva, "Economic Inequality and Insecurity: Policies for an Inclusive Economy," report prepared for commission chaired by Olivier Blanchard and Jean Tirole on major future economic challenges, Republic of France, June 2021, https://drodrik.scholars.harvard.edu/publications/economic-inequality-and-insecurity-policies-inclusive-economy.

53. One possible reason sectoral training programs have not scaled up is that they screen their trainees intensively, ensuring those that enroll are motivated and likely to succeed.

54. As Criscuolo et al. note: "Worker-centered policies, such as education and training, may need to be complemented by *firm-centered policies* that promote productivity in low-wage firms to effectively address concerns around high inequality and low productivity growth": Chiara Criscuolo et al., "Workforce Composition, Productivity and Pay: The Role of Firms in Wage Inequality," Institute of Labor Economics (IZA), Discussion Paper no. 13212, May 2020.

55. For a related discussion, see Joseph Parilla, Glencora Haskins, and Mark Muro, "Seizing the Moment for Place-Based Economic Policy: Implications for Practitioners and Policymakers from the Build Back Better Regional Challenge," Brookings, May 21, 2024, https://www.brookings.edu/articles/seizing-the-moment-for-place-based-economic-policy/.

56. "Birgit Klohs: Regional Development in West Michigan and the Grand Rapids Medical Mile," *Policy Works* podcast, episode 1, Reimagining the Economy Program, Harvard Kennedy School, https://www.hks.harvard.edu/centers/wiener/programs/economy/podcast/episode1-klohs. The quote is from a workshop at the Harvard Kennedy School in 2023.

57. James Fallows and Deborah Fallows, *Our Towns: A 100,000 Mile Journey into the Heart of America* (New York: Penguin Books, 2018).

58. Fallows and Fallows, *Our Towns*, 90.

59. "$1B Build Back Better Regional Challenge: Supercharging Local Econo-mies," US Economic Development Administration, https://www.eda.gov/funding/programs/american-rescue-plan/build-back-better; "Good Jobs Challenge: Getting Americans Back to Work," US Economic Development Administration, https://www.eda.gov/arpa/good-job-challenge; "Biden-Harris Administration Announces 22 Recompete Pilot Program Finalists," US Economic Development Administration, December 20, 2023, https://www.eda.gov/news/press-release/2023/12/20/biden-harris-administration-announces-22-recompete-pilot-program.

60. "Build Back Better Regional Challenge Awardee Profiles," US Economic Development Administration, https://www.eda.gov/sites/default/files/2022-09/Build-Back-Better-Awardee-Digital-Booklet.pdf.

61. On France, see Rodrik and Stantcheva, "Economic Inequality and Insecurity." On the UK, see Dani Rodrik and Huw Spencer, "Productivist Policies for the UK: How Productivism Can Build a New Economic Settlement," *IPPR Progressive Review* (Winter 2023), https://drodrik.scholars.harvard.edu/resource/productivist-policies-uk; and Vidit Joshi, Dani Rodrik, and Huw Spencer, "Creating a Good-Jobs Economy in the UK," Resolution Foundation, Economy in 2030 Inquiry, July 2023, https://drodrik.scholars.harvard.edu/publications/creating-good-jobs-economy-uk.

62. David Autor, "AI Could Actually Help Rebuild the Middle Class," *Noēma*, February 12, 2024, https://www.noemamag.com/how-ai-could-help-rebuild-the-middle-class/.

63. "Employment Projections," US Bureau of Labor Statistics, https://www.bls.gov/emp/. On the development of the nurse practitioner profession, see Eugene Levine, "What Do We Know about Nurse Practitioners?," *American Journal of Nursing* 77, no. 11 (November 1977): 1799–1803, https://www.jstor.org/stable/3424497; and Faye G. Abdellah, "The Nurse Practitioner 17 Years Later: Present and Emerging Issues," *Inquiry* 19, no. 2 (Summer 1982): 105–116, https://www.jstor.org/stable/29771476.

64. Alycia Bischof and Sherry A. Greenberg, "Post COVID-19 Reimbursement Parity for Nurse Practitioners," *Online Journal of Issues in Nursing*, May 31, 2021, https://doi.org/10.3912/OJIN.Vol26No02Man03.

65. Rosemary Goodyear, "The Nurse Practitioner in the US," in *Nursing Practice, Policy and Change*, ed. Marjorie Gott (Abingdon, UK: Radcliffe Medical Press, 2000): 93–113, http://ndl.ethernet.edu.et/bitstream/123456789/17577/1/68.pdf.pdf#page=106.

66. This discussion is based on Rodrik, "An Industrial Policy for Good Jobs."

67. Paul Osterman, "Improving Job Quality in Long Term Care," in *Creating Good Jobs: An Industry-Based Strategy*, ed. Paul Osterman (Cambridge, MA: MIT Press, 2019): 115–144. See also Ai-jen Poo and Ilana Berger, "We Need More Home Care Workers. But First We Have to Pay Them Enough," *New York Times*, March 30, 2022; Matthew Stevenson, "Demand for Healthcare Workers Will Outpace Supply by 2025: An Analysis of the US Healthcare Labor Market," Mercer Health Provider Advisory, 2018.

68. Osterman, "Improving Job Quality in Long Term Care," 124.

69. For experience in nursing homes, see Christine E. Bishop, "High-Performance Workplace Practices in Nursing Homes: An Economic Perspective," *The Gerontologist* 54, no. S1 (2014): S46–S52. In social services, Sabel, Zeitlin, and Helderman describe how the decentralization of youth care services in Utrecht, Netherlands, that empowered local actors to engage in experimentation enhanced delivery and performance: Charles Sabel, Jonathan Zeitlin, and Jan-Kees Helderman, "Transforming the Welfare State, One Case at a Time: How Utrecht Makes Customized Social Care Work," *Politics & Society* 52, no. 2 (January 2023), https://doi.org/10.1177/00323292221140710.

70. Heidi Anttila et al., "Towards Ethical and Sustainable Technology-Supported Ageing at Home in Finland—KATI Programme," *Proceedings of the Conference on Technology Ethics 2021*, vol. 3069, https://ceur-ws.org/Vol-3069/FP_03.pdf.

71. Minna Anttila et al., "How to Adopt Technologies in Home Care: A Mixed Methods Study on User Experiences and Change of Home Care in Finland," *BMC Health Services Research* 23, no. 1342 (December 2023), 7–8, https://link.springer.com/article/10.1186/s12913-023-10368-z#Sec2.

72. Osterman, "Improving Job Quality in Long Term Care."

73. Ton, *The Case for Good Jobs*, 189.

74. Erik Brynjolfsson, Danielle Li, and Lindsey Raymond, "Generative AI at Work," National Bureau of Economic Research, Working Paper no. 31161, April 2023, https://www.nber.org/papers/w31161.

75. Daron Acemoglu, David Autor, and Simon Johnson, "Can We Have Pro-Worker AI?," Shaping the Future of Work, MIT, September 19, 2023, https://shapingwork.mit.edu/wp-content/uploads/2023/09/Pro-Worker-AI-Policy-Memo.pdf.

76. Scott Abrahams and Frank S. Levy, "Could Savannah Be the Next San Jose? The Downstream Effects of Large Language Models," unpublished paper, June 23, 2024, https://papers.ssrn.com/sol3/papers.cfm?abstract_id=4874104.

77. Acemoglu and Restrepo, "Automation and New Tasks;" Daron Acemoglu and Simon Johnson, *Power and Progress: Our 1,000-Year Struggle over Technology and Prosperity* (New York: Hachette PublicAffairs, 2023); Owen F. Davis, "Artificial Intelligence and Worker Power," June 2024, https://ofdavis.com/ai.pdf.

78. Rodrik and Stantcheva, "Economic Inequality and Insecurity."

79. Rodrik, "An Industrial Policy for Good Jobs."

5: Fostering Economic Growth to Reduce Poverty

1. Jenni Marsh, "Employed by China," CNN, https://www.cnn.com/interactive/2018/08/world/china-africa-ethiopia-manufacturing-jobs-intl/; Zhang Zizhu, "Inside the Chinese Factory in Ethiopia Where Ivanka Trump Places Her Shoe Orders," Africa-China Reporting Project, January 30, 2017, https://africachinareporting.com/inside-the-chinese-factory-in-ethiopia-where-ivanka-trump-places-her-shoe-orders/.

2. "On the Path to Industrialization: A Review of Industrial Parks in Ethiopia," World Bank, 2022, https://documents1.worldbank.org/curated/en/099350011132228872/pdf/P1741950a12ef10560af5008750d1393b7c.pdf.

3. The need for a new growth strategy for developing countries is discussed in Dani Rodrik and Joseph E. Stiglitz, "A New Growth Strategy for Developing Nations," January 2024, https://drodrik.scholars.harvard.edu/publications/new-growth-strategy-developing-nations.

4. "Four Decades of Poverty Reduction in China: Drivers, Insights for the World, and the Way Ahead," World Bank, 2022, https://openknowledge.worldbank.org/server/api/core/bitstreams/e9a5bc3c-718d-57d8-9558-ce325407f737/content.

5. See, for example, Anne Krueger's contribution to the symposium: Mehrsa Baradaran et al., "What Comes after Neoliberalism?," *Project Syndicate*, June 4, 2024, https://www.project-syndicate.org/onpoint/what-comes-after-neoliberalism; and Hanning Fang, "Why Is China's Economy Slowing Down?," Tufts Now, November 20, 2023, https://now.tufts.edu/2023/11/20/why-chinas-economy-slowing-down/.

6. Jude Blanchette, "Confronting the Challenge of Chinese State Capitalism," Center for Strategic and International Studies, Global Forecast 2021 Essay Series, January 22, 2021, https://www.csis.org/analysis/confronting-challenge-chinese-state-capitalism.

7. Heilmann, Sebastian, "Policy Experimentation in China's Economic Rise," *Studies in Comparative International Development* 43, no. 1 (Spring 2008): 1–26.

8. On the Chinese reform strategy, see Lawrence J. Lau, Yingyi Qian, and Gerard Roland, "Reform without Losers: An Interpretation of China's Dual-Track Approach to Transition," *Journal of Political Economy* 108, no. 1 (February 2000): 120–143, https://www.jstor.org/stable/10.1086/262113; Yingyi Qian, *How Reform Worked in China: The Transition from Plan to Market* (Cambridge, MA: MIT Press, 2017); Yuen Yuen Ang, *How China Escaped the Poverty Trap* (New York: Cornell University Press, 2016); and Isabella M. Weber, *How China Escaped Shock Therapy: The Market Reform Debate* (London: Routledge, 2021).

9. "Housing Characteristics of Hong Kong Population," 2016 Population By-Census, https://www.bycensus2016.gov.hk/en/Snapshot-05.html.

10. The following discussion draws on Dani Rodrik, "The New Development Economics: We Shall Experiment, But How Shall We Learn?," in *What Works in Development? Thinking Big and Thinking Small*, ed. Jessica Cohen and William Easterly (Washington, DC: Brookings Institution Press, 2009): 24–48.

11. For example, most analysts would agree that "macroeconomic stability" or "good governance" are desirable things for economic development. The real policy question is how to achieve them. For a positive theory of the choice that governments face between experimenting through policy innovation and emulating "best practices" from elsewhere, see Sharun Mukand and Dani Rodrik, "In Search of the Holy Grail: Policy Convergence, Experimentation, and Economic Performance," *American Economic Review* 95, no. 1 (March 2005): 374–383.

12. Eva Vivalt, "How Much Can We Generalize from Impact Evaluations?," *Journal of the European Economic Association* 18, no. 6 (December 2020): 3045–3089, https://doi.org/10.1093/jeea/jvaa019.

13. Poverty can also be reduced by providing financial support and access to public services. But unless the productive capacity of poor households is raised, these policies entail treating merely the symptoms rather than the causes of poverty.

14. Dani Rodrik, "The Past, Present, and Future of Economic Growth," in *Towards a Better Global Economy: Policy Implications for Citizens Worldwide in the 21st Century*, ed. Franklin Allen et al. (Oxford, UK: Oxford University Press, 2014): 70–119.

15. Dani Rodrik, "Unconditional Convergence in Manufacturing," *Quarterly Journal of Economics* 128, no.1 (February 2013): 165–204. In recent years, there has been unconditional convergence in other sectors of the economy too, but the rate of convergence is very slow compared to what we observe in formal manufacturing: Dev Patel, Justin Sandefur, and Arvind Subramanian, "The New Era of Unconditional Convergence," *Journal of Development Economics* 152 (September 2021), https://www.sciencedirect.com/science/article/abs/pii/S030438782100064X.

16. For the story of a US textile mill that reopened and became competitive vis-à-vis imports with far fewer workers and significant automation, see Stephanie Clifford, "U.S. Textile Plants Return, with Floors Largely Empty of People," *New York Times*, September 19, 2013, https://www.nytimes.com/2013/09/20/business/us-textile-factories-return.html?pagewanted=all&_r=0.

17. Jonathan Tilley, "Automation, Robotics, and the Factory of the Future," McKinsey & Company, September 7, 2017, https://www.mckinsey.com/capabilities/operations/our-insights/automation-robotics-and-the-factory-of-the-future.

18. These numbers are from the company's form 20-F filing with the SEC: US Securities and Exchange Commission, Form 20-F, 142, NIO Inc., for fiscal year ended December 31, 2023, https://ir.nio.com/static-files/b9974b9f-e057-41aa-be67-97f41e5c0d82#page78. I am grateful to an anonymous reviewer for the reference.

19. Reijnders et al. document an increasing bias against less educated labor in global value chains: Laurie S. M. Reijnders, Marcel P. Timmer, and Xianjia Ye, "Labour Demand in Global Value Chains: Is There a Bias against Unskilled Work?," *World Economy* 44, no. 9 (January 2021): 2547–2571.

20. On the educational qualifications in Ethiopian industrial parks, see "Table 2: Average Number of Production Workers ('Machine Operators'), Education and Time Worked, by Industrial Park," in Christian Johannes Meyer, Eduard Krkoska, and Koen Maaskant, "Wages and Compensation in Ethiopia's Industrial Parks: Evidence from a Firm Survey," World Bank (April 2021): 5, https://doi.org/10.1596/35391; and "Table 5: Sample Characteristics by Sector, Skill Group and Company Origin," in Florian Schaefer and Carlos Oya, "Employment Patterns and Conditions in Construction and Manufacturing in Ethiopia: A Comparative Analysis of the Road Building and Light Manufacturing Sectors," IDCEA Research Report (2019): 25. On average education levels, see "Mean Years of Education in Ethiopia: Age Groups: Average Number of Years of Schooling Attained for the Age Group 20–24; Years: 2011," UNESCO Institute for Statistics, https://www.education-inequalities.org/indicators/eduyears/ethiopia#ageGroups=%5B%22eduyears

_2 (which gives a figure of 6.2 years for a youth in the twenty to twenty-four age bracket); and "Ethiopia: Human Capital Index 2020," Human Capital Project, World Bank, September 2020, https://databankfiles.worldbank.org/public /ddpext_download/hci/HCI_1pager_ETH.pdf (which cites 7.8 years for someone who enters school at age four).

21. Xinshen Diao, Mia Ellis, Margaret McMillan, and Dani Rodrik, "Africa's Manufacturing Puzzle: Evidence from Tanzanian and Ethiopian Firms," *World Bank Economic Review* 0 (2024): 1–33, https://doi.org/10.1093/wber/lhae029.

22. Anna Wiener, "Inside Adidas' Robot-Powered, On-Demand Sneaker Factory," *Wired*, November 29, 2017, https://www.wired.com/story/inside -speedfactory-adidas-robot-powered-sneaker-factory/; Adrián Hernández, "Learning from Adidas' Speedfactory Blunder," *Supply Chain Dive*, February 4, 2020, https://www.supplychaindive.com/news/adidas-speedfactory-blunder -distributed-operations/571678/.

23. "Global Robotics Race: Korea, Singapore and Germany in the Lead," International Federation of Robotics, January 10, 2024, https://ifr.org/ifr-press-releases /news/global-robotics-race-korea-singapore-and-germany-in-the-lead.

24. Dani Rodrik, "Prospects for Global Economic Convergence under New Technologies," in *An Inclusive Future? Technology, New Dynamics, and Policy Challenges*, ed. Zia Qureshi (Washington, DC: Brookings Institution, 2022): 65–82. The story is similar in Rwanda, a country where growth has been fueled by tradable services, which—like today's manufacturing—is skill intensive relative to the local labor force. Continued rapid growth is dependent on significant upgrading in education and skills. See Richard Newfarmer and Anna Twum, "Rwanda: Harnessing the Power of the Next Generation," in *New Pathways to Job Creation and Development in Africa: The Promise of Industries without Smokestacks*, ed. Haroon Bhorat, Brahima Coulibaly, John Page, and Richard Newfarmer (Washington, DC: Brookings Institution Press, 2025), https://rowman.com/ISBN/9780815740162 /New-Pathways-to-Job-Creation-and-Development-in-Africa-The-Promise-of -Industries-without-Smokestacks}.

25. Mauritius and Turkey are the only exceptions to this rule, which can be identified in the Groningen Economic Transformation Database on sectoral employment and value added: Gaaitzen de Vries et al., "The Economic Transformation Database (ETD): Content, Sources, and Methods," WIDER, Technical Note no. 2, 2021, https://doi.org/10.35188/UNU-WIDER/WTN/2021-2.

26. Dani Rodrik, "Premature Deindustrialization," *Journal of Economic Growth* 21, no. 1 (March 2016): 1–33.

27. Hagen Kruse, Emmanuel Mensah, Kunal Sen, and Gaaitzen de Vries, "A Manufacturing Renaissance? Industrialization Trends in the Developing World," WIDER, Working Paper no. 2021/28, February 2021, https://www.wider.unu.edu /publication/manufacturing-renaissance-industrialization-trends-developing -world. See also David Kunst, "Premature Deindustrialization through the Lens of Occupations: Which Jobs, Why, and Where?," Tinbergen Institute, Discussion Paper no. TI 2019-033/V, December 2020. This paper documents four stylized facts about premature deindustrialization. First, the jobs that have disappeared

are mostly of the unskilled type. Second, the disappearing jobs have tended to be concentrated among formal jobs, both within manufacturing and elsewhere. Third, premature deindustrialization has been driven by occupations that are intensive in tasks suitable to automation by information and communications technology (ICT). Fourth, high- and middle-income countries have been the most affected, while low-income countries appear to have avoided premature job losses in manufacturing so far.

28. The statistics are from the Development Research Center of the State Council of China.

29. Rajan and Lamba provide a similarly pessimistic take on the prospects of job creation in manufacturing in India. See Raghuram G. Rajan and Rohit Lamba, *Breaking the Mold: India's Untraveled Path to Prosperity* (Princeton, NJ: Princeton University Press, 2024).

30. See Peter Sheldon and Seung-Ho Kwon, "Samsung in Vietnam: FDI, Business-Government Relations, Industrial Parks, and Skills Shortages," *Economic and Labour Relations Review* 34 (2023): 66–85.

31. Thessa Lageman, "Remembering Mohamed Bouazizi: The Man Who Sparked the Arab Spring," *Al Jazeera*, December 17, 2020, https://www.aljazeera.com/features/2020/12/17/remembering-mohamed-bouazizi-his-death-triggered-the-arab.

32. Kaleb Girma Abreha, "Deconstructing the Missing Middle: Informality and Growth of Firms in Sub-Saharan Africa," World Bank Group Policy Research, Working Paper no. 10233, November 2022, http://documents1.worldbank.org/curated/en/099924211162242314/pdf/IDU0b070c6340f4d10403d08bd90f758ec6dcf49.pdf.

33. Matias Busso, Maria Victoria, and Santiago Levy, "(In)Formal and (Un)Productive: The Productivity Costs of Excessive Informality in Mexico," Inter-American Development Bank (IDB), Working Paper no. IDB-WP-341, August 2012, https://www.econstor.eu/bitstream/10419/89037/1/IDB-WP-341.pdf; Santiago Levy, "Dysfunctional Firm Dynamics and Productivity Stagnation in Mexico," unpublished paper, March 2023.

34. Louise Fox and Dhruv Gandhi, "Youth Employment in Sub-Saharan Africa: Progress and Prospects," Africa Growth Initiative at Brookings (AGI), Working Paper no. 28, March 2012, https://www.brookings.edu/wp-content/uploads/2021/03/21.03.24-IWOSS-Intro-paper_FINAL.pdf.

35. Gaurav Nayyar, Mary Hallward-Driemeier, and Elwyn Davies, "At Your Service? The Promise of Services-Led Development," World Bank Group, 2021, https://documents1.worldbank.org/curated/en/1557316311771398616/pdf/At-Your-Service-The-Promise-of-Services-Led-Development.pdf.

36. On India, see Tianyu Fan, Michael Peters, and Fabrizio Zilibotti, "Growing Like India: The Unequal Effects of Service-Led Growth," *Econometrica* 91, no. 4 (August 2023): 1457–1494, https://onlinelibrary.wiley.com/doi/abs/10.3982/ECTA20964. On the cross-country evidence, see Xinshen Diao, Margaret McMillan, and Dani Rodrik, "The Recent Growth Boom in Developing Economies: A Structural-Change Perspective," in *The Palgrave Handbook of Development Eco-*

nomics: Critical Reflections on Globalization and Development, ed. Machiko Nissanke and José Antonio Ocampo (Cham, Switzerland: Palgrave Macmillan, 2019): 281–334. See also Bhorat et al., eds., *New Pathways to Job Creation and Development in Africa.*

37. Nayyar, Hallward-Driemeier, and Davies, "At Your Service?"

38. Louise Fox and Dhruv Gandhi, "Opportunities for Youth Employment in Sub-Saharan Africa: Progress and Prospects," chapter 2 in Bhorat et al., eds., *New Pathways to Job Creation and Development in Africa.*

39. Linda Poon, "A Look at Street Vendors around the World," Bloomberg, November 13, 2015, https://www.bloomberg.com/news/articles/2015-11-13/for-international-street-vendors-day-a-look-at-street-vendors-around-the-world.

40. Details of this initiative come from Leonardo Iacovone and David McKenzie, "Shortening Supply Chains for Fruit and Vegetable Vendors in Bogota," *Finance & PSD Impact* 54 (August 2019).

41. This account is taken from Aneesh Mugulur, Gayatri Chandrasekaran, and Nikhil Nadiger, "Saksham Saarthi: A Unique Collaboration between the Government of Haryana and Cab Aggregators to Create Employment Opportunities," Samagra: Transforming Governance, Working Paper, May 2019.

42. For a useful taxonomy of different categories of firms and associated government programs in the context of South Africa, see Zaakhir Asmal, Haroon Bhorat, Alexia Lochmann, Lisa Martin, and Kishan Shah, "Supply-Side Economics of a Good Type: Supporting and Expanding South Africa's Informal Economy," CID Research, Working Paper no. 158, April 2024. The vocational training needs of enterprises of different sizes and characteristics in Tanzania are discussed in Antonio Andreoni, Sophie van Huellen, Lucas Katera, and Cornel Jahari, "How to Overcome Rent Seeking in Tanzania's Skills Sector? Exploring Feasible Reforms through Discrete Choice Experiments," *World Development* 182 (2024), https://doi.org/10.1016/j.worlddev.2024.106705.

43. This discussion draws on Dani Rodrik and Rohan Sandhu, "Servicing Development: Productive Upgrading of Labor-Absorbing Services in Developing Economies," Reimagining the Economy Program, policy paper, January 2025, https://drodrik.scholars.harvard.edu/publications/servicing-development-productive-upgrading-labor-absorbing-services.

44. Lucas Navarro, "The World Class Supplier Program for Mining in Chile: Assessment and Perspectives," *Resources Policy* 58 (October 2018): 49–61, https://www.sciencedirect.com/science/article/abs/pii/S0301420717301137; Jie Bai et al., "Search and Information Frictions on Global e-Commerce Platforms: Evidence from AliExpress," National Bureau of Economic Research, Working Paper no. 28100, September 2021, https://www.nber.org/system/files/working_papers/w28100/w28100.pdf.

45. For a study on services in Tanzania that examines such firms, see Mia Ellis, Margaret McMillan, and Jed Silver, "Employment and Productivity Growth in Tanzania's Service Sector," in *Industries without Smokestacks: Industrialization in Africa Reconsidered*, ed. Richard Newfarmer, John Page, and Finn Tarp (Oxford, UK: Oxford University Press, 2018): 296–315. See also Charles Sabel and Piero

Ghezzi, "The Quality Hurdle: Towards a Development Model That Is No Longer Industry-Centric," unpublished paper, May 10, 2021, https://charlessabel.com /papers/QualityHurdle_May-10-2021.pdf.

46. This was the result of a randomized experiment in Egypt: Gharad Bryan, Dean Karlan, and Adam Osman, "Big Loans to Small Businesses: Predicting Winners and Losers in an Entrepreneurial Lending Experiment," *American Economic Review* 114, no. 9 (September 2024): 2825–2860, https://doi.org/10.1257/aer .20220616.

47. This description is based on David McKenzie, "Identifying and Spurring High-Growth Entrepreneurship: Experimental Evidence from a Business Plan Competition," *American Economic Review* 107, no. 8 (2017): 2278–2307; and Muyi Aina, "Youth Enterprise with Innovation in Nigeria—YouWiN!" Federal Ministry of Finance, 2016, https://www.pdfnigeria.org/rc/youth-enterprise-with-innovation -in-nigeria-youwin/.

48. The description here draws on IntraHealth International, "mSakhi: An Interactive Mobile Phone-Based Job Aid for Accredited Social Health Activists," Manthan Project, September 2013, https://www.intrahealth.org/resources /msakhi-interactive-mobile-phone-based-job-aid-accredited-social-health-activists; and A. Kumar, M. E. Khan, and G. Bora, "mSakhi: Making the 'm' Work for Community Health Workers," in *Articles from the 13th World Congress on Public Health* (2013): 249–254.

49. For sources on Harambee that this account draws on, see Rodrik and Sandhu, "Servicing Development."

50. Franklin D. Roosevelt, "Franklin D. Roosevelt Speeches: Oglethorpe University Address: The New Deal," May 22, 1932, https://publicpolicy.pepperdine .edu/academics/research/faculty-research/new-deal/roosevelt-speeches /fr052232.htm.

51. Angela Tritto, "How Indonesia Used Chinese Industrial Investments to Turn Nickel into the New Gold," Carnegie Endowment for International Peace, April 2023, https://carnegieendowment.org/research/2023/04/how-indonesia -used-chinese-industrial-investments-to-turn-nickel-into-the-new-gold?lang =en; Rick Mills, "Indonesia and China Killed the Nickel Market," Mining.com, March 4, 2024, https://www.mining.com/web/indonesia-and-china-killed-the -nickel-market/; Per Elinder Liljas, "Cheap Coal, Cheap Workers, Chinese Money: Indonesia's Nickel Success Comes at a Price," *The Guardian*, April 10, 2024, https:// www.theguardian.com/world/2024/apr/11/cheap-coal-cheap-workers-chinese -money-indonesias-nickel-success-comes-at-a-price; Teesta Prakash, "Indonesia's Nickel Supremacy: China's Backing and Australia's Decline," *Australian Outlook*, February 16, 2024, https://www.internationalaffairs.org.au/australianoutlook /indonesias-nickel-supremacy-chinas-backing-and-australias-decline/.

52. Nicholas Stern and Joseph E. Stiglitz, "Climate Change and Growth," *Industrial Corporate Change* 32, no. 2 (April 2023): 277–303, https://doi.org/10.1093 /icc/dtad008.

53. Hans Peter Lankes, Rob Macquarie, Éléonore Soubeyran, and Nicholas Stern, "The Relationship between Climate Action and Poverty Reduction," *World*

Bank Research Observer 39, no. 1 (February 2024): 1–46, https://academic.oup.com/wbro/article/39/1/1/7504628.

54. Namrata Kala, Clare Balconi, and Shweta Bhogale, "Climate Adaptation," *VoxDevLit* 7, no. 1 (June 2023), https://voxdev.org/sites/default/files/2023-09/Climate_Adaptation_Issue_1.pdf.

55. Sam Butler-Sloss, Kingsmill Bond, and Vikram Singh, "The Energy Transition and the Global South: A More Attractive Energy Future for All," Rocky Mountain Institute, November 2022, https://rmi.org/wp-content/uploads/dlm_uploads/2022/11/the_energy_transition_and_the_global_south.pdf.

56. Heidi Garrett-Peltier, "Green versus Brown: Comparing the Employment Impacts of Energy Efficiency, Renewable Energy, and Fossil Fuels Using an Input-Output Model," *Economic Modelling* 61 (February 2017): 439–447, https://doi.org/10.1016/j.econmod.2016.11.012.

57. Vera Songwe and Jean-Paul Adam, "Delivering Africa's Great Green Transformation," Brookings, February 16, 2023, https://www.brookings.edu/articles/delivering-africas-great-green-transformation/?b=1.

6: A Productivist Paradigm

1. Dani Rodrik, "On Productivism," Harvard Kennedy School, March 2023, https://drodrik.scholars.harvard.edu/publications/productivism.

2. Dani Rodrik, "Milton Friedman's Magical Thinking," *Project Syndicate*, October 11, 2022, https://www.project-syndicate.org/commentary/milton-friedman-s-magical-thinking. Friedman borrowed the pencil story from Leonard E. Read.

3. Keith Bradsher, "Once Elusive, Orchids Flourish on Taiwanese Production Line," *New York Times,* August 24, 2004, https://www.nytimes.com/2004/08/24/business/once-elusive-orchids-flourish-on-taiwanese-production-line.html; S. Wei, C.-C. Shih, N.-H. Chen, S.-J. Tung, "Value Chain Dynamics in the Taiwan Orchid Industry," *ISHS Acta Horticulturae* 878, International Orchid Symposium (2010): 437–442, https://www.actahort.org/books/878/878_56.htm.

4. Akio Hosono, "The Chilean Salmon Industry Takes Off: From the Commercialization to the Early Development Phase," in *Chile's Salmon Industry: Policy Challenges in Managing Public Goods*, ed. Akio Hosono, Michiko Iizuka, and Jorge Katz (Tokyo: Springer, 2016): 45–74; Manuel Agosin, Nicolas Grau, and Christian Larrain, "Industrial Policy in Chile," Inter-American Development Bank, Working Paper no. IDB-WP-170, December 2010, https://www.econstor.eu/bitstream/10419/89154/1/IDB-WP-170.pdf.

5. Amir Lebdioui, "Chile's Export Diversification since 1960: A Free Market *Miracle* or *Mirage*?," *Development and Change* 50, no. 6 (October 2019): 1624–1663, https://onlinelibrary.wiley.com/doi/pdf/10.1111/dech.12545.

6. Josh Lerner, "The Boulevard of Broken Dreams: Innovation Policy and Entrepreneurship," LSE Growth Commission, Institute for Government, https://cep.lse.ac.uk/LSE-Growth-Commission/files/LSEGC-lerner-innovation-policy-entrepreneurship.pdf.

7. William H. Janeway, "What Drives Innovation?," *Project Syndicate*, January 20, 2023, https://www.project-syndicate.org/onpoint/innovation-technological-and-market-risk-key-role-of-the-state-by-william-h-janeway-2023-01. For insightful case studies of US industrial and innovation policy, see Fred Block and Matthew R. Keller, eds., *State of Innovation: The U.S. Government's Role in Technology Development* (Boulder, CO: Paradigm, 2011).

8. The scholarly literature on whether industrial policy works is discussed in Réka Juhász, Nathan Lane, and Dani Rodrik, "The New Economics of Industrial Policy," *Annual Review of Economics* 16 (August 2024): 213–242, https://doi.org/10.1146/annurev-economics-081023-024638. As we discuss in this article, until recently, the empirical evidence was generally negative, suggesting that industrial policy does not produce the intended effects. The newer literature, paying closer attention to issues of causal identification and ranging from historical cases to place-based policies in Europe to East Asian policies, yields much more positive results on the efficacy of industrial policy.

9. Barack H. Obama II, "Remarks by the President on the Economy," Solyndra Inc., Fremont, California, May 26, 2010, https://obamawhitehouse.archives.gov/the-press-office/remarks-president-economy-0. The account here is based on Dani Rodrik, "Green Industrial Policy," *Oxford Review of Economic Policy* 30, no. 3 (Autumn 2014): 469–491.

10. Heather Zichal, "Keeping America Competitive: Innovation and Clean Energy," White House, January 31, 2011, https://obamawhitehouse.archives.gov/blog/2011/01/31/keeping-america-competitive-innovation-and-clean-energy.

11. Cited in Anjani Datla, "Shaping the Future of Solar Power: Climate Change, Industrial Policy, and Free Trade," Harvard Kennedy School case written under the direction of Robert Lawrence, January 2012.

12. Rodrik, "Green Industrial Policy."

13. Nick Turse, "The Wild and Strange World of DARPA," History News Network, no date given, https://www.historynewsnetwork.org/article/the-wild-and-strange-world-of-darpa.

14. The four projects are salmon farming, Pacific oysters, boxed beef, and raspberries and blueberries.

15. Dani Rodrik and Charles Sabel, "Building a Good Jobs Economy," November 2019, https://drodrik.scholars.harvard.edu/publications/building-good-jobs-economy.

16. A subsequent congressional report stated, "The lack of available competitor information for Solyndra and the rapidly dropping price of polysilicon and panel prices should have prompted DOE to reconsider the Solyndra loan guarantee or, at the least, postpone the Solyndra closing so it could examine how the Solyndra loan guarantee would be impacted by the Chinese pricing pressures": Majority Staff Report for US House of Representatives Committee on Energy and Commerce, "The Solyndra Failure," 112th Congress, August 2, 2012, 132. See also Ronnie Greene, "Recurring Red Flags Failed to Slow Obama Administration's Race to Help Solyndra," Center for Public Integrity, September 13, 2011, https://publicintegrity

.org/politics/recurring-red-flags-failed-to-slow-obama-administrations-race-to
-help-solyndra/.

17. Majority Staff Report, "The Solyndra Failure," 135.

18. See Carol Browner, Ron Klain, and Larry Summers, "Briefing Memo: Renewable Energy Loan Guarantees and Grants," White House, October 25, 2010, https://www.documentcloud.org/documents/265143-summers-renewable -energy-memo2010.html, for the text of an October 2010 memo from three senior administration economists to President Obama on possible options for the loan program.

19. John McArdle, "Solyndra Spent Liberally to Woo Lawmakers until the End, Records Show," *New York Times*, September 16, 2011, http://www.nytimes .com/gwire/2011/09/16/16greenwire-solyndra-spent-liberally-to-woo-lawmakers -unti-81006.html.

20. See Majority Staff Report, "The Solyndra Failure," 145.

21. On the reasons for and consequences of treating inequality as a negative externality, see Morten Nyborg Støstad, "The Power of Treating Inequality as an Externality," *VoxEU*, Center for Economic and Policy Research, June 18, 2024, https://cepr.org/voxeu/columns/power-treating-inequality-externality.

22. For an argument for green industrial policies based on this kind of reasoning, see Philippe Aghion, Lint Barrage, David Hémous, and Ernest Liu, "Transition to Green Technology along the Supply Chain," INSEAD, Working Paper no. 2024/15/EPS, January 2025.

23. Economists make a distinction between horizontal and vertical policies. Horizontal policies are general public goods and macroeconomic policies that don't have a sectoral focus, while vertical policies (such as industrial policies) target a particular sector or technology. Many public goods, such as those discussed in this paragraph, however, are vertical in the sense that they benefit particular sectors.

24. Timothy J. Bartik, *Making Sense of Incentives: Taming Business Incentives to Promote Prosperity* (Kalamazoo, MI: W. E. Upjohn Institute for Employment Research, 2019), https://doi.org/10.17848/9780880996693.

25. Piero Ghezzi, "Mesas Ejecutivas in Peru: Lessons for Productive Development Policies," *Global Policy* 8, no. 3 (July 2017): 369–380, https://onlinelibrary .wiley.com/doi/abs/10.1111/1758-5899.12457.

26. Peter B. Evans, *Embedded Autonomy: States and Industrial Transformation* (Princeton, NJ: Princeton University Press, 1995): 12.

27. Elizabeth Thurbon, Sung-Young Kim, Hao Tan, and John A. Mathews, *Developmental Environmentalism: State Ambition and Creative Destruction in East Asia's Green Energy Transition* (Oxford, UK: Oxford University Press, 2023): 5.

28. Thurbon et al., *Developmental Environmentalism*, 128.

29. For some of the early problems with the pilot cities program in EVs, see Christopher Marquis, Hongyu Zhang, and Lixuan Zhou, "China's Quest to Adopt Electric Vehicles," *Stanford Social Innovation Review* (Spring 2013): 52–57, https:// www.hbs.edu/ris/Publication%20Files/Electric%20Vehicles_89176bc1-1aee-4c6e -829f-bd426beaf5d3.pdf.

30. Hongyang Cui and Hui He, "Liuzhou: A New Model for the Transition to Electric Vehicles?," International Council on Clean Transportation, December 18, 2019, https://theicct.org/liuzhou-a-new-model-for-the-transition-to-electric-vehicles/; Thurbon et al., *Developmental Environmentalism*, 106–134.

31. Thurbon et al., *Developmental Environmentalism*, 133.

32. Matthew Freedman, David Neumark, and Shantanu Khanna, "Combining Rules and Discretion in Economic Development Policy: Evidence on the Impacts of the California Competes Tax Credit," *Journal of Public Economics* 217 (January 2023), https://doi.org/10.1016/j.jpubeco.2022.104777. The promise about working with firms to avoid breach is in the *CalCompetes Application Guide*, FY 2022–23; video at https://www.youtube.com/watch?v=NmEmeJsCA94.

33. Charles F. Sabel and Jonathan Zeitlin, "Experimentalist Governance," in *Oxford Handbook of Governance*, ed. David Levi-Faur (Oxford, UK: Oxford University Press, 2012): 169–183.

34. A comparative study of Latin American productive interventions loosely modeled on the experimentalist governance framework found that capture and manipulation by firms was much less of a problem than the authors had initially feared. See Eduardo Fernández-Arias, Charles Sabel, Ernesto Stein, and Alberto Trejos, "Overview: Public-Private Collaboration on Productive Development Policies," in *Two to Tango: Public-Private Collaboration for Productive Development Policies* (Washington, DC: Inter-American Development Bank, 2016): 1–29.

35. This summary is based on Sabel and Zeitlin, "Experimentalist Governance," 169–183.

36. Ricardo Hausmann, Dani Rodrik, and Charles F. Sabel, "Reconfiguring Industrial Policy: A Framework with an Application to South Africa," August 2007.

37. See Juhász, Lane, and Rodrik, "The New Economics of Industrial Policy," for a good discussion emphasizing the endogeneity of state capacity.

38. Rodrik and Sabel, "Building a Good Jobs Economy"; Fernández-Arias et al., "Overview: Public-Private Collaboration."

39. Charles F. Sabel and David G. Victor, *Fixing the Climate: Strategies for an Uncertain World* (Princeton, NJ: Princeton University Press, 2024).

40. Sabel and Victor, *Fixing the Climate*, 19–30. These authors blame the resistance to adopting similar processes in climate change on the desire to keep firms at arm's length, in keeping with the technocrats' perceived model of governance.

7: Remaking Globalization

1. The data are from the World Bank's online data query tool.

2. Public attitudes on China have taken a sharp turn for the worse in the US. In 2005, more Americans viewed China favorably than unfavorably. By 2019, only 26 percent of Americans had a favorable view of the country. These feelings are reciprocated in China, where 75 percent of respondents now hold negative views about the US: Laura Silver, Kat Devlin, and Christine Huang, "U.S. Views of China

Turn Sharply Negative Amid Trade Tensions," Pew Research Center, August 13, 2019, https://www.pewresearch.org/global/2019/08/13/u-s-views-of-china-turn-sharply-negative-amid-trade-tensions/; Adam Y. Liu, Xiaojun Li, and Songying Fang, "Unpacking 'the West': Divergence and Asymmetry in Chinese Public Attitudes towards Europe and the United States," *Journal of Current Chinese Affairs* 52, no. 1 (2023): 119–133, https://doi.org/10.1177/18681026221139301.

3. Jake Sullivan, "Remarks by National Security Advisor Jake Sullivan on Renewing American Economic Leadership at the Brookings Institution," April 27, 2023, https://www.whitehouse.gov/briefing-room/speeches-remarks/2023/04/27/remarks-by-national-security-advisor-jake-sullivan-on-renewing-american-economic-leadership-at-the-brookings-institution/. The Sullivan speech is the clearest articulation of the abandonment of hyperglobalization by the US establishment.

4. A much-anticipated 2024 report prepared for the EU by former Italian prime minister and European Central Bank president Mario Draghi strikes a very similar line to Jake Sullivan's speech. In the report, Draghi argues that EU trade policy should be subservient to EU industrial strategy, rather than vice versa—a remarkable reversal in the European approach to the global economy: Mario Draghi, "The Future of European Competitiveness," European Commission, September 2024. See also Draghi, "Radical Change—Is What Is Needed," Speech at the High-Level Conference on the European Pillar of Social Rights, Brussels, April 16, 2024.

5. The treatment of intellectual property, tariff escalation, debt resolution, international taxation, and transfer pricing, which greatly favors major economic powers, are some examples. See Joseph E. Stiglitz and Dani Rodrik, "Rethinking Global Governance: Cooperation in a World of Power," March 2024, https://drodrik.scholars.harvard.edu/publications/rethinking-global-governance-cooperation-world-power.

6. White House, "National Security Strategy," October 2022, https://www.whitehouse.gov/wp-content/uploads/2022/10/Biden-Harris-Administrations-National-Security-Strategy-10.2022.pdf.

7. The first Trump administration blocked the appointment of judges to the WTO appellate body, paralyzing the institution's dispute resolution system. President Biden followed the policy.

8. Dani Rodrik, *The Globalization Paradox: Democracy and the Future of the World Economy* (New York: W. W. Norton, 2011); Dani Rodrik, "Who Needs the Nation State?," *Economic Geography* 89, no. 1 (January 2013): 1–19.

9. Nilüfer Çağatay, "Beggar-Thy-Neighbour," in *The New Palgrave Dictionary of Economics* (London: Palgrave Macmillan, 2018), https://doi.org/10.1057/978-1-349-95189-5_607.

10. Consider a small economy that has no market power on world markets. The government would have no reason to apply a trade restriction for purposes of exercising market power. But it may still want to use tariffs for protective reasons.

11. Thomas Tørsløv, Ludvig Wier, and Gabriel Zucman, "The Missing Profits of Nations," *Review of Economic Studies* 90, no. 3 (2023): 1499–1534, https://gabriel-zucman.eu/files/TWZ2022Restud.pdf.

12. There are some special circumstances under which this may not be true. In a two-country world, one nation may still be left better off when both sides apply optimum tariffs, if there is a sufficiently large asymmetry in size.

13. For an argument that the US should not pursue primacy over China, see Ben Rhodes, "A Foreign Policy for the World as It Is: Biden and the Search for a New American Strategy," *Foreign Affairs*, July/August 2024, https://www.foreignaffairs .com/united-states/biden-foreign-policy-world-rhodes. On weaponized interdependence, see Daniel W. Drezner, Henry Farrell, and Abraham L. Newman, eds., *The Uses and Abuses of Weaponized Interdependence* (Washington, DC: Brookings Institution Press, 2021), https://www.jstor.org/stable/10.7864/j.ctv11sn64z.

14. This framework is based on an initiative that was led by Jeffrey S. Lehman, Yang Yao, and myself. See Lehman et al., "US-China Trade Relations: A Way Forward," US-China Trade Policy Working Group, Joint Statement, October 2019, https://www .inet.econ.cam.ac.uk/files/us-china_trade_joint_statement_2019.pdf. The framework is extended beyond trade to the global system in Dani Rodrik and Steve Walt, "How to Construct a New Global Order," *Oxford Review of Economic Policy* 40 (2024); and Dani Rodrik and Steve Walt, "How to Build a Better World: Limiting Great Power Rivalry in an Anarchic World," *Foreign Affairs*, September/October 2022.

15. Sullivan, "Remarks by National Security Advisor Jake Sullivan."

16. Janet L. Yellen, "Remarks by Secretary of the Treasury Janet L. Yellen on the U.S.-China Economic Relationship at Johns Hopkins School of Advanced International Studies," April 10, 2023, https://home.treasury.gov/news/press -releases/jy1425.

17. Yingfan Chen, Hamilton Chen, and Dingding Chen, "The Broadening Strategy of U.S. Technological Restrictions on China," *The Diplomat*, April 4, 2024, https://thediplomat.com/2024/04/the-broadening-strategy-of-u-s-technological -restrictions-on-china/.

18. "China Lashes Out at Latest U.S. Export Controls on Chips," AP News, October 8, 2022, https://apnews.com/article/technology-business-china-global -trade-47eed4a9fa1c2f51027ed12cf929ff55; Edward Luce, "Containing China Is Biden's Explicit Goal," *Financial Times*, October 19, 2022, https://www.ft.com /content/398f0d4e-906e-479b-a9a7-e4023c298f39?shareType=nongift; Gregory C. Allen, "Choking Off China's Access to the Future of AI," Center for Strategic & International Studies, October 11, 2022, https://www.csis.org/analysis/choking -chinas-access-future-ai.

19. Reportedly, TikTok gave many assurances to the US government to forestall legislation that would ban its app from the US, including offering a unilateral "kill switch" in case the company was found to be violating its commitments. It claims the US government did not engage with the Chinese company on the assurances or the offer: Imran Rahman-Jones, "TikTok Confirms It Offered US Government a 'Kill Switch,'" BBC News, June 21, 2024, https://www.bbc.com/news/articles /cxwwz7l02j0o.

20. Pinelopi Goldberg, Reka Juhasz, Nathan Lane, Giulia Lo Forte, and Jeff Thurk, "Industrial Policy in the Global Semiconductor Sector," unpublished paper, June 27, 2024.

21. Robert Z. Lawrence discusses how a regime with greater policy autonomy along these lines can be rendered compatible with the WTO: Lawrence, "How to Save the WTO with More Flexible Trading Rules," Peterson Institute for International Economics, Policy Brief 22-15, December 2022, https://www.piie.com/publications/policy-briefs/how-save-wto-more-flexible-trading-rules.

22. Dani Rodrik, "Don't Fret about Green Subsidies," *Project Syndicate*, May 20, 2024, https://www.project-syndicate.org/commentary/green-subsidies-justified-on-economic-environmental-and-moral-grounds-by-dani-rodrik-2024-05.

23. White House, "Fact Sheet: President Biden Takes Action to Protect American Workers and Businesses from China's Unfair Trade Practices," May 14, 2024, https://www.whitehouse.gov/briefing-room/statements-releases/2024/05/14/fact-sheet-president-biden-takes-action-to-protect-american-workers-and-businesses-from-chinas-unfair-trade-practices/.

24. Specifically, the rules of origin specified that at least 40–45 percent of auto content had to be produced by workers earning at least $16 per hour.

25. For a proposal along these lines, see Dani Rodrik, "Towards a More Inclusive Globalization: An Anti-social Dumping Scheme," Economics for Inclusive Prosperity, February 2019, https://econfip.org/policy-briefs/towards-a-more-inclusive-globalization-an-anti-social-dumping-scheme/.

26. Dani Rodrik and Arvind Subramanian, "Why Did Financial Globalization Disappoint?," *IMF Staff Papers* 56, no. 1 (March 2009): 112–138; Davide Furceri, Prakash Loungani, Jonathan Ostry, and Pietro Pizzuto, "Financial Globalization, Fiscal Policies and the Distribution of Income," *Comparative Economic Studies* 62 (2020): 185–199, https://doi.org/10.1057/s41294-020-00113-4.

27. For how such a tripartite deal can be worked out, see Reza Baqir, Ishac Diwan, and Dani Rodrik, "A Framework to Evaluate Economic Adjustment-cum-Debt Restructuring Packages," January 2023, https://drodrik.scholars.harvard.edu/publications/framework-evaluate-economic-adjustment-cum-debt-restructuring-packages.

28. Julie McCarthy, "The New Global Tax Deal Is Bad for Development," Brookings, May 16, 2022, https://www.brookings.edu/articles/the-new-global-tax-deal-is-bad-for-development/. See also Stiglitz and Rodrik, "Rethinking Global Governance."

29. Gabriel Zucman, "A Blueprint for a Coordinated Minimum Effective Taxation Standard for Ultra-High-Net-Worth Individuals," commissioned by the Brazilian G20 presidency, June 25, 2024, https://www.taxobservatory.eu//www-site/uploads/2024/06/report-g20-24_06_24.pdf.

30. Emmanuel Saez and Gabriel Zucman, "Progressive Wealth Taxation," *Brookings Papers on Economic Activity* (Fall 2019): 437–533.

8: A New Progressive Agenda

1. I have written about these tensions in Dani Rodrik, *Has Globalization Gone Too Far?* (Washington, DC: Institute for International Economics, 1997); Dani Rodrik, *The Globalization Paradox: Democracy and the Future of the World Econ-*

omy (New York: W. W. Norton, 2011); and Dani Rodrik, *Straight Talk on Trade: Ideas for a Sane World Economy* (Princeton, NJ: Princeton University Press, 2017).

2. James Carville, "I Was Wrong about the 2024 Election. Here's Why," *New York Times*, January 2, 2025, https://www.nytimes.com/2025/01/02/opinion /democrats-donald-trump-economy.html.

3. Amory Gethin, Clara Martínez-Toledano, and Thomas Piketty, "Brahmin Left versus Merchant Right: Changing Political Cleavages in 21 Western Democracies, 1948–2020," *Quarterly Journal of Economics* 137, no. 1 (February 2022): 1–48, https://doi.org/10.1093/qje/qjab036.

4. Jason Stanley, "The End of US Democracy Was All Too Predictable," *Project Syndicate*, November 7, 2024, https://www.project-syndicate.org/commentary /trump-election-inequality-meant-that-us-democracy-was-doomed-by-jason -stanley-2024-11.

5. A pollster asked Hispanic voters in Texas before the 2024 presidential election what they saw as the number one problem with the Democratic Party. The main complaint he heard was not about cultural issues or "wokeness." It was that the "Democratic Party [is] the party of welfare benefits for people who don't work." See "The Book That Predicted the 2024 Election," *Ezra Klein Show*, November 9, 2024, https://www.nytimes.com/2024/11/09/opinion/ezra-klein-podcast -patrick-ruffini.html.

6. Michael J. Sandel, *The Tyranny of Merit: What's Become of the Common Good?* (New York: Farrar, Straus and Giroux, 2021).

7. Sandel, *The Tyranny of Merit*, 206.

8. Roberto Mangabeira Unger provides such an agenda: "Imagine three stages in the deepening and spread of such a knowledge economy for the many. In the first stage, the focus falls on the uplift of the small and medium-sized firms of the backward economy, on the transformation of self-employed service providers into technologically equipped artisans, and on the discovery and dissemination of the most fertile productive practice—a twenty-first-century equivalent to nineteenth-century agricultural extension. In a second stage, a distinctive institutional arrangement begins to emerge out of the effort at uplift: a form of partnership or strategic coordination between firms or individual economic agents and national or local governments that is decentralized, pluralistic, participatory, and experimental, and that advances in tandem with cooperative competition among the firms or agents. In a third, speculative stage, far into the future, the productive assets of society would be vested in social funds controlled neither by the government nor by private investors. These funds would run a rotating capital auction, auctioning off the productive assets of society, for limited times, to whomever could offer the funds that held them the highest rate of return. We might describe such a regime as 'capitalism without capitalists.' Its point would be to ensure that finance serves the productive agenda of society rather than serving itself and that its most important responsibility, the making of new assets in new ways, not remain, as it is today, no more than a tiny part of the business of the capital markets": Unger, "Overthrowing the Dictatorship of No Alternatives," *American Affairs* VIII, no. 1 (Spring 2024): 123–140.

INDEX

Page numbers in *italics* refer to illustrations.

unconditional convergence in, 133. *See also* automation
Mao Zedong, 125, 126
McTague, Erica, 90
McTague, Thomas, 90
Mearsheimer, John, 61, 62
mercantilism, 40, 43, 53, 96, 209
methane, 65, 66
Mexico, 54–55, 126, 131, 142, 156, 203, 206
Michelin, 114
micro-enterprises, 21, 125, 147–148
middle class: democracy linked to, 3, 5, 13–14, 93; erosion of, 2, 13, 99; labor movement linked to, 98; manufacturing jobs and, 15, 20, 97; rebuilding of, 7, 23, 35, 36, 220; requirements for, 13–14
minimum wage, 41, 58, 105, 107
modeling, in economics, 41–42
monopoly, 43, 188
monopsony, 104
Montreal Protocol (1987), 175
moral hazard, 167
mortgage-backed securities, 177
Multfiber Arrangement (1974–1994), 189
multilateral governance, 194
Musk, Elon, 121
mutual negotiations and adjustments, 192

Namibia, 153
national security, 37, 101, 163, 169; hyper-globalization's disregard of, 62; sanctions against China linked to, 34–35, 189, 194–195
national vs. global solutions, 29–32
nationalism, 5, 18, 220; in Germany, 91, 212
nationally determined contributions (NDCs), 74–75, 81
neoliberalism, 5, 6, 33, 35, 49, 60; backlash against, 211–212; center-left support for, 213; Chinese advances linked to, 125–126; elements of, 40; productivism distinguished from, 176
Netherlands, 91, 157, 212
New Deal, 27, 44
New Zealand, 74, 81
nickel, 84, 85, 151
Nigeria, 143, 148–149
Nine West (fashion brand), 123
Nio (electric vehicle company), 67 68, 135
Nixon, Richard, 39
Nortel, 175
North Atlantic Free Trade Agreement (NAFTA), 54, 57, 202

North Korea, 136
nurse practitioners, 116–117
nursing, 102, 116

Obama, Barack, 159–160, 162, 163
Ola (Indian ride-sharing company), 146
optimum tariffs, 188
orchids, 157
Organization for Economic Co-operation and Development (OECD), 49, 95
Ørsted (wind power producer), 66
Osterman, Paul, 117–118
ozone-depleting substances (ODSs), 175

Pakistan, 63
pandemics, 2, 5, 29, 30, 51, 194. *See also* COVID pandemic
Paris Accords (2015), 74–75
patriotism, 220–221
pencil manufacture, 156–157
pensions, 97
People's Party (US), 46, 92
Per Scholas, 112
Peru, 168–169, 186
photovoltaic (PV) products, 69, 71, 85
Piketty, Thomas, 213
Pinochet, Augusto, 158
Poland, 93
policy experimentation, 27–27
populism, 5, 24, 46, 59, 60, 92–93
Portugal, 131
poverty reduction, 7, 17–23, 123–154, 219; in China, 2, 19, 36, 125–126, 131; economic growth linked to, 3, 19, 36, 125, 131, 140, 144, 150; education linked to, 26; global cooperation linked to, 4, 29; as global public good, 186; green economy compatible with, 220; hyperglobalization linked to, 52; productivity linked to, 131, 144
premature deindustrialization, 21, 138–139
press freedom, 92
presumptive development strategies, 129–130
principal-agent model, 173
procurement, 69
productivism, 3, 36, 122, 155–176
productivity, 5, 15, 218–219; in manufacturing, 98; measurement of, 108; obstacles to improving, 109; of poor households, 19, 95; poverty reduction linked to, 131, 144; in service sector, 16–17, 21–22, 36, 107–108, 115, 117–118, 142–143, 154; wage and employment regulation linked to, 106

Sullivan, Jake, 179, 194–196
Sweden, 44, 91

Taiwan, 19, 55, 62, 101, 128, 157, 191
Taiwan Semiconductor Manufacturing
  Company (TSMC), 100–101
tariffs, 124; Biden's use of, 16; optimum,
  188; reduction of, 46, 56, 192; Trump's
  use of, 6
tax havens, 189, 207
taxation, 13, 20, 50, 120; electric vehicles
  and, 85; efficacy of, 111–112, 113; global
  agreement on, 31, 51; international, 207–
  209; intra-European frictions over, 182;
  for investment and job creation, 111–112,
  167, 171–172; progressive, 92, 209; race to
  the bottom in, 59. *See also* carbon pricing
technology transfer, 88, 186
telemedicine, 118
Tesla Inc., 68, 121, 136, 161–162
Texas, 12, 79
textiles, 47, 96, 120
Thailand, 157, 206
3D printing, 135, 136
Thurbon, Elizabeth, 68, 69–70, 80, 170
Tingley, Dustin, 78, 79
Ton, Zeynep, 106, 119
tracking, of employees, 107, 119, 120
trade adjustment assistance (TAA), 57
training, 112–113, 149–150, 168
transgender rights, 214
Trump, Donald, 14, 212; as authoritarian, 2;
  China targeted by, 16, 177, 197; climate
  change disregarded by, 6, 11; as dema-
  gogue, 92; Hispanic support for, 214–215;
  incoherent policies of, 6, 11, 177–178,
  184; international cooperation disdained
  by, 30, 34–35; manufacturing renewal
  promised by, 15, 16, 99–100; renewable energy disdained by, 66, 76, 89;
  self-destructiveness of, 184, 210; tariffs
  imposed by, 177–178; working-class support for, 90–91
Trump, Ivanka, 123
Turkey, 93, 101, 124, 131
turnover, in workforce, 106, 124

Uber, 146
Ukraine war, 77, 85, 191
Uncertain Futures (Gazmarian and Tingley),
  78, 79
unconditional convergence, 133
unemployment, 48, 57, 95, 107, 122, 187–188
unemployment insurance, 95, 97

Unger, Roberto Mangabeira, 261n8
United Auto Workers (UAW), 98
United Nations, 31
universal basin income (UBI), 165
urbanization, 99
USMCA (United States–Mexico–Canada
  Agreement, 2018), 202, 203
utility, 96

venture capital, 120, 158–159, 161
vertical policies, 256n23
Victor, David, 175
Vietnam, 86, 139–140, 153
Vivalt, Eva, 130
voluntary export restrictions (VERs),
  47, 189

Waldman, Adelle, 102
Washington Consensus, 27–28, 35, 129
water frame, 120
water quality, 28, 151, 175
Watson, Thomas J., 28, 161
The Wealth of Nations (Smith), 42–43
wealth tax, 13, 87, 208
welfare state, 14, 40, 44–45, 47–48, 122, 165,
  176, 216
Westinghouse Electric Corporation, 100
When Work Disappears (Wilson), 57
Williamson, John, 227–28n21
Wilson, William Julius, 57
wind energy, 10–11, 65, 66, 69, 70,
  76, 101
Wisconsin Regional Training Program
  (WRTP), 112
World Bank, 31, 86–87, 145
World Trade Organization (WTO), 54, 182,
  189, 202, 204; Chinese membership in,
  61, 71, 127; GATT replaced by, 47, 49;
  proposals for, 88; public indifference
  toward, 31; Seattle meeting of (1999), 38;
  subsidies limited by, 198

xenophobia, 2, 14

Yellen, Janet, 71
YouWIN! (Nigerian entrepreneurship
  program), 148–149

Zambia, 143, 206
Zeitlin, Jonathan, 172
Zenawi, Meles, 123
Zhang Huarong, 123, 126
Ziblatt, Daniel, 92
Zucman, Gabriel, 87, 208